M000209741

ANCIENT
EGYPTIAN
MAGIC

Cassandra Eason is the author of more than 50 books on a variety of subjects, including parenting, psychic power, ancient wisdom, magic and ritual and tarot. She has been acknowledged as a world expert on parent/child intuitive links and her expertise in this area has led to many appearances on television and radio. Cassandra is also a practising druidess and has lectured on the paranormal at several universities in the UK. She has five children and lives on the Isle of Wight.

ANCIENT
EGYPTIAN
MAGIC

CLASSIC HEALING AND RITUAL FOR THE 21ST CENTURY

CASSANDRA EASON

Text © Cassandra Eason 2003

All rights reserved. No part of this book may be reproduced, stored in a retrieval system or transmitted in any form or by any means, electronic, mechanical, photocopying, recording or otherwise, without the prior permission in writing of the copyright owners.

ISBN 1-84333-634-0

A catalogue record for this book is available
from the British Library

Published in 2003 by
Vega
64 Brewery Road
London, N7 9NT

A member of **Chrysalis** Books plc
Visit our website at www.chrysalisbooks.co.uk

Managing editor: Laurence Henderson
Editor: Rob Dimery
Designer: Roland Codd
Jacket: Grade Design, London
Index: Indexing Specialists
Printed in Great Britain by CPD Wales

CONTENTS

THE LIVING PAST

Ancient Egyptian magic is the oldest form of magic in the world. Much of our modern knowledge of magic and rituals can be traced back more than five thousand years to the great first civilization that sprang up along the banks of the mighty, life-giving River Nile. This magic still survives in modern Egypt – though secretly – in the homes of some devout Muslims and Egyptian Coptic Christians. When I stayed in Cairo, I met people living near the Great Pyramids of Giza, or the older site at nearby Saqqara on the edges of the Sahara, or who had worked as students excavating the tombs further south. All recounted strange experiences and powerful feelings, often of past worlds when they had lived or worked in the employ of a great king or temple.

Many of the incenses and perfumes sold in Cairo's colourful bazaars are the same fragrances that were used in the Pharonic courts and temples, and – now as then – can be used to raise levels of awareness and provide experiences of other dimensions. Older even than the chakra or psychic energy centre systems in use today – which are based on Indian philosophy – is an ancient Egyptian system that associated certain traditional fragrances, such as lotus, papyrus and jasmine, with different psychic energy spots in the body. This is mainly an oral tradition; I learnt of it from an Egyptian perfumer whose family had created perfumes for hundreds of years. Other sources too have suggested that the idea of psychic energy centres originated in Africa and Ancient Egypt long before records began and passed into India with early migration.

A number of Bedouin, or desert people, have moved to towns near the edge of the great deserts that still form much of the modern Egyptian landscape, bringing with them ancient arts of sand and stone reading carried out by wise grandmothers. Today, some of the descendants of this nomadic people are still able to read the future in the residue left in a cup that has held the thick, Turkish-style coffee favoured in Arab countries. This is an art that certainly began in the sixth century CE in the Yemen, though it may be even older, and which has been passed on via traders in the early bazaars and markets of Egypt. This is just one way the ancient magical traditions, or *heart* reading as I heard it called in Cairo, have survived in the modern Egyptian world.

What is magic?
According to the ancient Egyptians, *heka* or *hike* – old words for magical power – was a gift from the deities to humankind to improve their lives and protect themselves and their families. Christian Jacq, a French scholar who has written a number of works on the magic of the old world, has defined ancient Egyptian magic as 'the essential energy which circulates in the Universe of the Gods, as well as in that of humans'.

In ancient times, religion and magic were not separated as they are now and healing was part of the whole spiritual concept, with prayers, rituals and spells being an integral part of remarkably advanced medical knowledge. Today, we are becoming increasingly aware that these old physician priests and priestesses who practised in the Temple of Sekhmet the lion goddess, and under the protection of other deities, understood something that modern doctors are only just rediscovering: the mind and spirit are crucial to the healing of even those problems that seem purely physical.

From past to present

The people of Egypt still carry the old ways in their hearts, and perhaps their genes, but there are conflicts as to how this can be reconciled with their religious beliefs. This is what Fatima, a businesswoman in modern Cairo, told me:

> *I was with a group of students from Cairo who made a field trip to the temples at Luxor. It was very intense. We were studying hard and often spent the night in temples waiting for lectures that might begin at four in the morning. It could be very strange sitting in those rooms and feeling the old magic around you. After the trip many of us began having dreams about Bast the cat goddess.*

Bast is depicted as a cat, or as Bastet a cat-headed woman, and she is fiercely protective, especially towards women.

The Goddess Bastet

At that time I was in a very serious relationship with a man. We were about to get married and had even started choosing the colours of the furnishings of the new home we were about to set up.

Then I had the cat dreams of Bast in her cat form. In one of them, I was in a lift with that man and I was going to press the button to take us down to the ground floor. But a small cat appeared and stopped me. When I put out my hand to press the button, she pushed my arm away.

I didn't know what the dream meant at first and forgot about it. Then it happened again. I dreamed I was walking down the street with my boyfriend and the cat pushed against my legs to stop me walking with him.

Then I dreamt I was in a car and my boyfriend, to whom I was shortly to be married, had left me there to sleep the night. The cat appeared and this time she spoke to me and said that she didn't want me to sleep here alone. I told her that I couldn't sleep with her in the car and reached down to throw her out. But when I reached down to pick her up and throw her out of the window, she had changed into thousands of tiny cats. I threw the cats out of the window and they changed into the figure of the man in my life, who was running away.

I understood what the dream meant when I did not hear from my boyfriend for weeks and then he suddenly deserted me without an explanation.

On the Egyptology course I visited a small temple between Luxor and Aswan. It is a strange place with a false door; a door which engineers say could not have possibly been built where it is built. It seemed to me that the pictures on the wall were moving.

I was in the birthing room where Egyptian queens went to give birth. It seemed to me that I could see and hear the queen and she was talking to me.

I have met other Egyptians who like Fatima are devout Muslims, who nevertheless have connections with the old world of Egypt. For some, these experiences can cause problems because of their religion, but others are aware that the power of the old world is still strong and that as with Fatima's experiences, most are entirely benign and protective.

Making the connection

It is not just Egyptians who feel the pull of this most magical ancient world. People from around the world have described the sensation of coming home when they land at Cairo or Luxor airport. Maria, now a television astrologer told me this:

The soul of the world I believe is buried beneath the ground in the Middle East.

Having spent many years both living and travelling in this part of the world I was familiar with the way of life. I had never though been to Egypt when I was invited to a wedding in Cairo.

Some months earlier, when I was still running my family business a woman called Alison walked into one of our shops. I immediately felt a strong rapport with her. Until that time I had only dabbled with astrology along with various other psychic avenues. Alison ran a small healing centre and I decided to have a regression to try and put my life into focus.

The regression itself was very powerful, I found myself standing barefoot on dry rough grass, close to water. I could hear the lapping of waves; it was not the sea. The sun was burning my back and right shoulder. I was wearing a one-shoulder gown that was soft and came to my feet, which were bare. I was arguing and was planning to commit murder by poison. Alison decided it was too distressing for me to stay in this part of the regression so brought me out of the trance. At my next regression, immediately I knew I was in a tomb. I had taken the poison myself and was now buried.

Months later, I visited the ancient pyramids at Saqqara and I walked along the pathways that would originally be corridors I had a powerful flashbacks again like snapshots in time, of priests, in long robes, chanting. Later a guide confirmed that it was here that the ancient priests walked to the temple with incense and offerings. By now I was beginning to feel psychic energy that seemed to be awakening. Still, at this stage my regression of the previous year did not surface.

Such was the emotion I experienced on this trip that I felt compelled to return in the summer, this time to Luxor and the Valley of The Kings. The hotel I chose completely at random, so imagine my amazement when after arriving late afternoon I was standing barefoot by the side of the pool. Behind me the Nile flowed and across the water was the Valley of the Kings. The grass was coarse and dry beneath my feet, the sun was burning my shoulder and the Nile was lapping by the edge of the hotel. Even though it was still hot I felt a shiver run through me and I knew instantly I was standing in the exact position I had stood in my regression, where I believe I had once been thousands of years previously.

Following on from this, I made regular journeys to Egypt until, unknown to me, I made what was to be my last trip. I went on a cruise from Luxor to Aswan to visit my favourite sites.

The most powerful and possibly [the most] intense encounter occurred to me at Philae. Philae is a beautiful temple dedicated to the goddess Isis. I took with me an offering for the goddess, a large rose quartz crystal and some incense. The temple lies in the centre of a lake, [and is] approached in small boats. I dropped the rose quartz into the lake. I wanted to be able to link in with the crystal when I was many miles away back in the UK.

By the time I left the little harbour and entered the temple, it was dark. The temple was beautifully lit. It was very quiet and I was almost alone.

I reached the inner sanctum where the altar stood dedicated to the goddess Isis. The lighting here was low. I stood completely alone and silent, feeling the immense power contained in that room. I placed my hands palms down onto the altar, crushing the incense into the altar. At that very moment all the lights throughout Philae went out. I stood in complete blackness at the altar. At that moment I knew I was not alone but with all the other women who had come here to pray and make offerings.

Sceptics would obviously say that Egyptian power cuts are commonplace. But the lights went out at precisely the moment my hands and incense came into contact with the altar.

That night on the boat a dream or visitation occurred, so powerful I can still recall it vividly today. A pharaoh or priest stood above me and then he pressed himself on top of me, almost suffocating me. I could feel his breath upon my face and the weight of his body. I sat up in bed and he was gone.

I still feel the energy, I still see the stars so brilliant and know that a part of me still belongs there. Within 12 months my life had totally changed as a knowledge that until then lay buried inside was truly awakened and I now work professionally as an astrologer.

The living past

The architecture, the statues and the rituals recorded on papyri, on tomb and temple walls and on stone offering tablets, have preserved so much knowledge of the ancient Egyptian civilization. This has been made possible by the preservative power of the sand and also because of an almost universal fascination with the only evolved civilization to remain relatively unchanged for more than three thousand years. The latter was a double-edged sword for the Egyptians, because of the desire of the outside world to take these fabulous treasures back to their own lands. The first tourists to record their impressions of the country, as well as invading it, were the ancient Greeks and the great general Alexander claimed that the supreme god Amun had acknowledged him as a son.

However, it does mean that wherever we live, we can see priceless statues of the deities, protective amulets or charms dating back five thousand years or more. They can be found in national museums all over the world as well as in situ in Egypt, where a number of the people still live in ways not dissimilar to those of their distant ancestors. The donkey carts laden with melons hold their own with the manic microbuses spilling passengers in modern Cairo. Young children play safely in the sandy courtyards in the cool of the late evening. Tiny shops making shoes, clothes or selling vegetables, trading late into the night, are gathering places for the old women who often occupy the ground floor of family apartments, caring for young children while the younger women work. You can still see the farmers using oxen to plough the narrow fertile strip of land alongside the irrigation canals built by the pharaohs, animals cooling themselves in the water, the women baking the traditional breads in clay ovens and effortlessly carrying huge jugs on their heads.

Like Fatima, modern Egyptians listen to their dreams as sources of wisdom, as they did five millennia ago. One lady I met at an ancient monument told me the salutary tale of a cynical tour guide who regularly visited a temple of Hathor near Luxor and made disparaging remarks about the long cow ears of the goddess. One night he had a vivid nightmare that the goddess told him he was no longer welcome at her temple if he behaved so disrespectfully and that he would receive a warning if he attempted to go again. In the light of morning he dismissed the dreams as imagination and set off with his group. As he walked on the causeway to the temple a small Egyptian boy came up to him and in perfect English told him: 'The lady has sent me to tell you that you may not go into her temple.' Then the child disappeared. When the guide asked the group, no one had seen the child. Needless to say, he diverted his tour and has never spoken disparagingly since of the ancient world.

The Goddess Hathor

Working with the magic of Ancient Egypt

If you can manage even a few days in Cairo, or further south at Luxor to visit the tombs and temples of the Valleys of the Kings and Queens, you will be able to tap into the living heritage there. And as you stand in the blazing heat, you will be able to understand why the sun deities were so important. You can see the rays radiating over the side of the pyramids, forming steps into the sky for the pharaoh's spirit after death.

As the blue Nile flows between marshes and strips of irrigated farmland, with the dusty desert extending endlessly on either side, it is easy to understand the importance of its fertility and the life-giving powers of the waters and its deities to the Ancients.

Yet, as I said, you can work with Egyptian treasures in every land and museums are increasingly making such artefacts more accessible. Cairo Museum regularly sends its treasures to museums and exhibitions worldwide and reproductions of the treasures are also appearing as tourist attractions around the world. There are also numerous television programmes on the history of Egypt, especially on the information-based channels on satellite and cable (such as Discovery, History or Learning), videos, CD-ROMs, books and magazines galore as well as countless Internet sites that reproduce ancient texts. You can buy statues of the Egyptian deities, some with their animal heads, or in their animal forms as a focus for ritual, from ethnic stores as well as museum shops, or you can download images from the Internet. A significant number of people from all lands do, like Maria, trace past lives back to Egypt. Whether actual or symbolic, these strong feelings suggest a powerful spiritual connection with the birthplace of magic.

Working with Heka

Heka was the god who personified the concentrated, flowing invisible power that we call magic. A funerary spell from a Middle Kingdom sarcophagus (coffin) may be found in one corner of Cairo Museum – a museum of which it is said that to see every exhibit would take many months. Here is a rough translation of the spell. By reciting the words you can absorb the magical power into yourself or, in more modern terms, awaken your own inner higher spiritual and magical mind power:

To become the god Heka

I am Heka, the one who was made by the Lord of All before anything, the son of he who gave form to the universe. I am the protector of what the Lord of All has ordained to be.

This spell can also be a good way to begin any ritual or divination.

For Heka represents the power by which, in one of the main creation myths, the creator god Ptah brought creation into being by uttering magical words. For this reason, believers in magic thought that saying words aloud would make wishes come true. This is similar both to the Christian concept of 'In the beginning was the Word', from St John's gospel, and also to the whole concept of speaking words aloud in magical rituals and indeed in prayer to bring what is desired into being or to banish fears and sorrow.

Heka also protected the sun god Ra, or Re, during his nightly journey through the Underworld. By his magical uttering, he defeated Apep, the evil serpent who tried to prevent the solar boat emerging at dawn to bring sunrise to the world each morning.

Order and chaos in magic

This nightly battle between the sun god and the evil serpent represented the triumph of order, represented by the daily passage of the sun overcoming the chaos of darkness. For, in contrast to the Christian view of overcoming and destroying evil, there is always a balance in these ancient Egyptian beliefs. Destructive forces or deities also had complementary powers: for example, Serqet or Selkit, the scorpion goddess, had power to protect against scorpions, to heal scorpion stings, and also to provide protection against monsters that might be encountered in the underworld.

The balance and order of the universe was maintained by the principle of universal harmony – Ma'at – personified as the goddess of truth, justice and right action. Indeed, apart from the sun, the essentially chaotic Nile represents the most important feature of the life of Egypt. The flooding of the Nile was regarded as being under the control of the god Hapy.

The floods caused chaos annually, as well as bringing fertility to the land, until the building of the Aswan Dam in Southern Egypt in 1966. This annual flood renewed the fertile soil along the flood plain of the Nile, but if the flood was too high there was great destruction of homes and fields to those living on the flood plain. If the flood was too low, there would be drought and the soil would not be sufficiently rich to support the people. But without the chaotic Nile there would be no fertile land at all.

Egyptian magic is about the balance between order and chaos. Today, we can use the rich symbolism of the Nile and the sun and the myths of the deities as a way of focusing on our own needs, and use the most benign and positive of the ancient magical arts to bring healing to ourselves and others and empower ourselves to make positive change in our own lives.

Making positive magic

Like any force capable of bringing positive effects, magic can also be used for destructive purposes. Therefore, any kind of magical work relies on personal responsibility. Because Egyptian magic is so powerful, it is doubly important only to use its forms for the good of others, or – if for one's own benefit – without harming anyone else.

We often do need to tone down Egyptian spells and rituals as they were written for far harsher times when threats – which might come in the form of invaders from other lands, disease, or scorpions and snakes – constantly threatened life and home. But essentially they are of value and have formed the basis for much modern magic.

If you read the original Egyptian spells, you will see a lot of names that you might not recognize. Many of these are names of demons from the Underworld, who belonged to another age. While I do not believe you will conjure up these creatures in Hollywood B-movie style by invoking their names, there is nothing to be served in using names that have no personal significance to us and which were linked to harmful effects. Rituals are most powerful if they are personal to us.

During the last hundred years we have become aware how important it is to avoid negativity in magic, for what we send out we get back three times. We can and should harm no one by magic.

Kings and priests who used power against enemies would argue this was a legitimate form of protection. Spells that seemed to make the magician assume the form of the deity, and thereby assume also his or her powers, or which threatened the deities that if they did not help they would not be given offerings, can in modern terms be regarded as symbols through which existing personal mind power can be amplified and channelled.

In the following chapters, I will describe ways in which the old forms can be adapted to modern needs without losing either power or beauty. I was lucky enough to talk to people who were able to explain what some of the old rituals meant, but I have not identified them because of their own religious beliefs. I have also used myths and suggested ways of using the all-powerful word as well as charms and symbols to weave your personal – and always positive – rituals. Many of the spells and rituals I have used were either translated for me by contacts I made in Egypt or are amalgamations of a number of different and often conflicting versions of ancient papyri. If you do want to read originals there are many translations on the Internet. Many modern writers and magical practitioners use the books of the Egyptian scholar E.A.

Wallis Budge as a basis. Most importantly, write your own spells and rituals using the deities and forms of rite that I suggest, or that you read of elsewhere. In this way you can combine the beauty of the past with the needs of the present.

Using the book

After Chapter 1, which deals with the question of how to begin working with Egyptian magic, you can read the chapters in any order, as they are all relatively self-contained. At the back is a list of deities and their qualities that you can refer to for speedy reference or if you have not yet read the main deity chapter. I have also given a chronology of Egyptian dynasties so that you are not slowed down by unnecessary dates in the main book. Often, especially with myths or spells, the originals were recorded hundreds of years after they were first used and the different deities merge. This makes precise dating difficult.

Each section is largely practical and features exercises and rituals or divinatory forms with which you can experiment. In time, you may settle upon a few basic ritual forms from which you can develop your work. I have also listed other books on the subject. But in essence you can adapt tools and material you have already around the home and garden and I have suggested alternatives at every stage.

The visions of Egypt

The most powerful tool at your disposal is your imagination, which you can use to visualize blue or hazy skies, bright sunlight, vivid sunrises and sunsets with orange rubber ball solar discs – especially the further south you go in Egypt – and skies of jewel-like stars over the desert. There is much we do not know about Ancient Egypt. Its secrets are daily being discovered and the pieces carefully fitted together, but there will always be mysteries about that bygone era. Who were the deities? How could such an advanced civilization have emerged, seemingly, from simple nomadic peoples who settled in the lush valleys around the river after the rains receded in Neolithic times? What can we learn from this rich spirituality about the immortality of the spirit, or where we go after death, or how far we can change our lives by words and ritual and connect ourselves with powers whose origins are lost in prehistory?

My favourite words on this subject are those of the historian Kenneth Clark, who wrote: 'By evolutionary standards it should have taken millions of years for the primitive hunter with low forehead to turn into the graceful intelligent-looking man we find in the earliest Egyptian sculpture. In fact, it took only about 500. By the year 2750 Egypt had developed nearly all the qualities that we value, or used to value, in our own civilization.'

Whether we watch the sun rise over the desert as we speak words of empowerment or sit in our specially created Egyptian place in a corner of the garden or a room in a suburban home, we can connect with a beautiful and effective form of magic that can illuminate our lives, heal and join our own spiritual essence with the wellspring of ancient wisdom.

1

BEGINNING EGYPTIAN MAGIC

The temple was the house of the god or deities, where the *ka*, or soul, of the god dwelled. Its form and rituals were considered a reflection of the universe and a way of maintaining order over chaos. Temples, especially those of creator deities (see chapter 7), were built on high ground to represent the first mound rising from Nu, the water of chaos. Because the king – or pharaoh as he was called from the time of the New Kingdom, circa 1500 BCE (see Appendix 2 for the dates of ancient Egyptian dynasties and periods) – was regarded as the representation of divinity on Earth, the high priest in every temple made the daily offerings in the king's name. After death, the king would himself be worshipped in ritual so that he would make the land harmonious and fertile. Those who were sufficiently wealthy also prepared for their death by arranging for mortuary temples to be built, for it was believed that the *ka* of the deceased dwelled here, guarding the body. If offerings were made to sustain the *ka*, the spirit of the deceased would ensure for family members that the deities met their needs.

How can this principle work today? We no longer literally believe that the spirit of a god, or indeed of one of our ancestors, dwells within the statues or altars we set up. But they can act as a focus, just as visiting the grave of a loved one helps us to remember them when they were alive, and focuses our love.

In the same way, we can work within a home or garden temple we have created with the specific energies and strengths of the deities that exist in a less evolved form within us, waiting to be brought out. We can also set up a small place where we remember the family ancestors in a positive way, demonstrating that we are not just creatures of the here and now but are connected with an unbroken line of past, present and future and that we believe that the human spirit does not just cease to be after death.

By means of rituals using water, perfume and incense, we can establish an harmonious rhythm to bring order and serenity in our lives to stand against the frantic activity of the modern world. We can create a time and place of stillness where we can formulate our inner needs, reorder priorities and – through slow, repetitive steps and words – draw on those strengths we need not only for ourselves, but to make the world better. So, in setting up our Egyptian altar and working with it, we are not summoning spirits or ancient deity forms, but continuing a process that was established thousands of years ago to create a small place of harmony in an inharmonious world.

The temple in ancient Egyptian tradition

Only royalty and nobility were allowed within the temple precincts. In these areas were found statues of the deity or deities to whom the temple was dedicated, along with statues of the king, pharaoh or rich person who had endowed the temple. Outside the temple there might be images of the pharaoh, placed there so that he could act as intermediary for the ordinary people with the gods. There would also be private shrines where people might make petitions to the deities, especially protective ones – such as Hathor or Isis for women. Here, offerings were left on tables for the priests to take into the inner sanctuary: bread, onions, incense, perfume, flowers and linen together with petitions for magical intervention or healing.

Inside the temple was the raised sanctuary devoted to the main deity. This was the holy of holies, where the statue of the deity was kept in its covered shrine, often in the form of a wooden boat that would be carried through the streets in procession on festivals. Here the high priest would daily open the special doors, anoint the statue, wash it, burn incense and make offerings. Apart from the priest, only the king himself might enter this sacred place.

People also had their private shrines at home, dedicated to the household deities, especially Bes, the dwarf god of protection and joy, and Tauret, goddess of fertility, with the body of a hippopotamus and the tail of a crocodile. Like Bes she protected the family and all women, especially those in labour. But households might also feature small statues to Hathor, Isis or a local god or goddess and perhaps a statue of a noble ancestor on the home altar.

In both temple and home it was believed that the *ka* of the deity or ancestor resided within the statue and guarded the body in the tomb. So it was important to ensure there were sufficient offerings both to sustain the *ka* and to persuade the deity to remain within the statue. The Egyptians also left letters to their ancestors asking for help. Often these were written around the rim of a pottery bowl that would be filled with offerings.

Creating your own temple

If you live in a warm, dry place, you can create an outdoor sanctuary shielded by trees. But it may be easier to have an indoor place where you can be dark and private. You may have an attic or a basement that you could adapt for this purpose; alternatively, you can curtain off an area of bedroom or workroom for your special place. You can even improvise a setting in your bedroom using a table. Mothers in particular tend to be very generous with space for other people – perhaps this might be manifested in a playroom for their child, a television room or a shed for a partner's hobbies. It is not selfish to try to claim space for what is important for you. Garden chalets can be bought relatively cheaply or you can adapt a garden shed with windows.

It is not that your tools are spooky or would harm children. The reasons are purely practical. It is also important to create a private place of stillness and sanctity where you can go to draw strength from the ancient world and gradually build up the power through ritual.

Making your special place

If possible, paint your ceiling blue and either use transfers to add stars or use the luminous paint that will shine in the dark to invoke the protection of Nut the Sky Mother, whose body is covered with stars (see page 207). If the weather is good you can work under the stars. Use a square or rectangular table or large piece of stone supported on bricks for your altar. It should be high enough to sit or kneel in front of while facing south.

If you want a cloth, use a square of white linen or cotton that does not quite cover the table top.

When the altar is not in use, have a curtain or screen in front of it. You can pick up old-fashioned screens quite cheaply at a garage or car boot sale, or simply use a curtain. You may wish to leave an area behind the curtain in front of the altar where you can work during special, private times.

The tools of Egyptian magic

You will need a statue or a picture of one or more of your favourite deities or a pottery or stone animal to represent their animal form if they have one, for example a cat for Bast, the cat goddess who cares for you as a cat does her kittens. Statues of Bast often include her kittens. Indeed, when I was outside the Cairo Museum, I saw a cat and her kittens poke their heads out from beneath a statue of Mother Isis. Another kitten emerged from the shade of a sarcophagus. I felt this was a good omen.

The easiest place to purchase statues and other Egyptian artefacts at reasonable prices is from a museum shop. Increasingly, they are also sold by mail order and on line.

I have found that it is best to have different images for different needs. For example: Thoth for wisdom, Horus for healing and Tauret for fertility. Consult the list of deities and their attributes in Appendix 1. You can build your collection of pictures and statues over time. If you do not have a deity form, draw one or write his or her name on linen or white card as a focus and let the image of the god or goddess build up in your mind.

Altar artefacts

▲ A deep pottery bowl in which to place fragrant daily offerings such as flowers, pot pourri, incense, herbs or spices. Place this in the centre of the table or altar.

▲ An oil lamp – choose a simple one, with a wick or a beeswax candle to represent the element of fire. Set this in the south of the altar.

▲ Fill a small tray with soft yellow sand, some heaped in the centre to form a pyramid mound. Use either the kind of sand children have in sand pits or rich, dark soil. This can stand in the north; it represents the first earth that rose from the waters. Alternatively, you can buy a small, squat pyramid in crystal, calcite or metal, representing the stairway to the stars.

▲ An incense burner. Sometimes, when you are in a hurry, you will want to use incense sticks or cones in a deep container. But when you have time for a ritual or want to spend the evening quietly, use loose incense powder or flowers in an incense censer or holder. You can buy relatively ornate ones with a heat-proof chain so you can waft the incense around. You will also need round charcoal discs (see page 146 for instructions on lighting incense) to burn in the bottom of the censer, on which to scatter the incense. Loose incense and charcoal are widely available in New Age stores or by mail order. Place the censer in the east to represent the sky or air.

▲ A small ceramic bowl for water. No temple is compete without its lake to represent the primal waters from which life came and as a reminder that in ancient Egyptian thought the waters still surround the Earth and heavens. You can set a bowl of water in the west. Use mineral water, as it is for purification in rituals. You can also use it for floating oils or ink on water, both traditional methods of divination.

Your own wand

The most common kind of ancient Egyptian wand resembled an Australian Aboriginal boomerang. This was no coincidence, for it was based on the throwstick used by ancient Egyptian wildfowlers. Both the latter and the original Australians – though separated by 10,000 miles of ocean – realized that if you were trying to knock down a wild bird with a thrown stick, you would achieve far greater accuracy if the stick was slightly curved. The Australians took it one stage further and developed the tricky stick that will come back when you throw it (rather like the magical hammer of Thor in the very different culture of the Vikings).

The ancient Egyptian wildfowlers would hide in the reeds of the Nile waiting for passing ducks and geese. In Egyptian art, flocks of wild birds were used to represent the forces of chaos. So by extension, the throwing stick was seen as a force for bringing chaos back under control.

You throw your stick against them. A million fall: green-throated geese, laughing geese, whistling pintails.

Hieroglyphic inscription honouring Tutankhamun

The throwstick was so highly thought of by the Egyptians that they used it as a hieroglyph to mean 'throwing'. The wand based on the throwstick – the device that brought order from chaos – was used to protect the home, and in particular women who were pregnant or in labour. It was decorated with various protective amulets or charms and deities and is held in the power hand – the one you write with – to amplify power either by sending energies into the universe or when flicked away from you as a defensive device to fend off malevolence. You can set this in the north-east of your altar.

The museum in Cairo has a fascinating exhibit: three cases of ancient Egyptian throwsticks, plus some Australian models for comparison (there is a similar display in the Pitt-Rivers Museum in Oxford, England). Early examples of these wands, dating back to 2800 BCE, have little decoration and have points that end in the heads of animals.

Seven hundred years later there was a change in style: wands became decorated with elaborate carvings on one or both sides, often depicting protective deities such as Tauret, the hippopotamus goddess, and Bes, the lion-headed dwarf. Egyptologists refer to this type of wand as apotropaic, which means it was used to fend off evil.

So how can you get one of these wands? I'm afraid they're not common in museum shops or even in the bazaars of Cairo, which sell most things ranging from the mundane to the mystical. The best of these items were made from hippopotamus ivory, but hippos cannot even be found on the banks of the Nile, let alone the Isle of Wight, where I live. Thankfully, too, ivory trading has been banned in most parts of the world. I made my wand from environmentally friendly balsa wood. This has the multiple virtues of being easily obtainable from craft shops, light in weight and easily cut into a boomerang shape with a craft knife. Balsa wood is a reasonably cheap material to use and you might wish to make a selection of wands, decorating them with different gods and symbols according to the magic you wish to work.

Use a strip of balsa wood 30 cm (about 12 in) long by 7.5 cm (about 3 in) wide. (You can make it larger or smaller as required.) Cut it into the classic boomerang shape.

Decide on the symbols you want on your wand and trace them from this book.

Lay the tracing paper on the wand and, pressing hard, draw over the tracings. As balsa wood is soft, you will leave an indentation that you can draw over with a felt-tip pen or paints. Practise first on scraps of balsa to get the feel of working with this soft wood. You might like to try writing spells in hieroglyphics on balsa wood to get the indented feel of carved stone (without the need to become a master mason). Balsa wood spells can then be burned or buried as the ritual requires.

You may find this wand too lightweight for your tastes. An alternative is to use Milliput, a modelling putty used for restoring porcelain, ceramics and other antiques. There are similar brands in different parts of the world. You can get it from DIY stores or direct from the Milliput company at the following address: Unit 8, the Marian, Dolgellau, Mid Wales LL40 1UU (tel: 01341 422 562).

The Milliput I used comprised two tubes containing a putty and a hardener that have to be mixed together to produce a clay-like substance that, within eight hours, will set as hard as stone. It does need to be mixed thoroughly, so wear gloves during the process. The putty is pliable enough to be formed into the boomerang shape. Then you can draw your gods, goddesses and symbols of power on the wand using a blunt stylus. When the putty has set, you can paint it.

However, advance planning is needed, because what you do in the first hour is literally set in stone once the Milliput has dried.

My DIY efforts always look home-made, but personally crafted artefacts are very magical, because they are imbued with the essential self.

Your own sistrum

A sistrum is a metal rattle that is used to begin and end ceremonies and to enhance power through sound. It was often seen in the hand of Isis or Hathor or Bastet.

Temples would have a senior priestess, sometimes a royal person, who would play the sistrum at ceremonies. The instrument is meant to resemble cow horns bent round to form a loop. Threaded through three holes on each horn were three thin metal rods.

You may be able to buy one on the internet or from a museum store or something similar from a musical instruments shop. I was unable to find one in shops so I created a rough version myself. For reference, this is how you go about the task of making your own sistrum:

Sistrum decorated with the head of Hathor

▲ Buy a thin sheet of tin and three long thin copper rods. You should be able to find these materials in a craft shop.

▲ You will also need tin snips – similar to pliers – so that you can cut the tin. These slash through tin like dress-making scissors through cloth, and are available from DIY stores.

▲ Begin by cutting a piece of tin 30cm (1ft) by 7.5 cm (3 in). Use heavy gloves during the cutting, because the edges of tin are sharp. For the same reason it is worth turning over the edges with a pair of pliers.

▲ The two ends of the metal for the sistrum need to be tapered at the ends so that they can be fixed to a handle.

▲ The fixing tabs on the tin will need to be less than the width of the wood.

▲ Punch six holes, three at each end, with an awl or even a screwdriver – tin is very easily worked. They will need to be equidistant, so that when you bend the tin into the cow-horn shape and insert the copper rods, they run straight across.

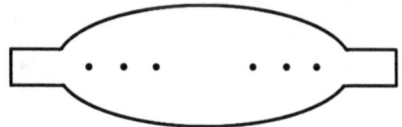

Sistrum template

▲ Fold the tin into the shape of a cow horn.

▲ Cut the rods to the required length with the tin snips and insert them through the sets of holes, bending them to stop them from falling out.

▲ You can use an old wooden handle and force the ends of the metal in or use a rounded stick and tack the ends to the top. I used a piece of broken-off branch from a local forest.

▲ If you wish, you can make small discs of tin, punch holes into them, thread on the copper rods and sit the discs in the middle of the sistrum. I omitted the extra rattles, as some Egyptians did – the rods make a surprising amount of noise on their own.

If you cannot make a sistrum, you can improvise with a hoop of bells wound around a bent and twisted metal coat hanger. When cleansing a space, you can ring the sistrum clockwise around a room or artefact, to psychically drive away negative energies. Ringing the sistrum around yourself will remove the tensions of the day and other people's negativity. Set the sistrum and your wand in the north-west of your altar.

Perfume

I have written a full chapter on perfumes elsewhere in this book. To contain the perfumes, you can buy small glass perfume bottles with a stopper or adapt an old perfume or cologne bottle with a stopper or lid. You can even use your favourite cologne or a rose or lavender water, though traditionally, one of the pure essences was used, such as lotus or papyrus. If you do go to Egypt, you can visit a traditional perfumer and smell the most amazing pure essences, undiluted by alcohol. Prices do tend to be very high, but you can buy a small quantity and the essence is so powerful that a drop or two is sufficient. Sometimes perfume in bazaars can be simply oils of not particularly high quality.

Perfume is used in Egyptian magic both for personal anointment and to sprinkle or spray in the four main directions – south, west, north and east – to purify the altar (see page 18). Set your perfume in the south-west of the altar.

For altar work you will need small balls of cotton wool and four very tiny dishes to hold them, one to be placed in each of the main directions on your altar.

Mirrors

These were sacred to the goddess Hathor – patroness of women, music and dance – and was originally a round or oval hand mirror, often decorated with Hathor or the eye of Ra or Re, the Sun-god from which the first Hathor mirror was formed. It was originally made of silver, highly prized in Egypt because it was quite rare and was thought to be the material out of which the bones of the deities were made. The mirror was highly polished on one side. I watched a jeweller in the market at Cairo buffing silver with a cloth and then washing it in warm water before polishing it again. Often the mirrors were trimmed with gold, Hathor's own metal.

You can use the mirror to catch the light – traditionally the rays of sunset – on your altar and to reflect the power into an amulet or charm or to remove pain and for divination (see page 114). You can set this in the south-east of your altar if you wish, or just add it for sunset or scrying ceremonies to the centre of the table.

Working with the four directions

Egyptian magic can be thought of in terms of the four directions that marked the concepts of time and space.

Time forms a horizontal line from the rising of the sun in the East to the setting of the sun in the West. The geography of Egypt provides the North/South axis. The river runs south/north with the source of the Nile in the south, rising in the Eastern Highlands, and ending in the Delta in the North, where it runs into the Mediterranean.

Egyptian magic differs from the westernized version of magic, in which we tend to face either north or east and begin there in ritual. The Egyptians looked to the all-important source of the Nile in the south. Thus Upper Egypt was in the south and Lower Egypt was in the north, towards the Nile Delta.

In ritual face south so that you are looking towards the source of the Nile and the noonday sun. This means that the east – the rising sun – will be to your left and the west – the setting sun – to your right. For this reason, temples were built on the east bank of the Nile – the direction of sunrise and rebirth – and tombs were built on the west – the region of the dead.

The symbol of the north and Lower Egypt is the hieroglyph for a papyrus plant:

North papyrus symbol

Upper Egypt and the south is represented by the blue lotus, represented by the following hieroglyph:

South lotus symbol

As you face the four directions, you can visualize the pool of lotus in the south, the sunset in the west, the papyrus marshes in the north and the sunrise in the east.

Personal preparations

Buy or make a long white loose kaftan robe with short sleeves to avoid the dangers around candles and burning oils. The traditional white pleated kilt for men and virtually topless transparent female garbs are not appropriate in the modern world and self-consciousness or a sense of dressing up can take away from the spiritual focus needed. A kaftan can be worn by a man or woman or you can buy a traditional gallabeah, the long loose-sleeved garment popular in Middle Eastern countries today.

A cloak can be useful for working outdoors, in a plain material or perhaps the star-spangled ones worn in honour of the sky and star goddess Nut by her priests and priestesses. These should be kept only for magical work and regularly washed, pressed and hung up ready to use.

Before working in your special place, take a bath or shower using either jasmine or rose essential oil or shower gel, to calm yourself and to distance yourself from the world.

Preparing the temple for ritual

▲ Check you have all the artefacts you will need on your altar table. If you are using an incense censer, light the charcoal five minutes before you need it.

▲ Each time you begin a ritual you will need to purify the altar. You can use one or more of the following methods, according to the time of day and the ritual (see below).

Purification by water

▲ Take the bowl of water on the altar and scatter a few drops of water at the four corners of the altar, beginning in the south-west corner and proceeding clockwise. At each corner say:

'With the waters of the celestial Nile, I purify this altar and this ritual.'

s Facing south, next hold your dish of water between your hands and raise it over the centre of the altar and say four times, one for each of the main directions:

'I purify this water by the sacred lotus, the setting sun, the wise papyrus and dawning of the new day. May only goodness and light enter herein.'

▲ Now sprinkle a drop of water in each of the four cardinal directions on the altar in turn – south, west, north and east, saying:

'So does the sun rise each day and life is renewed.'

▲ As you do so, visualize at each the symbol, for example the lotus flowers on the shimmering pool in the noonday sun for the south.

Perfume purification

▲ Another method of purification is one that does not appear in westernized magic, but it is a truly spiritual experience and one that I have found enables me to work at a much deeper level than I can with westernized systems.

▲ Use either a perfume in a bottle with a stopper or an all-purpose essence such as lavender, jasmine or rose water.

▲ Holding the bottle in your hands, face all four main directions in turn, starting in the south.

▲ Inhale the scent and place a single drop on your brow and then place a further essence drop on a cotton wool ball in a tiny dish in each of the four directions. Say at each of the directions:

'With fragrance I purify this altar and my work. May only goodness and light enter within.'

▲ For a very special ceremony, you can use four bottles: frankincense for the south, jasmine for the west, rose for the north and lavender for the east. If you have a small cup of instant coffee granules, you can inhale this in between to clear your senses.

Purification by incense and fire

▲ Light your oil lamp or candle and incense stick, if you are using one. Otherwise, sprinkle powdered incense on the hot charcoal block in the censer.

▲ From the East, pass the incense smoke clockwise round the edge of the altar in a continuous circle saying:

'With incense I purify this altar and my work. May only light and goodness enter within.'

Offerings

The altar is now ready and you can place offerings of flowers or loose incense and tiny fresh fruits in the offerings dish, giving thanks first for the blessings of your life, however small, and then asking first for others and then for yourself a simple request, either aloud or written on paper that you can burn in the candle flame or leave in front of the lamp.

Creating ritual

Sometimes this will form a ceremony in itself and you may wish to sit quietly before the oil lamp or candle and allow images to form of an earlier world. Alternatively, perhaps you would prefer to imagine words from one of your favourite Egyptian deity forms. In the early days if you are unfamiliar with the deities, you may see one that regularly forms in your mind's vision who in time will identify him or herself and may act as your special deity.

You are not summoning spirits, rather focusing on ideal qualities that you need in your life (see Appendix 1 for a list of these). At other times you may decide to practice divination or carry out a more formal ritual based on one of those that I suggest in the following pages.

Ending the ceremony

▲ When you have finished, let any incense burn through and clear away the ash. Extinguish the candle or lamp and prepare a fresh candle and oil for the next time you use the altar.

▲ Sweep the altar with a tiny brush and if necessary remove the linen cloth to be washed.

▲ Leave the offerings until just before the next ceremony, then either dispose of them or, if they are usable, place them around the home.

Honouring the wise ancestors

You may also wish to remember a member or members of your family who have died and to whom you feel particularly close. Alternatively, you may focus on a family hero or heroine who brought the family from the countryside to find work in the city hundreds of years ago, or who journeyed across an ocean, or who was a sailor, a missionary or a wise healer.

A spiritual ancestor

You may also focus on someone from the ancient Egyptian world with whom you feel kinship. You may have read about a particular character in Egyptian history, dreamed about them or experienced a flash of a past life in Egypt. In a museum you may see a statue or a tomb painting, showing someone whom you resemble physically, or with whom you sense great sympathy. I found my Egyptian alter ego in a brightly painted statue of the wife of a scribe in Cairo Museum, with whom I felt an instant spiritual link. Hossam, my guide, commented how much she resembled me physically. I use her image to connect me when I feel alienated spiritually. This character may appear more and more frequently in your dreams as you build up the psychic link and can act as a wise guide during scrying (crystal gazing) or rituals if you experience visions of yourself in Ancient Egypt.

Making the place of the ancestors

▲ Set a small side table to the west of the altar or push one against a west wall. West is the direction of the ancestors.

▲ Have a photo, a family treasure or if you prefer a vase of white flowers as a centrepiece, plus a symbol such as a crystal, a small pyramid or picture of your wise Egyptian kin and guide or favourite Egyptian historical character. You can paint or draw the Egyptian you see in dreams and set that in the place of the ancestors. Do not worry if you are not artistic.

▲ Set a small offerings dish in front of your personal and your spiritual ancestor.

▲ You need not place this table behind the curtain.

▲ Make the offerings quite personal when you are recalling a known ancestor – for example, a beloved grandmother's favourite perfume in a small bottle or a few of her favourite chocolates or flowers.

▲ For the Egyptian kin, offer incense, small fruits, crystals or dried flowers in the bowl.

▲ You need not purify this table, but you should keep the offerings fresh and change them every few days, stopping to touch the focal symbol of your ancestors and allowing wise words to come into your mind.

The Book of Egypt

Much of the magical knowledge of Ancient Egypt was recorded either in beautiful hieroglyphic writings or in shorthand form hieratic script, whether on a coffin or the walls of a tomb, on stelae, ceremonial tablets or on papyri. It might be helpful to begin your own book of knowledge, in which you can record your personal ceremonies, lists of deities, dream work, divination, relevant myths, perfumes and oils you find useful and chants you invent, plus work relating to your past life. You can use a loose-leaf folder so that you can add to your symbols and work regularly or keep a working notebook or computer files and then write the most important ones carefully in black ink on the pages. You can download or trace images of special deities and your experiences of working with them, plus any museum information or holiday pictures and over the years the book becomes a personal record and a gift for future generations.

Timings

Traditionally the most important ceremony of the day was at sunrise, followed by the ones at noon and at sunset. The hour before sunset was considered especially good for divination.

Midnight was also a time for protective magic and the banishing of sorrow and problems and for encouraging prophetic dreams. Sunrise was a special healing time and sunset was a good time for empowering charms and protective amulets.

A few minutes in your temple at dawn, when even the town is quiet and the air pure, can be a wonderful way to start the day. In the summer especially, I take advantage of the early sunlight and then make up for lost sleep with a short rest either during the day or in the early evening. But you can carry out your work whenever you need or wish with different kinds of natural and artificial light.

Occasionally, when you have a whole day or two free, carry out all four purification ceremonies, at dawn, noon, dusk and midnight. If you have a sistrum, you can ring it at the beginning of each ceremony and again to close the ceremony.

Dawn

This ceremony is especially dedicated to Horus, the falcon-headed god, and you may like to add his statue or image to the altar (see pages 94–5 for working with Horus).

▲ Open the curtain round the altar.

▲ Work facing the east or the direction of the sunrise, as it is only true east on the spring and autumn equinoxes (March 21 and September 21 in the northern hemisphere and the other way round in the south). Do this even if you cannot see the sunrise directly.

▲ Carry out the basic purification with water.

▲ On a roll of white paper write in black ink the names of any people you know who are ill, or animals or places that need healing.

▲ Read them aloud one by one and ask:

    'Horus, hawk of dawn, may he/she/it be healed and restored as the day is renewed.'

    You can ask for yourself to be healed from worries as well as from actual illnesses.

▲ Roll and secure the paper with a white ribbon and leave it all day on the altar.

▲ Leave the curtain open so that the light may fill the altar, only closing it if you cannot return before sunset.

Noon

If you did not carry out the dawn ceremony, pull the curtain right back so that light shines on the altar. This is the special time of Ra, the Sun-god (see Appendix 1) and you may like either to use a statue of him with the sun disc on his head or a metal sun disc, image or golden ball. I have a golden Chinese medicine ball model that is perfect.

▲ Purify the altar with water, even if you did so at dawn.

▲ Fill a large glass bowl with water and set it in the centre of the altar so that it fills with light. If it is a dull day, supplement the available light with gold candles.

▲ Encircle the bowl with white flowers. Use silk or paper if you cannot get real ones.

▲ Light frankincense, orange or rosemary incense sticks, fragrances of the sun, one at each of the four cardinal directions of the altar. Set them in tall holders (bottles will do).

▲ Facing south, take the southernmost incense stick (use a broad, firm-based one that can be easily carried) and walking clockwise around the altar nine times (the sacred number three by three), say:

> *'Lord Ra, blazing fire of the noonday sky, fill me likewise with power and light and bless my altar and my life.'*

▲ Still facing south, splash the sun-filled water on your face and make three declarations of power or confidence concerning your life. These can be for yourself or others. For example:

> *'By the power of the high sun, I will overcome prejudice and I will work and gain promotion. By the power of the high sun, I will prevent by legal means the wildlife marsh from being drained for a landfill site. By the power of the high sun I will stop overloading my body with caffeine.'*

▲ Take your wand in your power hand, the one you write with, and as you speak, raise it and bring it in front of you, flicking it from left to right in a slashing movement, saying after each empowerment:

> *'So I speak and so it shall be done.'*

If you do not have a wand, use your arm in the same way.

▲ Tip the rest of the sun water in clear glass bottles for use in your bath and to revive plants.

Dusk

This is my favourite ceremony and can be adapted any time after coming home from work, ideally as the rays of sunset filter on to the altar.

This is the time of Hathor and so you might like to use a statue of her with the sun disc between her horns or her image as a cow. Hathor was sometimes called Lady of the West.

▲ Face west or the direction of sunset as you work. If this is the first ceremony of the day, draw back the curtain to receive the last rays of light.

▲ This time, purify the altar just with perfume. Rose was the scent of Hathor and as this is her special time it is very potent for sunset work.

▲ Sprinkle the four directions at the edges of the altar clockwise, with single drops of rose cologne or water, or anoint the cotton wool. Begin from the west, saying:

> *'With your fragrance, Lady Hathor, I welcome the light of evening and with it let flow away all sorrow and regrets for what was not fulfilled, keeping joy in what was achieved.'*

▲ Now set your mirror in the centre of the altar and if you cannot see the sunset, light orange and red candles, the colours of Hathor.

▲ Sometimes you may wish to incorporate mirror divination at the end of your dusk ceremony (see pages 113–14 for Hathor mirror divination).

s But first breathe in the light of sunset or the candlelight slowly and gently through your nose. Then equally slowly and gently, blow the light after each in-breath in a gentle, invisible, ever-radiating circle of swirling red, purple, pink and orange light reflected in the mirror, enclosing in protection yourself, your altar and your home and family. Once you get into the rhythm, sigh the words:

'Bless and protect all, Lady of the West'

▲ on the out breath. Use also your gentle breathing to remove pain or sorrow from yourself and others, by continuing the gentle breathing, adding:

'Bless, protect and heal'

▲ to the outward breath. Then sit quietly, allowing the visualized sunset to swirl around you, taking away all unresolved conflicts and tensions.

▲ When it is dark, extinguish any candles and close the curtain, saying:

'Rest within the womb of your mother, weary sun, to be reborn in the morning. May I do likewise.'

Midnight

You can perform this ceremony late in the evening if you do not wish to stay awake till midnight.

If it is a clear night, draw back the curtain – if you have not done so already – so that you can see the stars. If you don't have a window in your temple room, focus on your starry ceiling. This is the time dedicated to Nut, the Sky-goddess whose body was arched over the Earth and covered with stars and within whose body the Sun-god and his solar boat travelled the night to emerge at dawn. You can obtain many beautiful pictures of her arched over the Earth.

▲ Light your oil lamp or a large white or beeswax candle.

▲ Purify the altar with incense. Use jasmine or mimosa, scents of the night or sandalwood, another traditional night fragrance, as a stick or in a censer.

▲ Face north, the direction of midnight and the northern constellations that so fascinated the ancient Egyptians (see Chapter 14).

▲ With the incense stick or censer smoke, make a clockwise circle round the outside of the altar, enclosing yourself also in a continuous smoke stream, saying:

'Wise Nut, Mother you absorb all into gentle sleep. Bring sleep to me also and all who also lie awake in pain or in anxiety or have no place to rest their head.'

▲ Gaze into the bubbling oil or candle and visualize pictures.

▲ If you are working by candlelight, drop coloured essential oils into a small bowl of water, or drop dark fragrance oils on the water's surface, and let images form spontaneously that will answer questions you did not even know you were asking (see pages 112–13).

▲ Even if you do not wish to carry out a divination, minutes spent gazing into the candle or lamplight and inhaling a night fragrance slowly and gently (see also pages 135–6) from your incense stick can mark the transition between day and night and the conscious and unconscious world.

▲ It is a good time for past world visions, perhaps while holding a statue or ancient Egyptian symbol. Even those of us who did not have a direct link with the ancient Egyptian world can, in the stillness of the night, tune into other lives there that can shed illumination on present situations and future possibilities (see pages 145–6). At this time you may talk to your wise Egyptian ancestor.

▲ Close the curtain when you are ready and go to sleep.

Adding to ritual

This chapter gives you an outline and template so you can begin to introduce ceremony into
your life. If you have no time even to purify your special area, spend just a minute or two in
your Egyptian sanctuary drawing strength and perhaps anoint yourself with a drop of perfume
on your forehead, brow and wrists, saying softly at each anointment:

> *'Bring to me and to this sacred place the power of the old land, the fertility of Kemet (the rich
> dark silt of the Nile), the warmth of the sun and the life of the waters.'*

As you read the following chapters you will be able to enrich your ceremonies with knowledge
of words of power, of amulets and charms, colours, oracular practices, traditional ancient
Egyptian healing powers and detailed knowledge about the individual deities whose myths
are central to many of the ancient spells. You will write your own hymn to the sun and also
one to the sacred water.

Most amazingly, at some point you will find you are speaking words you did not know and
carrying out rituals that you feel you have known all your life. You are not being possessed or
even guided by spirits – the process is entirely natural and positive. For ancient Egyptian
magic, more than any other kind, helps you to gain or regain your deep connection with the
wisdom that is universal, the gift of wise people that we can tap into because of our own
historic roots back to the first humans and, perhaps, to the realms of spiritual wisdom that are
personified or given form as the ancient deities.

Whether you are reading this in the frozen northern world, in America, Europe or
Australia, your spiritual if not actual kinship does extend to the land of sun and water where
magic was born and lives still and can be experienced wherever and whenever you move away
from the mundane to the mystical.

2

THE MAGICAL POWER OF IMAGES

The magic of Egypt is centred on the use of both symbols and words of power. Chapter 3 focuses on using chants and statements of power for turning desires into reality and amplifying personal psychic energies to drive away danger and fear. Chapter 4 deals specifically with protective amulets or charms, which were such a major feature of Egyptian magic. It suggests methods of making and empowering them plus a method of divination using your personal hieroglyphic amulets.

But first I will introduce more general ancient Egyptian magical symbols and the materials used so that you can add them to the daily ceremonies of the previous chapter and carry their powers in your everyday world.

Wax and clay

Wax and clay figures excite more speculation and negative attention than almost any other aspect of Egyptian magic. This kind of ill-wishing has persisted in negative magical systems throughout the world right through to the present day, not least in the infamous example of the wax doll that was stuck with pins and melted. This practice originated in prehistoric magic, but was developed to a high level of sophistication: figures of enemies were burned, drowned or beheaded to bring success. One apparently historical account tells how an irate husband created a miniature wax crocodile and by magic transformed it into a huge live crocodile in order to kill the lover of his unfaithful wife (see pages 43–4). In museums containing artefacts dating back to the Old Kingdom in Egypt, we have archaeological evidence of figures stuck with iron pins.

So is it safe to use images in modern magic? Like magic itself, a piece of melted wax or a lump of clay is essentially neutral; legend tells that the God Khnum formed humans from the clay of the Nile on his potter's wheel.

If you wish to make an image of a would-be lover and stick it full of pins so that the real person cannot resist you, or send clay scorpions to people you do not like, you are offending the laws of common morality as well as a number of religious codes. Generally, if something is wrong morally then it is also wrong magically and if you go reciting very ancient texts about smiting your enemies or grinding them underfoot, you are using the power of your feelings to ill-wish someone. The use of an image on which to focus the power makes the act even nastier. That is not the purpose for which this book is intended.

However, there are many ways we can use the basic concepts of this idea – as, indeed, some ancient Egyptian magicians did – for good, for healing and to banish unwelcome aspects of our lives. The ancient Egyptians lived in very different times, when there was real danger from scorpions, serpents and enemies who might try to invade your land and destroy your young. Their response was to use magic as one means of defence, as in the example of the queen in an Egyptian legend who, when all the men were gone, defended the young and the other women by using statues of soldiers that she set around the walls of the town and brought to life when danger threatened.

The other factor in any kind of magic or morality is that we cannot override the free will of anyone else. We can, I think, morally prevent someone from harming our loved ones by turning their attention aside magically or casting a screen of protection and psychic invisibility around the loved one. However, we should not compel anyone to stop loving someone else, to desire only us or to compel a noisy neighbour or spiteful colleague to leave. All magic evolves according to the times, and those who still practise ancient Egyptian magic, at least those I met, are aware of the limits imposed not only by the power of magic but also by personal responsibility. But there are ways we can use the old rituals to turn aside jealousy or unfair criticism.

Making clay images

By actually forming a figure, or an animal, etching words of power on the clay or dough and then reciting them, you can without offending the laws of morality, focus your own intentions and concentrate your personal power. Equally, you can destroy an image representing an addiction or destructive emotional bond and thus you can psychically as well as psychologically banish fear and awaken determination to be free.

In making an image of yourself for healing or to gain strength you are endowing it with your essential self, your emotions, hopes and dreams, so it is a very powerful form of magic. Equally, in forming the image of a lover or family member you can send them protection, healing or courage.

An image can represent someone you want to love you, or who you wish would love you more, a child who is being bullied, a baby you desire, a prospective employer you wish to impress or something in yourself you wish to improve or banish. So you might, for example, make a figure of a soldier to represent yourself if you need courage, or an animal in order to absorb its unique properties (see pages 118–31).

▲ Use either the kind of clay you buy in a craft store, or children's play clay, or dough. You can make a basic dough with plain flour, water and a little cooking oil – such as sunflower oil – to make it pliant. You can keep clay wrapped well in damp plastic, and dough placed in a sealed container will remain pliable for a few days if it is stored in your fridge.

▲ As you create the basic mix, or work a lump of clay after buying it, make sure you work in sunlight, or at least daylight, and move your fingers rhythmically, saying:

'Light enter into this clay/dough that I may create beauty and goodness and work only for higher purposes without malice or malevolence.'

▲ Whisper this over and over in a steady rhythm. This stage is important. You need make or store only small quantities of the clay or dough.

▲ Place the prepared clay or dough in a lidded bowl and have a flat wooden board to hand, the kind used for cheese or bread, plus moulding tools. Avoid sharp knives and where possible used wooden implements.

▲ Add a second square of linen to avoid staining the altar cloth. Alternatively, if you have a low altar you can set your board on the ground.

▲ After purification of the altar space with water (see page 18), open the clay or dough and sprinkle a few drops of water over it, then a few drops of perfume. Finally, pass incense over the image four times clockwise, and at each pass say:

'*I purify this clay and my heart from all negative intent. May only good reside within.*'

▲ Since the ancient Egyptians believed that a *ka*, the soul part, might reside in statues, make your figure with kindness and gentleness.

▲ You can buy different shades of modelling clay if you wish, or add natural food colouring to the dough, so that you can incorporate colour symbolism into the ritual (see pages 33–7).

▲ Alternatively, you can form a circle of dough and draw a symbol in it – a flower such as the lotus if you need health, a pile of loaves for abundance at home or for money, a wall enclosing representations of you or your family, a boat for travel of all kinds, a bird for freedom, a tool for learning new skills, a papyrus scroll for learning. It need only be a rough representation and if you keep within the kind of symbolism used in Ancient Egypt, then the magical connection with this form of magic will be easier, a sun disc for regeneration of enthusiasm or opportunity. For example, you might use the hieroglyph for strength and support. This was depicted as the symbol for the backbone of the Underworld God Osiris. The backbone was one of the most essential parts of Osiris's body to be found by his wife Isis after Osiris was murdered and dismembered by his brother Set, also known as Seth. It meant Isis could recreate Osiris's strong form and so become pregnant with his son Horus, who would avenge his father's death. The hieroglyph was an important symbol of strength throughout Ancient Egypt, and is known as Djed or Tet (see pages 65–6 for its significance and for other hieroglyphic images of power).

Djed

Take inspiration also from images from Ancient Egypt in books, on television programmes and videos and the Internet. Begin a symbol collection in your personal Book of Egypt and in time you will produce an alphabetical list to which you can refer for future inspiration.

Wax images

These are even easier to form.

▲ All you need is a small, squat candle, or several candles in different colours set directly on to a metal tray so that the melted wax will form a circle on the tray that you can engrave and then cut out. Buy candles in which the colour goes all the way through (see pages 33–7 for the very important symbolism of colour in Ancient Egypt).

▲ Purify the altar with water and set your candles in the centre.

▲ Before you light the candle(s), rub a very tiny quantity of pure virgin olive oil upwards into the wax. Ask that only the highest powers of goodness and kindness will enter the wax and make an assurance that the use, like the intention, will be pure. The candle will be more flammable when you rub it with oil, so take extra care.

▲ Focus on your needs while the candle melts and, breathing quietly and gently, watch the candlelight through half-closed eyes. Play music if it helps you to relax. You may be able to obtain some Coptic music, which is beautiful to listen to.

▲ Once the candle is burned through, you can engrave it with the symbol, or with words of power, or perhaps cut a figure of a person into the wax – two people for lovers.

▲ While the wax is still warm and soft, you can etch hieroglyphs of power and protection (see pages 61–72) around the image if you wish.

Empowering images

Once you have created and engraved the dough, clay or wax, you can empower it with the purpose of the ritual.

▲ Take your incense censer or stick, using a cleansing sacred fragrance such as cedar or myrrh, and facing south pass it in a cross from south to north and then east to west over the stick, then south-east to north-west and south-west to north-east, to form a star shape in smoke. As you do so, say:

   'Be for me the strength/love/power/protection.'

▲ Add the name of a protective deity if you wish, such as Tauret, Isis or Hathor.

Using the image – a protective ritual

After you have empowered your image, you can use its energies magically to resolve an issue or to give yourself energy or healing. The ancient Egyptians frequently linked their spells to a deity name and/or myth. For example, Serqet or Selkit the Scorpion-goddess was considered the protective deity against scorpion stings and her golden image was one of the four protective goddesses who guarded coffins and shrines in which they were kept (see page 97). In the modern world she is often called to protect against spite and malice, especially in the family but also against unkind ex-lovers or gossiping neighbours.

▲ Gently holding the empowered image, state the specific purpose of the ritual, for example:

   'I seek protection from Elaine whose image I have created that she may stop

spreading spiteful gossip about me at work. Mother Isis as you protected the young Horus from his uncle Set in the papyrus marshes, and you golden Serqet who guards against the scorpion sting, make me pass from the scrutiny of Elaine and may she and I live in peace.'

▲ Waft incense around the figure to obscure you from its view and then gently wrap the figure in soft white linen and place it in a drawer.

▲ You can repeat the smoke and the words over the figure at regular intervals, rewrapping it in clean white linen.

This is much better for you than sending scorpions to sting the vicious Elaine, who already is being poisoned by her own mental venom (see also the magic of the seven arrows of Sekhmet on page 45).

The power of the image

Whatever the purpose for which you created the image, you will need to decide what to do with it after the ritual. The previous spell gently wrapped it and put it away. It may be unwise to break it, even if – for example – the form represents a bad habit or destructive emotional hold someone has over you.

If you feel that, therapeutically it would be good for the image to be destroyed, then a compromise is to let nature take her course.

▲ If it is a destructive image, make your dough with less oil so that it is quite dry and will crumble naturally. Breaking off bits of ourselves symbolically can be unbelievably painful. The crumbling method is especially good for removing chronic pain or a deep-seated sorrow.

▲ If it is an image to attract love, health or happiness, you may wish to leave it open on your altar with fresh flowers and anoint it regularly with perfume to give yourself, or another person, strength or courage. The ancient Egyptian fragrance of cinnamon was considered a tonic for giving an individual the fire to fight back and also to increase passion.

▲ Other figures, for example those that represent someone who is ill or unhappy, you may wish to anoint daily on your altar, with healing oils, such as cedar, myrrh or frankincense (see also pages 148–52).

▲ When you wish to gently end a relationship, focus on the feelings rather than the person. You can create two images, one for you and one for your lover. As you make them, however, state that they represent the feelings of you and your lover, not your lover him- or herself, and move them gently apart a little each day. Finally, wrap your (hopefully) now ex-lover's feelings in linen and keep the image in a drawer until it crumbles naturally, at which point it can be buried. In this case keep your own image separately wrapped in silk. You can bury your own feelings when they crumble, but remember before you do so to create and empower a new, strong image of yourself to keep on the altar and stud it with clear quartz crystals for new vitality and joy (see page 168).

Fertility images

Fertility figures – for example, a couple making love or a baby being held on a bed and suckled by its mother, or a woman with swollen breasts and belly – have been found in their thousands at the Temple of Hathor at Dendara. This Egyptian goddess was especially associated with women and fertility, as was Isis. Isis and Hathor wore head-dresses on which the sun disk was set between two cow horns to show they were the nurturing mothers of Egypt. Clay phallic symbols were also made to bring the petitioner a potent husband, or to aid potency in marriage. They represented the erect phallus of the fertility god Min (see page 205).

Fertility figures were also placed on domestic altars, often of a woman wearing a necklace, a girdle slung round her hips and with a prominent pubic triangle. They were sometimes fashioned from faience as well as clay. These domestic altars were dedicated to Bes, the dwarf protective deity, and Tauret, the hippopotamus goddess, as well as to Hathor.

The figures were also occasionally found in tombs, with inscriptions such as: 'May a child be born to your daughter.' Other fertility figures in tombs were believed to assist rebirth.

In the modern world, with all its attendant pressures, anxiety can block fertility even if there are no physical problems. Ancient Egyptians were also under great pressure: couples were expected to produce strong sons, as well as many daughters to care for the old and to make offerings at the family tombs. Such figures existed from the pre-dynastic times right through to the Roman period in Egypt and I have seen a number of examples in the British Museum in London.

A moon ritual for conception

Before I introduce the following ritual, I should stress that I am not offering it as a guaranteed means of becoming pregnant. Infertility can come about for a host of reasons and its treatment will vary according to the source of the problem.

For the image of a baby you might wish to create a leaf cradle and bring it out only in moonlight or when you make love.

▲ Alternatively set an image of a baby on your altar surrounded by greenery and with a statue of Hathor, if you have one, or a ceramic cow image. This should be done during the period from the night of the crescent moon (about two and a half days after the new moon) until the night of the full moon. As it is a lunar spell, you may prefer to work with the Egyptian Moon-mother and goddess Isis and use a representation of her as a focus.

▲ Each evening purify the altar with perfume (see page 18) and then pass a rose incense (for Hathor) and a lily or lotus incense (for Isis) over it in a circle clockwise, saying:
    'You who have been mothers, Isis, Hathor and Sky Mother Nut, mothers three, let me likewise this night be granted the blessings of a child.'

▲ If you are a Christian, you might like to pray to Mother Mary, who took over the role of Isis, or you can simply focus on all mothers everywhere.

▲ Make love when you wish on the nights from the crescent to the full moon.

▲ Carry the image into the bedroom on the night of the full moon and leave it on the
   window ledge open on white silk while you make love.

▲ After the night of the full moon, wrap the image in white silk and keep it in a drawer until
   the next crescent. You may find that your cycles begin to harmonize with those of the
   moon and you relax into conception.

Knots

Knot magic is one of the oldest and most potent forms of symbol magic. The knot in Ancient
Egypt represented a concentration of power that can be released when needed. According to
the Leyden Magical Papyrus, seven knots were especially powerful. Knots were used to
fasten charms and amulets around the ankle and neck.

One of the knot's main functions was to act as a magical barrier, both as protection against
harm and illness. One spell in the Leyden Magical Papyrus tells of a strip of linen on which
12 deities were drawn. The strip was then tied into 12 knots, the final creating a circle, and it
was worn as a necklet. According to the ritual the linen was blessed with beer, bread and
incense, dedicated to the gods.

Knots can also be used to hold energies until the specific time that they are required.
Again, they were sometimes attributed to a deity.

Of course, you do not have to choose 12 deities. You can work in threes, perhaps a family
of father, mother and child, such as Osiris, Isis and Horus, Ptah, Sekhmet and Nefertum from
Memphis or the Theban Amun, Mut and Khonsu, the Moon-god. Four for the four directions
and the sacred seven, which works well for spells where you wish to undo one every day for
a week, were also popular in Egyptian knot magic.

You do not need to dedicate knots to a deity. Instead, you can name specific powers or
strengths you need, as the power of speaking words aloud in ancient Egyptian magic is a way
of making wishes come true – in this case, the wishes or powers you are tying up in your knots.

Knot deities

There are three deities specifically associated with knots:

i) **Anubis, the jackal underworld/rebirth god** – because of his association with binding the
    mummy rules knots for preservation and protection. His knots are black.

ii) **Isis** – with her famous knotted girdle – the tjet that was a hieroglyph, associated with
    menstrual and life blood – rules knots for increasing energy, prosperity and for fertility and
    a good patroness of active knot magic that release power. Her knots tend to be made from
    red cord, or thin red or natural linen.

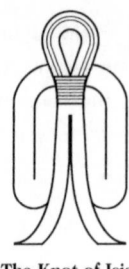

The Knot of Isis

iii) ***The seven daughters of Hathor*** – the sisters of fate, were represented by seven separate ribbons or cords of red and these were used both for love knots and to drive away or bind those who would do harm, especially against young children and women. The seven Hathors were called Lady of the House of Jubilation, Lady of the Stormy Sky, Lady from the Land of Silence, Lady of the Black Earth, Lady with Hair of Fire, Lady of the Sacred Land and Your Name Flourishes Through Power.

Thoth, god of Wisdom and Amun, Supreme Creator god, were also popular foci of knot tying.

Knot tying

If you have a task to do, or perhaps a week coming up when you will need particular strengths, you can use your deity knots not only to protect you and act as a barrier but – by untying one a day – to release its strengths.

If you use strips of linen for knot tying you can draw or write the names of the deities along the strip in fabric marker pen at regular intervals and tie knots over them. You can also draw deity symbols, for example an ostrich feather for Ma'at, goddess of truth and wisdom or a cat for Bast.

Name aloud the purpose of each knot you intend to tie and also the time scale. They can be a multiple sequence in gaining a particular strength, a number of steps or the same wish over and over if it is a vital or ongoing issue. For example, if you are doing a seven-day spell tie the seven ribbons together – but don't join them at the ends to make a circle.

Love knot ritual

Though dawn is a good time for knot work to increase power, for love and protection it is best to work later in the day. Though you can use the separate Hathor names for each knot, for simplicity let's use the basic Hathor name. If a woman wanted a husband, she prayed to Hathor in particular and left offerings for her.

You can use the ritual yourself to work for either a known or an unknown lover. Men as well as women can use the spell. Similar spells are still used in Egyptian popular folk magic.

▲ Light a red Hathor candle just before sunset – her special time.

▲ Purify the altar with perfume if you are carrying out a love ritual. If it is a Hathor fertility ritual use just incense to purify the altar. For all other kinds of knot magic sprinkle water over the altar as the purification substance.

▲ Set seven separate ribbons for the daughters of Hathor.

▲ Light your incense – on this occasion, a stick – using frankincense or sandalwood for any knot work if possible. However, rose is a good substitute for love magic.

▲ Have two offering bowls to hand also – one for crumbs of bread and the other for beer, wine or dark fruit juice. Beer in Ancient Egypt was very nourishing and not as alcoholic as it is today.

▲ Work in the hour before dusk and light a Hathor candle – a red or orange one.

▲ As you tie the knots, speak the following lines:

Knot 1: That he/she may come to me, Hathor guide the way.

Knot 2: That he/she may see and like me as I am, Hathor guide the way.

Knot 3: That he/she may be kind and gentle in word and action, Hathor guide the way.

Knot 4: May he/she grow to love me more each day, Hathor guide the way.

Knot 5: May he/she be faithful and never give me cause to doubt. Hathor guide the way.

Knot 6: May our love grow deeper with the years, Hathor guide the way.

Knot 7: May there be always unity through bad times as well as good so long as the water flows and the sun shines. Hathor guide the way.

▲ Do not join the ends together.

▲ Anoint both ends – first left, then right – of the knotted ribbons with a single drop of rose essence or water. Then anoint the five remaining knots, from left to right, saying:

'Fragrance of Hathor, perfume of love, bring and preserve love within these knots.

▲ With your incense, reproduce the knots from left to right over the ribbons in smoke, repeating the knot chant.

▲ Leave the incense to burn and the knotted love cord on the altar.

▲ Begin on the next dawn, or when you wake and it is light. Untie the knot to the far left, reciting only its chant, and leave the loose ribbon(s) on the altar.

▲ Continue until you have all seven ribbons free on the seventh day and bury them beneath a living tree, traditionally a fruit bearing one.

▲ Wait a week and if your love has not come, then repeat the spell. Then if it still does not work, wait a month and repeat, as the energies are building. Make sure you do go out as usual, perhaps finding new interests, but do not actively seek love – for example, in a singles bar. Egyptian magic tends to be slow but powerful.

You can also adapt this spell for protection. List a fear, or aspects of specific hostility, for each knot, and say for each of them:

'Hathor protect me today.'

Again, untie one knot each day, but this time bury the seven ribbons beneath a bush that is dying or in unplanted earth.

Colour magic

One of the most powerful forms of symbolism in magic is colour and in Egyptian art and sculpture colours were rarely used randomly – except, for example, in an action scene where darkness and light were used as contrast for less significant characters. Indeed, for every man and wife you see in Egyptian art, the man will have a red skin to represent the fact that he works out in the sun (even noblemen were shown like this) while the female was white, indicating she remained indoors. Sometimes worker statues of women were shown with red skin.

Red and white together symbolized completeness, as with the red and white crowns of Lower and Upper Egypt that were joined in the King.

To the Egyptians, colour was part of the essential nature of a person, deity or object and so it was an extremely powerful form in magic.

Amulets and charms would be made from particular coloured crystal or stone or painted in a particular colour to indicate the magic power (see chapter 5).

The colours of magic

The colours used in Ancient Egypt have survived thousands of years, mainly because they were created from mineral compounds. They can still be seen on statues from tombs and from paintings on tomb walls.

Black (*khem, km* or *kem*)

This had none of the gloomy or evil connotations of black in the modern world. Indeed its name, called *km*, is linked with *kmt* or *kemet* and means 'the Black land'. This was one of the names for Egypt, referring to the rich silt deposited by the Nile Flood. Therefore black was primarily a colour of fertility and rebirth. Life came from the dark primordial waters.

It also was the colour of the Underworld and specifically of Osiris, the underworld god who caused the constant cycle of regeneration and was instrumental in giving the blessed dead rebirth. Osiris was also sometimes shown as green.

Anubis, the god who was responsible for embalming the body, was depicted either as a black jackal or dog, or a black jackal-headed figure with gold limbs (see below).

A number of fine ancient Egyptian statues were painted black, especially the statues of kings. For example, the wooden statue of King Hor in the Cairo Museum is black; the raised arms on his head formed the symbol of his *ka*, or soul. This statue was created during the 13th Dynasty, around 1700 BCE. Most famous of all are the statues in pure black and gold that guard the entrance to Tutankhamun's tomb, and which represent the *ka* of the young king. At one time the statues stood in front of the naos, the gold shrines that enclosed Tutankhamun's coffins. I saw the black and gold *kas* in Cairo Museum and realised what a vital colour black could be.

Blue (*khesbedj* or *irtiu*)

Blue is a very powerful colour, used in Ancient Egypt to represent the sky, especially the starry heavens and the body of Nut the Sky-goddess, as well as the waters of the Nile.

Beautiful papyri paintings, and those on coffin lids, depict a rich lapis lazuli blue (the pigment was made from the crystal) studded with golden stars and the original waters. So, deep blue and gold can be used in ritual to symbolize Nut.

Surprisingly the benu – the heron or phoenix that was the first creature to perch on the mound that rose from the primeval waters (see pages 126–7) – is also blue . The bird is associated with the Sun-god Ra, especially when placed on top of pyramids or obelisks with a pyramid top. Blue is also the colour of Thoth, the god of wisdom and writing, in the form of a blue baboon.

So, blue can be used for wisdom and also for the power of the sky and flowing waters. But it also stands for powerful protection.

Amun or Amen the creator god was sometimes depicted with a blue face; the head-dress of Ptah, another creator God, was also blue. The hair of the deities was depicted in lapis lazuli.

Green (*wadj*)

This colour was primarily associated with, and often made from, the green crystal malachite – itself of the copper family (see pages 167–8). Green symbolized life and growth, and the green strip of land growing on either side of the Nile that even today is ploughed by bullocks and tilled by hand using implements that date back thousands of years.

Green is particularly associated with the green papyrus stem and leaves (which is itself the hieroglyph or sign for green), a plant used in making papyrus for writing. Uadjet, the serpent goddess, was protectress of Lower Egypt. Her symbol was the papyrus and she too was sometimes also called the green one.

Osiris was depicted with a green face and skin to represent the regrowth of the crops and his power over vegetation. Deceased people were likewise depicted with a green skin on coffins and on tomb walls, to signify their rebirth.

Green was a popular colour for amulets, especially the healing and life-giving ones (see chapter 5).

The colour turquoise, associated with Hathor and the rising sun, also signified rebirth (see chapter 5). It was also the colour of the heart scarab, which represented the heart, seat of the intelligence, conscience and emotions, an association that has continued into modern chakra or energy centre work.

Other references to this colour in ancient Egyptian life include the field of reeds in the afterlife, which was sometimes described as the malachite fields. Horus's wings were also depicted as green.

Red (*desher*))

Red is a mixture of power and danger. This was the colour associated with the desert on either side of the black fertile land, known as Deshret, the Red Land. Even today as you drive along beside the irrigation canals, you will see beyond the strip of fertile land that runs on either side of the canal, that the land suddenly changes from fertile to arid as it becomes the Sahara desert. Red ink was used in writing to indicate someone who was an enemy. In its negative aspect, it was associated with Set, god of evil, chaos and storms, though he was a necessary force in creating balance in the universe.

However, red was not only a colour of danger. It signified victory and was also creative and life-giving in its forms of fire and of blood, especially the menstrual blood of Isis, whose amulet tjet, her girdle (see above) was often in red jasper or carnelian.

Red is also the colour of Hathor, signifying fertility and especially passionate love and deep feelings in a long-term relationship. Mummies of the pharaohs contained a red crystal heart that was placed in the heart cavity in case the actual heart perished or was damaged.

Like gold, red is a solar colour, associated with the rising and setting sun, and so it also represents the sun gods, especially Ra. Kings were regarded as the sons of Ra in Ancient Egypt, and royal statues were also made in golden and red stone to emphasize this solar link.

White (*shesep* and *hedj*)

This was perhaps the earliest colour to be used in Ancient Egypt. It was an important colour in such a hot country, since it reflected the light.

From prehistoric times, white was associated with purity, sanctity and of course ritual and so was the natural colour for priestly and kingly robes. Even the soles of priestly sandals were white

The name of Memphis, a sacred city for thousands of years, translates as 'the city of white walls', because a white wall originally enclosed it. The statues still shimmer white in the sunlight.

White alabaster or calcite was used both in temple construction and for objects used in ritual while the Great Pyramids at Giza were once coated with white limestone to radiate the sun and form a symbol of the Sun-god and life.

Silver, a rare metal and regarded as the substance of the bones of the gods, was also called hedj and was a symbol of lunar light. Silver and gold together symbolized the moon and sun. Isis in her moon aspect and Khonsu the Moon-god often wear white. The lunar Thoth was a white ibis with a black face.

Yellow (*kenit* and *khenet*)

This was another solar colour and a symbol of all that was permanent and could not be destroyed. Gold was Ra's colour and the colour of the flesh of the gods. It was also the colour of pharaohs after death, since it was believed they had become deities, hence the traditional gold funerary masks and coffins. But all of the deities were created in gold to indicate their power and divinity and you can think of the solar lion goddess Sekhmet as golden yellow, a fierce protectress and healer (see page 208).

Working with Colour

There are countless ways you can use colour symbolism in your magical work, as the ancient

Egyptians did. One important method that I have described extensively on pages 61–2 is to use coloured crystals and on them etch or paint a hieroglyph of power (see pages 63–72) as a charm. Alternatively, you could use the crystal as a symbol of a particular power in a spell, for example green malachite for strength, fertility and growth in your life, perhaps after a setback.

You can use colour symbolism in any ritual, whether for power, healing (see chapter 12) or protection. Adapt coloured clay or dough (children's modelling clay comes in many colours and is very pliant) to mould a symbol of an object or a person, or make a circle and on it inscribe a deity name (see pages 199–210) or symbol .

As with the Hathor knot spell, you can use cords of a particular colour to represent your desire or fear, for example deep blue for wisdom or positive power or yellow or gold for the pure energy of the sun and the Sun-god Ra, promising a new beginning at dawn or achievement at noon. You can combine colours, knotting different cords together. Or, as the ancient Egyptians so loved to do, you can work with a profusion of coloured flowers and greenery to signify the qualities and strengths you seek in your life. Finally, you can use the all-purpose white linen, or indeed any white paper, and draw in the appropriate colour e.g. silver for Isis, a deity image or name or words that you will recite or burn in a candle flame to empower. We will use all these methods throughout the book.

Overcoming Chaos

But first, let's put together all the aspects of magic we have met in this chapter in a modern version of the Overcoming of Apep or Apophis. *The Book of Overcoming Apep* was fifteen chapters long and was taken from the funerary papyrus of Nesi-Amsu of Thebes. The book is full of spells, incantations and instructions, for as I mentioned earlier, every night Ra sailed the night solar boat through the duat, the underworld stream, identified in many papyri with the womb of Nut, from west to east. The World Serpent Apep, who represented the forces of Chaos, blocked his emergence. So Ra and the deities, such as Bast and the blessed dead who accompanied him had to fight a nightly battle so that the sun would shine again over the earth and heavens and order be restored. The king's priests and the priests of Ra or Amun would carry out magic and recite the chapters of the book each night to assist this crucial battle, while the deceased was prepared in advance with instructions of what he should say and do.

In the modern world, the image of Apep is a good one to represent our own forces of chaos that threaten to overwhelm us. These might be manifested in a particular problem – such as debt, hostility at work, unhappiness at home, a particular person, or an illness or problem you can't beat such as smoking that you need to give up for health reasons. Sometimes you won't have an Apep in your life, but most of us go though periods when we do feel overwhelmed and need a sun deity or two to help us fight off fears and worries that may keep us awake at night.

I have adapted a little of the basic Apep incantations but if you want to read original translations there are a number online, including one by Sir Wallis Budge in his *Archaeologia* –

hard going, but worth the effort.

If we are to allow Egyptian magic to evolve, it can be helpful to adapt and devise our own rituals, based on versions of the old spells, that do not involve threats – even against those who persecute us with demons; such actions can play havoc with the modern psyche.

A ritual for overcoming the forces of chaos and restore harmony in your life

Egyptian rituals can seem a little like performing a play. The narrative and actions were viewed as the way the power was transferred from the earthly plane to the magical plane where it was amplified by cosmic energies, thus creating the dynamic flash of power that would bring about the desired change.

As I mentioned earlier, the ancient Egyptians spat upon, trampled, stabbed, speared and burned both models of the Chaos snake and, in some spells, models of their enemies. Today we are aware that even justifiable symbolic destruction of enemies is morally wrong and psychologically as well as psychically dangerous since direct bad wishing rebounds on the sender. There are people who argue that those who, for example, harm children should be stopped by any means, but once you start acting as judge and jury you are setting in motion all kinds of destructive emotions. I believe we should focus purely on the bad actions of others and leave the person to their own karma.

You will need red coloured clay or dough to represent the serpent, a cord in this case in red for binding and overcoming the chaos serpent, a green pen and white paper to represent the new life and a yellow pen for the triumph of the Sun and order.

▲ Start by purifying the altar using water and perfume. As with binding and banishing spells, you will be releasing a fair number of personal negative vibes and so the water and perfumed altar will absorb them.

▲ Work just before dawn. You may like to place a Bastet statue or a pottery cat on the altar as extra protection against the symbolic snake, as this goddess traditionally helped to defeat Apep as the serpent wrapped himself round the boat.

▲ First make your clay serpent. For this work you may find it easier to have a white wood or ceramic chopping board, the kind you use for cheese or cutting bread, so that you do not stain the linen on the altar.

▲ Light protective incense, such as lavender or myrrh, and use a stick for easy manoeuvrability.

▲ As you work, name your personal serpent, being careful to name only the bad qualities and fears and not the person causing the problem. Thus, your Apep can represent the overload you may be experiencing at work because of lazy colleagues or at home from inert, unhelpful teenagers, but not the offenders themselves.

▲ Allow negativity or bad habits (your personal Apep who makes you smoke to much for example) to flow from you and feel yourself visibly cleansing and lightening.

▲ At this point, pause to pass the incense stick anti-clockwise around your head and body in spirals, from head to foot, saying:

'Go from me, flow from me, Nile water carry me, leave only harmony.'

▲ Your serpent can be as large or small, as complex or simple as you wish.

▲ Now, in traditional manner, you are going to draw your serpent in green ink on paper, once more naming your chaos or what you wish to bind or lose.

▲ Take your red cord and, rolling your paper, tie the cord round it in four protective knots, one for each of the four protective knot deities often used in anti-chaos rituals of this kind. Say:

'Isis, Sekhmet, Amun and Thoth, bind this Apep snake of Chaos. By Isis, Sekhmet, Amun and Thoth, be bound. Apep, go back to your dark places. Ever, victorious Ra, Ra, Ra, come forth.'

▲ Unroll the scroll and tear it into pieces, burning them in a white metal bucket or large silver-coloured pan half-filled with sand or on a metal tray in which you have placed a yellow or gold candle.

▲ Finally burn the cord, saying:

'Hate turn to love, bitterness to gentleness, sorrow to joy, Ra come forth from the womb of your Mother, triumphant that the day may begin.'

▲ Roll your clay serpent back into a ball, pass the incense over it and say softly:

'Apep, go back to your dark place, to defeat me no more. I turn my face to the morning. I have overcome the enemy of fear.'

▲ Sit and wait for the light to flood in. Then tidy away your altar, disposing of the used ball of clay, which now has lost all power.

▲ Have a shower and shake your fingers and toes, your head and shoulders and if possible try to wear white that day and perhaps carry a Shen (the sun rising over the horizon charm (see page 64).

Remember, the battle against Apep was fought nightly, so if your resolve weakens or the old problems come back, be gentle with yourself. As you become more skilled in magic, so will your compassion grow and you will understand increasingly that spite and malice often come from the unhappiness or emotional ills of the perpetrator. In time you may even wish to add healing of those who hurt you at the end of the ritual, perhaps by blowing out the candle or extinguishing the fire in which you burned the cord and sending light to them – but, as I know, that is not easy.

3

THE MAGICAL POWER OF WORDS

One of the major creation myths tells that Ptah thought the world in his mind and then created it by speaking magical words or *hekau*. This power he used was *heka*, which represents the power equivalent to the life force, as well as the god of that name. This power animates everything, as it did at the first creation. So, to the ancient Egyptians, every act of magic was a recreation of that first act of creation. By using words, both spoken and written, thought could once again be brought into actuality as spells, invocations and ritual prayers, recalling events when the deities manifested the powers sought by the magician. Indeed by recalling a mythical event ritually and speaking as though you were one of the deities involved, you could bring the same power into yourself. It was also a way to symbolically animate wax or clay images (see the crocodile story below). In modern terms we can call this awakening the deity power within you.

Horus was the god of scorpions or crocodiles and so may be invoked to help us deal with the symbolic crocodiles and scorpions in our lives. We are not summoning up spirits when we say, 'I, Horus, drive you crocodile (of fear) back into the water never to return', but focusing archetypal or idealized parts of our potential and higher nature.

The spoken and written word were also important for redressing the balance when chaos threatened to overwhelm order. Some of the gods and goddesses were particularly associated with magical power: Isis, Mistress of Enchantment, Sekhmet and Ra, the Sun-god.

The power of names

While every word contained power, the name of a person was considered to be especially magical. The name of a child was chosen with great care to reflect those qualities desired in the child. Sometimes a compound name would contain a deity name, indicating that the child was under the protection of the deity. The name was also important because it would appear on tombs and so be used for eternity in the land of the blessed. The prefix Nefer – as in Nefertiti, the beautiful wife of Akhenaten – was the hieroglyph for beauty and harmony. The nefer was probably an oud, the forerunner of the lute that is still played in Egypt today. Some Coptic Christian tunes are said to be descendants of music played to the pharaohs. Tutankhamun's name contained the words 'ankh', the hieroglyph and symbol of eternal life, and 'Amun', the name of the supreme creator god. 'Tut' is also a form of Thoth, and its inclusion in the name was thought to add the wisdom of this senior god of knowledge to the young pharaoh. Originally, his name was Tut ankh aten, named after the sun deity worshipped by his predecessor, but whose power was swiftly eradicated (see pages 73–4). Kings, scribes and nobles were blessed with the name Amenhotep, which means 'Amen' or 'Amun is at peace'. Kings and pharaohs had nomen' or coronation names, which added weight to their claim to sovereignty, usually by claiming kinship to a deity. So Queen Hatshepsut's coronation name was Maat- ka- Ra, taking on the rank of the ka or soul of Ra, and of the authority of Ma'at the goddess of truth and wisdom. The former identified her as a manifestation of the Sun-god himself and thus increased her legitimacy to rule in her stepson's place.

The Ren

So important was the name that it was given a special separate title as part of the components of the essential person and was included in funerary texts, originally on the coffin and later on tomb walls and funerary papyri.

Of course, the power of names could also be a terrible weapon since it was believed that every part of the body, soul and spirit was interdependent and so to erase a name from a tomb was to destroy the spirit in the afterlife.

For example, Thutmes or Thutmoses III, the son of Thutmoses II and a concubine, was proclaimed pharaoh on the death of his father in 1478 BCE. However, the widow of the king, Hatshepsut, became regent for the young king and reigned as pharaoh herself for 29 years. She effectively excluded him from power. On her death, Thutmoses III had his revenge by disfiguring her statues and deleting her name from all her monuments. Those whose names were not spoken at the offerings table in mortuary chapels or shrines by relations would, it was believed, cease to be in the afterlife and so a prayer was often set over the shrine so that passers-by might also recite it.

In life, too, inscribing the name of an enemy on a pot or wax image and then destroying it was believed to destroy the living person. This is not to be recommended, though you can – as I mentioned in the last chapter – write the name of a sorrow or fear or threat and destroy that.

Secret names

In Ancient Egypt, it was said that if you knew someone's secret name, you would have power over them. This belief persisted in magic right through to the occult societies of the early twentieth century. Deities had five secret names, which were associated with the elements, the heavenly stars and planets and particular strengths or qualities.

Magicians, too, would have a secret name by which they addressed themselves in magic, though they would not write it down.

The power of the secret name is demonstrated in a myth that tells of how Isis won her great magical power by tricking the Sun-god Ra into revealing his secret names to her. When the god was old, she secretly collected some of his spittle and fashioned it into a serpent that she left in his path to bite him. The bite left him in intense agony and he called upon the other gods to cure him. But because the serpent had been created from Ra's own substance, none of the other deities could relieve his pain. Isis said that she could cure him if he would reveal his secret names to her. At first he tried to give her false names, but she persisted and as his agony grew worse, he agreed. Isis cured him, but because she knew his secret names, she gained all his magical knowledge.

Some authorities say the myth was created by the Romans to discredit Isis, as they had become so worried about the popularity of Isis. We know she was a powerful magician in her own right. One myth tells of how she threatened to stop the sun's course when her infant son was stung by scorpions; none would aid her until at last the magician supreme, Thoth, healed him. She also cured headaches suffered by Ra and Thoth (see page 154).

Creating power names

You may like to create your own five power names that describe the person you would like to be. You may choose the name of a deity whose qualities you admire, the name of an animal or a star, or you may describe your own potential strengths in a different way.

For example, you might say:

'I am the lotus flower that opens at dawn to welcome the sun. I am Nut, woman covered all in stars. I am she who never turns from a challenge or danger. I am Sothis, star who heralds in the fertile flood with my radiance. I am the wise cobra who stands guard over her young and those in need, she who stings and can cure the most fearsome bite.'

If you need inspiration read the deity lists on pages 199–210.

Write your secret names in blue ink on white paper, recite them when you are alone, and when you have learned them, burn the paper in a blue candle in a bucket of sand. You are not destroying your name, because you can recite it as it burns and say:

'May my names live as long as the sun endures and the waters flow.'

You can recite your power names at the beginning of every ritual, at dawn when you greet the sun and at twilight. You can also whisper or say the names in your mind whenever you need courage.

Protective and empowering force of words

A prayer to Nut from the pyramid of Pepi 1 in Saqqara, dated around 2260 BCE, says:

The Sky-goddess, your mother, spreads herself above you.
She hides you from all evil.
The Sky-goddess protects you from all evil.

These and similar prayers and chants were meant to be recited to activate the inherent power and protection in nature and of the deity form invoked. Not only priests and priestesses used words as conductors of cosmic energies. Mothers recited them over infants' cradles or over the beds of sick relations or sisters in labour, invoking the appropriate deities. Men used them as house blessings and to keep illness and misfortune from the home. Kings and soldiers used them to keep enemies at bay, speaking words of power over model soldiers and boats to animate them and repel threatened invasion. Alexander the Great used this tactic to fill him with the confidence to conquer much of the known world.

Prayers and mantras or chants have continued in other religions but few faiths or cultures endowed their prayers with the emphasis that when the word was spoken so the Sky Mother actually enfolded her wings round the home. If this seems strange, think of it in modern terms as your own inner power store or protective instincts being strengthened by being plugged into cosmic powers.

There is great debate over exactly how words of power were spoken, because we do not know how the ancient Egyptians actually spoke their language. The pronunciations that experts give us are, at best, informed guesses. However, a modern Egyptian I met who had trained as an Egyptologist told me that he believed the invocations were spoken confidently and slowly with even pace and emphasis on each syllable of the word, rather than increasing in speed and intensity rising to a climax of power, as is the case with much modern magic.

Using words to animate a symbol

Let's look at this power in terms of an Egyptian story that may, of course, in itself be symbolic. There are many versions of this story, but this the one I like. It originally came from the Westcar Papyrus (papyri are named after the donors who present them to a collection or the original discoverers. The papyrus is dated from the Second Intermediate Period, about 1500 BCE), which can be seen in Berlin Museum. However, the story itself is probably much older and dates from the Fourth Dynasty, about 3830 BCE. This is a kind of Arabian nights format in which Prince Khafra, whose pyramid may be seen at Giza, was telling his father King Khufu a story. (We know Khufu as Cheops, although this is the Greek version of his name.) A magician – or in some versions, a Grand Vizier – called Ba-aner had a beautiful wife. But she was faithless and would meet her lover, one of King Nebka's soldiers, in a hut near the ornamental lake. (Nebka was a Third Dynasty king who may have been the intended owner of the unfinished pyramid at Saqqara.) The husband discovered that his wife's lover bathed in the lake at sunset after love-making. So he took wax from a special ebony box and fashioned a model crocodile seven handspans long and spoke magical words over it. These words would bring the crocodile model to life when it was cast into the lake. Then it could be commanded in the name of Sobek, the crocodile god, to seize the young man.

The magician's chief servant took the crocodile to the lake and, seeing the youth swimming, cast the crocodile into the water, repeating the magical words and calling: 'I Sobek command you seize the prey.' The crocodile came to life and grew to seven cubits (about 3.5 m or 12 feet) long. It seized the young man in its mighty jaws and dragged his helpless body to the bottom of the lake. There the youth could not breathe, yet was unable to die.

On the seventh day, the magician told King Nebka of events and they went down to the lake where the magician called: 'I, Sobek, command thee, return thy prey and resume thy sleeping form.'

Sobek

The crocodile rose from the depths, carrying the youth, dropped him before the King and magician, then returned to his waxen form. The king, having seen this marvel, decided to grant the adulterous youth no mercy, and he commanded the magician to repeat the words of power and the crocodile carried the youth back to the depths of the lake, never to return.

The boatmen of the Nile were unable to animate crocodile figures – perhaps a good thing, as there might have been some very unpleasant score-settling – but they would carry out a ritual in which a ball of clay was cast into the Nile while they demanded in the name of Sobek that no harmful water creatures might come near. Folk custom continued this rite long after the old gods were gone.

Modern rituals of power and protection

Obviously you can't go around literally animating model crocodiles or scorpions against your enemies, tempting though it may be. But just as in the last chapter I suggested ways of using images for power and protection, so you can – for positive purposes – psychically animate any statue, or your home-made images, or even a written declaration in either hieroglyphs (see Chapter 4) or your own script that you then recite.

In this way you can set a crocodile against seemingly impossible odds in your life or ask a lion to help you develop your leadership qualities (see also section on animal magic). You could also fashion a heart to give you courage, a scarab for renewing hope, or a feather like the one on the head-dress of Ma'at, symbol of truth and justice to help you fight against injustice. You can ask for the powers of these animals and objects to be magically awakened in your words; you are limited only by the scope of your imagination.

As I mentioned earlier, magicians, like the one in the story, did assume the authority of a deity. While you should not literally believe that you have turned into Horus by saying: 'I am Horus', you can summon up the almost limitless power of the Sky-god to soar as a falcon above any obstacles, or call on the regenerative power of Osiris when you are weary, by saying:

'I, Osiris, awake, renewed, refreshed and reborn and like the green corn will spring to life. I am Osiris and I command and it shall be.'

A fierce god like Sobek offered very strong protection against attack in all forms – and not only on water (see page 208). It works wonders when the office dragon or the in-law from hell is bearing down on you if you can recite silently over a crocodile drawn on a crystal, or even visualized:

'I Sobek outface thee. With my mighty jaws, swift slashing tail and my razor claws I fear none, mortal or immortal. Yet shall I not attack thee. Slide back into the Nile slime and hide thy face in shame.'

The Seven Arrows of Sekhmet

Let's use the example of my own favourite, the lion-headed solar goddess Sekhmet, who both healed and destroyed wrongdoers and injustice. You can adapt this spell and method for any need, using the appropriate deity. The seven arrows of Sekhmet were one of the weapons the goddess sent out against her enemies and they make a wonderful protective device against any form of hostility. They can also be used to restore fortune after a setback. I have used them to effect with my youngest son as a way of overcoming his fear of playground bullies and also for an unfair dismissal from a job for another family member. But let's focus on a different example: the need to find a job when work is short in your area, as a result of which you or a partner may have become dispirited.

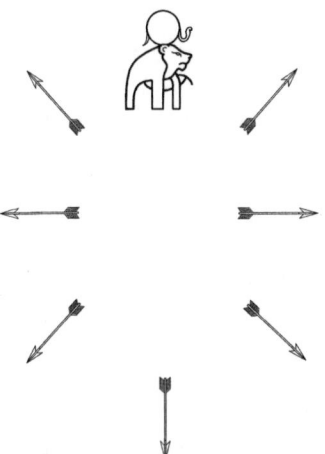

The Seven Arrows of Sekhmet

A Sekhmet employment spell

▲ Draw your seven arrows, tips facing outwards in red ink on white paper and within the circle write your empowerment. If, for example, you have lost your job and are having trouble finding another one, you might write:

'*I, Sekhmet, send forth these arrows against the misfortunes that have befallen me/my child/my partner. May they aim true and return victorious that right order may be restored. Sekhmet, Sekhmet, Sekhmet, Sekhmet, Sekhmet, Sekhmet, Sekhmet, arrows swift send out and swift return.*'

▲ If you have access to a bow and arrow, you could pin your drawing to the centre of a target and shoot seven real arrows at it, while chanting the words.

▲ You can fold the paper and carry it with you when you visit the local employment centre, or to an interview. Repeat the empowerment softly but clearly before entering. You can adapt the same approach for any other need where earthly efforts seem blocked or injustice has been done, remembering to send the words against wrong actions or words and not the perpetrator.

4

HIEROGLYPHICS AND MAGIC

To an ancient Egyptian, the fact that you are sitting here reading this book would mean that you were already a great magician. For writing was considered such a magical art that the sons of princes were proud to be trained as great scribes. The written word was the cement that held the empire together for thousands of years as scribes handled the huge and unwieldy bureaucracy of collecting taxes, paying the army and sending the decrees of the pharaohs the length of the mighty Nile.

One ancient text I saw in the Cairo Museum next to a statue of a scribe sitting with his palette says:

'You came endowed with great mystery. You are expert beyond your colleagues. The wisdom of your books is engraved on your heart. Your language is precious. A sentence from your mouth weighs more than three pounds.'

The scribe's painted limestone statue was found at Saqqara in the excavations of 1893 in the Old Kingdom and dates from the beginning of the Fifth Dynasty, in around 2475 BCE.

On a similarly dated statue the following line was written:

'As a scribe I am more profound than the Sky, the Earth and the Other World.'

Of course, scribes wrote these words, so we do have to allow for a little bias. But there is plenty of other evidence to demonstrate the awe with which the written word was regarded in Ancient Egypt. We find spells that were written on papyrus and worn in bags around the neck as amulets to ward off every evil, from colds to scorpion stings or invading armies.

The Egyptians themselves called hieroglyphs *medu netcher* – 'the words of the gods' or 'divine words'. Indeed, the Egyptians believed that the system had been developed by the god Thoth to preserve the words of Ra and to write down his own magical secrets. In fact, the ancient Egyptian phrase for writing means 'God's words', emphasizing the association between script and the power of the gods. Hieroglyphs contained not only meaning but were themselves repositories of the power they represented. For example, the ankh (see pages 63 and 64) is the symbol of the union of Isis and her husband Osiris. People would leave small bronze representations of them at temples to ask for favour, in this case for a fruitful marriage.

The ancient Egyptians were so impressed with the power of writing that they feared that words could literally jump off the page at them. The British Museum holds a funerary papyrus in which the name of Ra's serpent enemy is written in red ink. The final hieroglyph that makes up the name is struck through with knives to stop it harming the deceased.

The transcriber of the sound and words of the gods was the scribe par excellence Thoth, whom some myths say was present at creation and spoke the words of power that brought the world into being. Thoth is pictured as a man with an ibis head or as a baboon; baboons are very active at dawn and because of this the ancient Egyptians believed the animals were paying homage to Ra and were therefore sacred). Often Thoth is portrayed with a palette, a water jar, a reed pen and papyrus to take down the words of Ra or to record his own magical formulas.

It is well beyond the scope of this book to teach you to read and write hieroglyphics fluently – indeed, you may not have the time to study such a difficult subject. But because hieroglyphics are such an important part of Egyptian magic, I am including this rough guide. If you wish to study the subject further, a list of very useful reading can be found at the end of this book.

Working with hieroglyphics

Hieroglyphics began as simple pictures, which linguists call ideograms.

For example, this simple picture represented a mouth.

And this picture represented water.

But the scribes soon discovered that although you can say a lot with simple pictures, they are limited if you want to express more complex ideas – for example, spelling out a king's name or the name of a foreigner. What they needed was an alphabet like ours. They moved towards this goal by taking some of the more common ideograms and giving them character values. For example, their word for mouth was something like Re (we can't be sure because the ancient Egyptians, for reasons of their own, decided that they didn't need to bother to write down vowel sounds, so our Egyptian vowels are based on guesswork). The scribes decided that the ideogram would have the value of its first letter, so in the hieroglyphic alphabet, this figure stands for R.

The water ideogram had the value of N. So putting these hieroglyphics together formed the Egyptian word Ren, which means name.

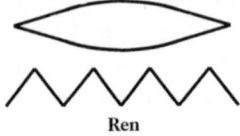

Ren

Hieroglyphics were assigned values for single consonants, as the table on page 50 shows. Some of the letters do not have equivalent sounds in English so this table is an approximation. There are other single consonant hieroglyphics, but I have left them out because they are for sound values that we do not have in English. You will notice that there are two extra characters – for the Sh sound, as in Sharon or Charlotte, and Ch, as in Charles or Cherry. The other peculiarity is that there are no vowels apart from an A and I. Although some books offer approximations of vowel sounds, the truth is that the scribes did not bother with vowels, using what is the equivalent of our speedwriting. So a sentence such as, 'What shall we do with the drunken sailor', would be written as 'Wht shll w d wth th drnkn slr'. Modern Arabic script is equally dismissive of vowels.

To add to the confusion, the scribes did not put spaces between words and put the hieroglyphics in combinations that looked attractive to them. It's no wonder that the secret of reading this script was lost for 2,000 years.

If you get no further with the study of hieroglyphics you can use the chart on page 50 to write your name or a rough phonetic equivalent. While in Cairo I bought my daughter Miranda a charm pendant as a souvenir and I was able to have her name put on it in hieroglyphics. This came out as Mrnd:

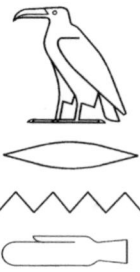

I have deliberately written the name vertically because that is how it appears on Miranda's long pendant and, conveniently, hieroglyphics can be stacked in this fashion. The rule in this example is that you read from top to bottom.

Hieroglyphics can also be read from left to right or right to left. One theory to explain this is that right-handed scribes using a reed pen found it easier to write as we do, dragging the pen across the paper from left to right. But right-handed masons, using a hammer and chisel to carve inscriptions on stone walls, found it more convenient to work from right to left. So how can you tell which way to read? The answer is to look for faces, see which way they are looking and read towards them. Take my name Cassandra, for example, which can be written

I have deliberately included the A sounds here to show the bird faces. They face left, so begin reading from the left.

But this version is equally valid:

This time, read towards the faces from right to left. Also note another change here. This time the N glyph has been put on top of the D glyph. Scribes would often stack small hieroglyphs in this way for neatness. When you come across a pile like this that you read from top to bottom.

To the ancient Egyptians, the simple act of writing their names in hieroglyphics was an empowering event. Try transcribing your own name and the names of friends and family into hieroglyphics using the chart. Don't worry about vowels. As I have said, my name could be written as Cssndr.

So Mark would become Mrk and Jennifer Jnfr. Think phonetically: the C in the chart is a hard C and can be used to write Kate or Karen. For Celia, use the S symbol. For Victor or Valerie, as there's no V, use an F. For X, use C and S. Experiment with writing from left to right, right to left or vertically and with stacking the hieroglyphics until you find a shape that is pleasing, just as the ancient scribes did. Usually names were enclosed in a frame, which is called a cartouche.

They could also be vertical.

There are many other types of hieroglyphics. One group represents two consonants: ankh, for example, represents N and Kh. Another type of hieroglyphic is the determinative, which is a 'silent letter' that helps to tell us what the word means. Imagine that you were writing to a friend using a vowel-less alphabet and wanted to tell him that you had gone down to the beach to buy a ht. How would he know whether you had bought a hat or a hut? One way to let him know would be to add the determinative. So if you wrote:

the picture of the hat would make certain there was no mistake while the picture of the house would tell him you'd bought a hut. However, if you wrote:

then the picture of the sun would indicate that the letters HT stood for hot or heat.

Two common determinatives are these:

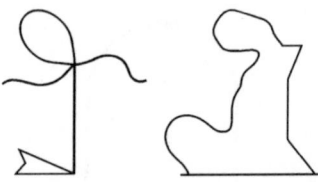

They stand for man and woman respectively and were often added to the end of a name to indicate the sex. When my *Handbook Of Ancient Wisdom* was translated into Czechoslovakian, I was surprised to find that my name had been translated as well, into Cassandra Easonova. A

Czechoslovakian friend told me that the *ova* was added so that people would know I was a female writer.

You might want to put such a hieroglyphic after a 'unisex' name such as Kim or Robin.

Once you are happy with your name, try writing a wish or an intention. You may decide to write it first in English, omitting the vowels until you become more practised.

Because hieroglyphics were considered magical and each letter has an associated object or animal you can, if you wish, create your own magical associations. I have suggested a few, based on ancient Egyptian ideas. While most of the alphabet letters are not strictly power words, making associations may help to strengthen their potency for you.

A is the vulture, a power amulet representing the protective power of Isis the divine mother, in death as well as life. Therefore it is a symbol of protection from a powerful external force.

B is the leg, which you could associate with swiftness of purpose.

C or K, the basket, is not a power word, but could be given a meaning of sustenance or gift. The alternative, the stair, could be a symbol of ambition or the desire for elevation in the worldly sense.

D is the hand – again, not a power amulet, although the hieroglyphic for two fingers is, representing Horus or Thoth in some versions helping his father Osiris up the ladder to heaven. By association you could therefore regard the hand as an instrument of help.

F, also V the Viper, unlike the snake, is not an amulet of power, but could nevertheless be regarded as swift, sharp defensive action, for the viper only stings humans if under attack.

G the Stand is also not a power word. A different hieroglyphic, the pillow, had the sacred power meaning of uplifting and so by indirect association the stand could be interpreted as lifting up or supporting someone in time of need.

H, the courtyard or quarter of a city, is not a power word, but could be regarded as the strength of hearth and home.

I and also Y, the single and double reeds respectively, were used to make papyrus for recording wisdom and so could be perhaps regarded as a symbol of knowledge and learning.

J, the serpent Buto or Uadjet, was regarded as the Snake-goddess and a serpent's head amulet was placed on dead bodies to prevent snakebite in the afterlife. A serpent rod was also used to open the mouth to free the soul, so again – by association – the serpent is a symbol of freedom.

L, the lion has for the modern world such an association with courage and nobility that this would be an obvious meaning. Plutarch reports that the lion was worshipped by the Egyptians, who decorated their doorways with open lion mouths as guardians to represent the rising of the Nile because the river began to rise when the sun was in Leo.

M, the owl, has traditionally been associated with wisdom, but is also a bird of warning, so the meaning might be to listen to your own inner warnings and wisdom.

N, water, is associated with the life-giving fertility of the Nile and so could legitimately be regarded as fertility.

P, the stool, could be seen as a respite, a resting place, and so might suggest temporary sanctuary.

Q is the hill – the primal mound. This could suggest a higher or different viewpoint.

R, the mouth, was vital after death so that the deceased person might utter the words of power that would enable him or her entry to the next world. Hence the ceremony of opening the mouth symbolically was so important after death. The mouth could, therefore, represent the power to communicate clearly.

S (which can also be used as a soft C, as in Celia) was the first letter of the word Seneb, which means health and was often used on its own in inscriptions for the whole word.

T, loaf, regarded in all ancient societies as the staff of life, could represent the possession of basic needs.

W, the chick, a symbol of young life, could be seen as innocence, enthusiasm and new beginnings.

In the next chapter, which deals with amulets and charms, we will work specifically with the true power hieroglyphics and use them in a system of divination for increasing their powers in your life.

Spells were often written in Hieratic, the cursive form of writing. Some of the scripts that survive today have been dated back to the Sixth Dynasty, but may be much older. As magic became more popular, spells were increasingly written in demotic script that began around the 25th Dynasty, about 900 BCE.

5

AMULET AND CHARM MAGIC

The Ancient Egyptians were the first to use amulets and charms in formal magic. They empowered symbols with magical words and substances such as incense, in order to carry with them power and protection that was regularly invoked from the cradle to the grave and then into the afterlife. This concept is just an extension of the word and image magic we have been working with in the previous three chapters.

In the previous chapters we created and empowered images of wax and clay and used them with spoken words of power in rituals. Then we learned the power of the hieroglyphic language and how by writing in it we could call different powers.

The next stage is to put together this knowledge to create more permanent symbols of power, healing and protection so that we can tap into the energies for a more sustained period when we cannot or would not want to carry out a ritual. Healing can be released over days, weeks or even months.

But amulets and charms are so much more than a slow-working spell. The more we use and carry them, the more powerful they become. For example, when we create or buy a prosperity or good luck charm, the charm becomes a giant psychic snowball. This is true whether it takes the form of one of the recognized magical hieroglyphs etched in wax, crystal, stone or on paper, or the image of a deity or animal energy made out of wood or crystal, or simply by writing our name on a crystal or wax as a statement that we exist and can make our own destiny. Whatever form it takes, the charm attracts extra luck or love.

So as well as using the specifically ancient Egyptian methods to create charms that I suggest in this chapter, you can also buy a tiny crystal, metal, pottery or wooden animal or make an animal or deity from wood or clay, or by drawing on crystal. Then you empower it and carry it, sleep with it or hide it in a secret place only you know and let the magic flow.

The power of amulets

There was a fundamental belief in Ancient Egypt that a statue or any image of a deity or one of its animal representations (see chapter 10), if magically charged and purified, could be a receptacle for part of the soul, or ka, of the deity. Wearing or carrying a tiny statue or picture of a deity or animal or a hieroglyphic, endowed the owner with some aspect, qualities or strengths of the divine power that was believed to dwell within the charged charm.

The power would last as long as the amulet, if the wearer remained pure of intent and kept the amulet magically cleansed. For this reason, durable materials such as crystals, gems and metals were used for charms and many have survived intact for thousands of years.

In the modern world, some people might find it disconcerting to walk round wearing – for example – a crystal on which was painted a vulture that represented the indwelling protective goddess Isis or the winged vulture goddess Nekhbet. But if we return to the concept of the divine or evolved soul within us all and think, as I have said before, of the deities as archetypes or idealized personifications of our very finest potential qualities, the idea is not at all alien. Indeed, if you make your own amulets you can empower them with your emotions and essential self.

The origin of amulets

It is most likely that amulets began as protection against very real dangers, such as serpents, scorpions, illness and situations in which people were vulnerable, for example during childbirth. The first amulets were models of animals. For example, the female hippopotamus, a creature of fierce maternal qualities, was often made into an amulet of blue glazed faience. Such amulets have been found dating from the later fourth millennium BCE, indicating that Tauret the hippopotamus goddess was an early goddess. Gradually these early amulets were replaced by the more complex statues of Tauret, with a hippopotamus head, a crocodile tail and a swollen belly, accompanied by Bes, the dancing dwarf god, who wore fierce expressions and wielded protective knives. These were used in the birthing room to protect the mother to be. She would also have with her a magical wand (see pages 13–14) in a boomerang shape engraved with protective deities and creatures.

Bes, the lion-headed dwarf

Early amulets date back before written records and it is likely that these were originally made of animal bones or tusks. Other less durable amulets for healing or short-term protection were made of herbs in a linen bag with a knotted cord. They would have been under the protection of the sisters Isis and Nephthys, who in legend wove the first linen, and the knotted cord was sacred to the weaver goddess Neith (see also page 206).

The Flinders Petrie Museum in London houses prehistoric figures of animals in stone, ivory and clay. Some of these were originally intended to be worn, for example a bone hair pin with an antelope on top and another with a bird on the pin head and a tiny ivory crocodile.

Development of amulets

By the Late Period, amulets were being created with quite complex symbolism. Items from this period include Thoth in the form of a bronze crouching baboon with a moon disc, a bronze striding ibis resting on the feather of Ma'at and a bronze figure of Bastet, in her cat-headed form holding a ritual sistrum. The Ashmolean Museum in Oxford has a comprehensive collection of cat mummies and Bast figures.

Gradually amulets were developed for many purposes – such as luck, money and love – and less elevated people began to learn or create folk magic spells and rituals to empower them.

Amulet power

Originally, amulets were not inscribed. Instead, words of power were spoken over them, whether the amulet was intended to protect the living or the deceased.

Gradually, amulets were engraved with spells to become tablets (often rectangular) featuring an image of the deity or power animal and the words of power. This made them even more potent, if less portable.

Those portraying a deity placed the wearer under their protection while charms in the shape of those of the pharaoh's sceptre, or even a pharonic head, had similar protective function. Some amulets were made in the shape of parts of the body – for example, a phallus to bring fertility. Another popular charm was a miniature leg or foot to prevent mobility problems. In death body part amulets were placed on the appropriate part of the mummy, for example a crystal or faience foot charm on the foot of the deceased so that he or she might move swiftly in the afterlife.

Colour was also significant for amulets (see pages 33–7).

Amulets and the afterlife

It was natural that even in simple early burials in huge pots during predynastic times, the deceased might be adorned or surrounded by the amulets he or she wore and loved in life, in the hope they would offer protection in the next world. Indeed, green schist (stone) animal amulets – especially scarab beetles, symbols of rebirth – were placed upon the breast of the deceased in these early graves, even before the practice of leaving elaborate grave goods with the body began.

Over time, as the ancient Egyptians' belief in the afterlife became more complex, amulets began to be regarded as having the power to protect not only the mummified body from corruption, but to guide and protect the deceased's spirit through the perils of the afterlife. Eventually, a crystal or gem amulet became assigned to protect each part of the body and in the most elaborate burials more than a hundred amulets might be placed between the different layers of linen during the mummification process.

Making amulets

Below, I describe a method of making wax amulets and for drawing amulets on parchment or white paper. As I suggested earlier, you can also craft animal forms from wood, or from clay which is then baked, or you can carry a bag of amulet herbs and spices with you in a white linen drawstring bag (see pages 160–1).

Once you have created your amulet, you need to endow it with power and protection. Strictly speaking, charged amulets are called talismans, but in practice the terms amulet, charm and talismans are interchangeable. Traditionally, an amulet acts to repel danger but does not attract power or good fortune until it is charged.

▲ Work on the night of the full moon to empower a charm, most magically just before sunset when you will see the moon and sun in the sky at the same time.

▲ Protective amulets of all kinds are traditionally made just after the full moon, as when it begins to wane it endows them with maximum protection.

▲ Any time after dusk is good for creating protective amulets. After you have dedicated them they can then be left on a window ledge or in a sheltered place outdoors until after dawn to absorb the rising energies of the early morning.

▲ The most powerful time of all is the evening before the summer solstice, as the amulet can then be left in a sheltered place to receive the dawn energies of the most powerful solar day of the year.

Hieroglyphic amulets

By far the most numerous amulets in the ancient Egyptian world were those representing a particular hieroglyphic, both for the living and the dead. These were engraved on crystals, gems or precious metals, or the symbols were made of faience or glass. For ordinary people who could not read the meaning of the hieroglyphic the magic was doubly powerful.

Drawing hieroglyphic amulets

Somewhere between the 11th to 22nd dynasties, the written amulet became increasingly popular, whether represented by a spell or an actual hieroglyphic. Traditionally these word charms were written on papyrus and if you visit Egypt and find a genuine papyrus store, you can still persuade the resident artist to create you a tiny papyrus featuring your name or a power word in hieroglyphic script, which you can wear in a thin gold tube or locket around your neck. Gold was the metal that represented immortality and eternity.

But you can just as easily draw your own hieroglyphic charms on parchment or good quality white or dark paper with fine coloured ink pens, paints and brushes – or, if you are very skilled, with a special scribe papyrus quill. You can follow the amulet colours listed on pages 63-71 or use your imagination, keeping to the six main colours used in Egypt (see pages 33–6). You can use a small white linen neck purse or carry your home-made hieroglyphic charm in a bag or pocket.

You can also create a hieroglyphic charm for a lover, a family member or a new-born baby.

You could write the name of the person in hieroglyphics (see previous chapter) and add one or two of the hieroglyphics of power listed below.

Making a wax amulet

On page 28 we created wax images as a focus for magic and then animated them to draw power and protection into ourselves.

You can use wax to create an amulet to release magical energies over a specific period (until the wax crumbles) and, like any amulet, over the days and weeks it increases in power. Wax amulets were very popular in Ancient Egypt, as although they did not last as long as crystal or stone, they are excellent for a short-term need where power must be concentrated. This is still true today, because you melt the power or protection into the creation process and so it is truly absorbed.

For example, there was an old spell in Ancient Egypt that involved melting wax while reciting the name of the desired person and saying:

'As the wax melts, so may her heart be molten to me.'

There were some nastier love spells involving figures with their hands tied behind their back or iron nails piercing the image, concepts that continued right up until the 19th century in Europe and Scandinavia and emigrants from those lands (and still exist among dark practitioners today). But if you love someone, you are not going to hurt their image – and certainly not in the name of love.

The ancient Egyptians did use beeswax when making their amulets. You may wish to seek some beeswax out at a craft store or through the Internet in naturally dyed colours as it is so fragrant and such a pleasure to work with.

There is no reason why you should not take advantage of the truly wonderful profusion of colours of modern candles available, though you may wish to retain some tradition by using only the six Egyptian colours: white, black, blue, green, yellow and red. Some people do not like black, in spite of the very positive Egyptian associations of the colour with fertility and rebirth.

Wax amulets are especially potent because they have been created from the four ancient elements: Earth – the candle itself; Air as the smoke rises; Fire – the flame; and Water – the melting wax. The union is said to create a fifth element, which is captured in the wax tablet.

Creating a personalized wax amulet

Once more, you are limited only by your imagination. You can create an animal shape by cutting it out of the wax (see page 28) or draw a circle and create a representation in it of a deity, or an animal. Alternatively, you might choose to create an image in the circle of wax of what you would like the amulet to bring you, for example an image of a baby or a lover. Using the hieroglyphic alphabet on page 50, you could even write your name, a word of power or the appropriate hieroglyphic for the strength you need (see pages 63-71) on the molten wax. You can create additional power and protection by endowing the amulet with a secret word of power or an adaptation of a deity name, for example, *Isis hidden in the marshes* – a reminder of the protective power the goddess showed to her infant son by concealing him in papyrus marshes from his murderous uncle Set, that you may want to invoke to hide you from potential hostility or confrontation. You never write this word down except in smoke and say it only in your mind. It is like the hidden files on a computer, there for back up.

▲ Set a small squat coloured candle directly on a fireproof tray rather than in a holder – secure it by dropping melted wax from the candle on to the tray.

▲ You can create circular amulets in a cake tray with a number of separate deep compartments, the kind you use for making small pies or cakes. Stand different coloured candles in the individual cake cups so you create a pool of wax. You can make several different amulets at once in this pool, perhaps one for each family member.

▲ Light the candle and state the purpose of the amulet, naming any deity who seems appropriate to the need, for example Osiris for any form of regeneration or rebirth after difficulty.

▲ Repeat in your mind – nine times – the secret words of power and protection or secret personalized deity name with which you will endow your amulet. It need not be the same deity to which you are openly dedicating the amulet.

▲ As the wax forms, light an incense stick in sandalwood or frankincense and write in smoke over the amulet in your normal script the secret words of protection and power.

▲ While the wax is still soft, mark out a circle or square and within it write the hieroglyphics with which you wish to endow it or draw the deity symbol using a small screwdriver, a paper knife or a metal nail.

▲ Then visualize the secret words burned into the wax or write them in incense smoke just over the surface without making an imprint.

▲ When the wax is set, ease it from the tray with a wooden spatula or, very gently, with a knife.

Dedicating amulets

You can use this method for dedicating any kind of amulet, whether bought or made. If a spell is urgent, you can also use this method for empowering an image you wish to animate (see page 28).

▲ Set your amulet on a fresh white cloth on the altar and enclose it with a square of white or beeswax candles at the four main directional points. These were traditionally dedicated to the four deities who guard the doors of the four winds: the south to Ra or Re, the Sun-god; the west to Isis, goddess of motherhood, women, and magic; north to Osiris, god of the vegetation and the underworld who ensured the continuing cycles of existence; and the east to Nephthys, sister of Isis and protective goddess, especially of the dead.

▲ Light the candles beginning in the south and proceed clockwise to each direction working clockwise – or sunwise, as it is called in magic.

▲ As you light each candle greet the directional deity saying:

'I purify this altar and this amulet with fire. May only goodness and light enter within this barrier of flame. I greet thee Ra/Isis/Osiris/Nephthys and ask thy protection and thy power.'

▲ Hold the last candle you lit over the amulet and name the purpose of the amulet, repeating in your heart the secret words.

▲ Beginning next in the west, take a small dish of perfume, such as lavender or rose water and proceed clockwise. Sprinkle a little perfume water at each direction point, saying:

'I purify this altar and this amulet with the fragrance. May only goodness and light enter within this barrier of fragrance. I greet thee Ra/Isis/Osiris/Nephthys.'

Scatter a few drops of perfume over the amulet; repeat the purpose of the amulet and then the secret words in your head.

▲ Take a tiny dish of either salt or white petals (you can also use pot pourri).

▲ Beginning in the north, scatter a few petals at each of the main directions, saying:

'I purify this altar and this amulet with this earth. May only goodness and light enter within this barrier of earth. I greet thee Ra/Isis/Osiris/Nephthys.'

▲ Scatter a few petals round the amulet; repeat its purpose and then the secret words in your head.

▲ Finally beginning in the east, light a frankincense or sandalwood incense stick and purify the four directions, saying:

'I purify this altar and this amulet with this smoke. May only goodness and light enter within this barrier of Air. I greet thee, Ra/Isis/Osiris/Nephthys.'

▲ Pass the incense over the amulet and name its purpose and deity focus, silently speaking the secret power words.

▲ Finally, leave the amulet, preferably outdoors in a sheltered place on a square of white linen to be empowered further by the dawn rays, especially during the period of the waxing moon.

▲ You can recharge your amulet weekly, or whenever it has been used a lot, by setting it on the altar after sunset on clean white linen. Beginning with the south, pass a candle, then scatter perfume, then petals and finally incense smoke over the amulet, rededicating by restating its purpose and finally saying in your head the secret words. Again, leave it in the open air until dawn if possible.

Hieroglyphic amulets for power, protection and divination

On page 64 are some of the most powerful hieroglyphics that came to have significance in the afterlife as well as in the world of the living. Because of this they took on the meaning of eternal life and immortality and were considered particularly lucky as charms.

I would suggest you make yourself a complete set by painting each hieroglyphic on an appropriately coloured crystal or stone (see pages 63–72). It's worth experimenting with different ways of making the marks: you might try special acrylic paint that will not rub off, or waterproof pen markers.

You can also etch the hieroglyphic symbol on to wooden discs with a pyrographic tool or – with care – a hot screwdriver and then paint the engraved hieroglyph black. Stain the wood. The discs should be round or tablet shaped with a flat bottom, about the size of a medium crystal, or small enough to carry in a purse. You could cut a very wide broom handle into pieces and stain it for this purpose, or you could use wood from a dry branch with a reasonably regular shape.

Crystal amulets do carry the additional power of the stone itself as well as the colour and you can carry the crystal hieroglyph charm with you in a small natural fabric purse or a knotted linen cloth to give you its particular strength all day.

Choosing the right hieroglyphic

Sometimes the choice of hieroglyphic charm comes easily. We do not always consciously realize the kind of power and protection we need in the day ahead, though. You can, however, allow your wise unconscious knowledge to help you. Try one of the following approaches:

▲ Place all your hieroglyphics in a drawstring bag and pick one at random to guide you during the day. This will tell you the strength you need for the day ahead and if you carry it with you, the chosen crystal will empower and protect you.

▲ You may find the same symbol appears regularly if a particular issue is dominant or specific opportunities are coming into your life. Sometimes it is a way of alerting you to an area of your life that you are ignoring.

Amulet divination

For a major decision, you can ask a question that is troubling you or a decision you have to make.

▲ Again place the marked crystals or discs in a drawstring bag, but this time draw out three at once.

▲ Consider the meaning of each and see how it applies to your life. The three together will answer either a specific question or tell you something about the days ahead.

▲ Through psychokinesis (mind power), your unconscious wisdom will ensure that you choose the relevant symbols to receive the message you need, which may or may not be the one you want or expect.

▲ You can then carry these three as you charm.

▲ For workplace decisions you could draw the hieroglyphics on white discs of card and set them face down on your desk. Mix them round, ask a question and pick one, two or three discs.

▲ Turn them over and allow your wise inner voice to guide you.

The Hieroglyphics of Power (see page 64)

Ankh

Ankh, the key, is the symbol of eternal life. This is the special amulet of Isis, representing her union with Osiris, thus uniting birth and death. It was her magical incantations that restored him back to life and potency.

The Ankh amulet was traditionally made of turquoise and can be painted on a deep blue crystal such as lapis lazuli as well as turquoise, also deep blue sodalite and blue howlite. It can be drawn in blue or white on blue paper.

It is the symbol of life, eternal life and the life force that runs through all creation. Almost every deity figure is portrayed carrying the ankh as symbol of immortality.

As an amulet use the Ankh for long life, for energy, for permanence in relationships or any aspect of life and as a luck bringer.

In divination the Ankh signifies success through personal creativity and so it may be a good time to persevere with an avenue that seems unpromising or breathe new enthusiasm into a stagnant relationship, rather than abandoning it.

The Ankh advises taking the long-term view of any relationship or venture and choosing what is of worth rather than the most exciting option or one offering instant returns.

▲ *Perseverance is the key.*

Ba or Spirit

The Ba is a hawk with a human head, representing the spirit of the deceased that flew out of the mummified body and gave life to the spirit body that dwelled with the Blessed Dead. It could return to the mummy at will and animate the ka. The hawk image linked it to Horus, the falcon-headed god.

The Ba amulet was traditionally made from gold, studded with gems – to indicate the immortality of its nature – and in death was placed upon the breastbone of the mummy.

You could use a sparkling yellow crystal such as citrine on which to draw the image.

As an amulet use the Ba to empower you to rise above restrictions and material concerns and to protect your spirit from those who would crush your optimism or individuality.

In divination it represents the need for time spent on the spiritual side of your life and also perhaps to spread your wings in your daily world. You are a creature of spirit and perhaps need to make more self time. This symbol also indicates awakening psychic powers.

▲ *Freedom is the key.*

The Boat

As the Nile was central to the life of the ancient Egyptians, the boat was the main means of transport – and not just for mortals. The Sun-god Ra crossed the sky each day in his solar boat. Ma'at, the goddess of truth and natural law, rode in the sun boat and even Ra was subject to her law and her allotting of the day and night, time and seasons.

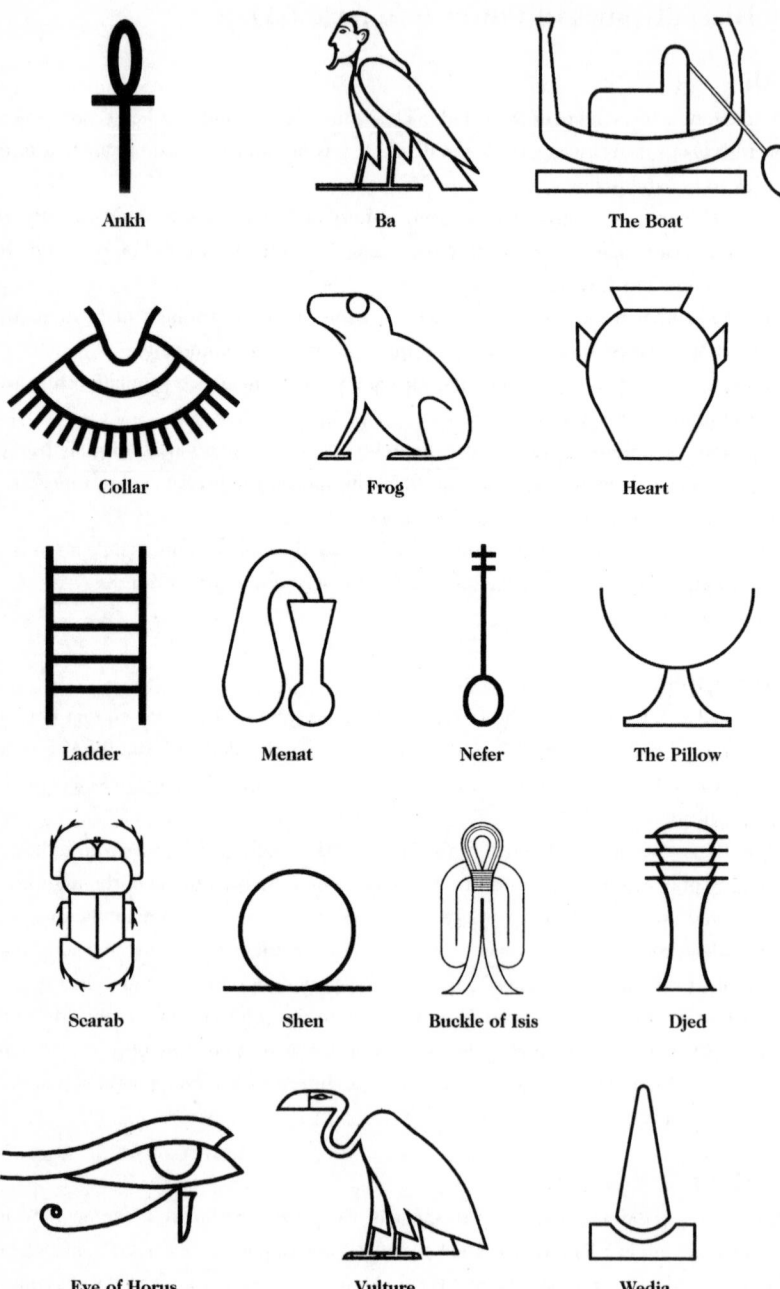

Ankh

Ba

The Boat

Collar

Frog

Heart

Ladder

Menat

Nefer

The Pillow

Scarab

Shen

Buckle of Isis

Djed

Eye of Horus

Vulture

Wedja

At night he travelled in his night boat and the Moon-god Khonsu also had a boat that sailed across the heavens.

The Boat amulet usually took the form of model boats placed in the tomb, made of wood, on which the deceased could sail following the sun. But you can draw one on a tiger's eye, the gold and brown gleaming stone that also symbolizes the sun. Alternatively, use a brown-banded agate.

As an amulet the Boat will protect you on journeys of all kinds and for new ventures – for example, a child going to school for the first time who may appreciate a Boat crystal sewn into the lining of a coat pocket. The amulet is also useful when time is an issue, helping you to prioritize.

In divination the Boat indicates that potential hazards which are worrying you, obstacles that you need to overcome, or even a major step that involves uncertainty, can be turned into success if you are prepared to expand your horizons. The solar boat was crewed by a number of deities, and in keeping with this you should seek practical help and support from people around you, as joint ventures are favoured.

▲ *Co-operation is the key.*

The Collar of Gold

The Collar of Gold was placed around a deceased person's neck on the day of the funeral to allow the spirit to escape from the earthly bindings in which the body had been wrapped. It was quite a late amulet, originating around the 26th Dynasty, and was made of pure gold. You can draw it on citrine or yellow jasper.

As an amulet the Collar of Gold is empowering and represents independence from stifling influences or situations and the ability to stand alone for principles or ideas.

In divination the Collar of Gold signifies the need to make your own decisions on a matter of importance and, if necessary, to cast adrift security in order to fulfil your personal destiny. Explore alternatives you may not have considered and perhaps change your routine if aspects of your life are no longer fulfilling.

▲ *Independence is the key.*

The Djed or Tet

The Djed, Tet or 'backbone of Osiris' represented the trunk of the plant that grew round the chest containing the body of Osiris. Empowered by his strength, it grew into a mighty tree. This tree, with the coffin inside it, was made into a column for the palace of the king of Phoenicia. Isis disguised herself to gain entry to the palace and, summoning up thunder and lightning, split open the column with her wand.

Thus Djed is a symbol of strength not of only Osiris – though in ritual it came to represent his backbone – but of Isis who, by her power and courage, was able to release the body of Osiris from imprisonment.

In life the Djed amulet was used to protect the spine and to cure back injuries. On the mummy it would also ensure the deceased would rise up and stand tall and that Osiris would carry their spirit. There are two forms of the hieroglyphic and you can use either: a column with four cross pieces on top, the symbolic tree, or a shorter T cross, to represent a spine. The Djed is often found with the Buckle of Isis, the Tjet, to balance male and female energies. The two are seen together on Tutankhamun's funerary beds.

Sometimes the eye of Horus, the son of Isis and Osiris, combined with the other symbols to form a triple amulet group of protection. The right hand of the deceased held the Tjet and the left the Djed.

The Djed, which was traditionally made of gold or wood, can be drawn on any deep blue stone such as lapis lazuli or sodalite. Alternatively, you can use the Osirian colours of black (perhaps an obsidian, jet or black jasper) or green (malachite).

As an amulet Djed represents the strength of Osiris and so is empowering as well as protective, keeping away doubt and fear as well as actual harm. It is good for increasing confidence, especially for young people or for anyone being bullied physically or emotionally.

In divination the Djed indicates that great inner strength is at your disposal and that any plan or relationship has firm foundations. If there have been setbacks the lessons learned will hold the key to future success. Stand firm and opposition will melt away.

▲ *Strength is the key.*

The Frog

The Frog is another Nile creature and as such is associated with abundance and fertility. The seemingly miraculous cycle of transformation from egg through tadpole to frog gave this creature strong associations with resurrection.

Heqet, or Heket, was the frog Goddess, wife of the potter god Khnum, who fashioned people from the Nile clay. In life her amulet brought fertility to women and in death promised resurrection. During the Greek and Roman occupation of Egypt, lamps in the shape of frogs symbolized new life and spiritual illumination whenever they were lit.

The amulet is good on a green stone such as jade, malachite (which was very popular in Ancient Egypt) or an aquamarine for water.

As an amulet the frog promises fertility in any venture. It can also be used to encourage the conception of a child and also to attract abundance to the home and the wearer.

In divination the frog indicates that you are entering a very creative, fertile period and that it is a good time to lay the seeds for future ventures in career or relationships. Welcome natural change points so that you can continue to grow spiritually and emotionally.

▲ *Fertility is the key.*

The Heart

The Heart was the source of good and evil intentions that, to the ancient Egyptians, were quite as significant as thoughts. As the seat of intelligence and intentions, it required special protection after death. Though some Egyptologists I spoke to told me that the heart was generally left in the body, some accounts – especially during later periods of Egyptian history – record that the heart was placed in a canopic jar (a vessel dedicated specifically to the storage and preservation of vital organs) to be preserved after death, hence the form of the hieroglyph.

A crystal heart or a heart scarab would be used in its place in the body or, when the heart was left in the body, to act as support for this all-important organ.

In the afterlife each heart was weighed on scales in the halls of the Dead against the symbolic feather of Ma'at. If the scales balanced, the heart was judged to be free from sin and the deceased joined the blessed dead.

You can use any red crystal, such as carnelian or red jasper for the heart amulet.

As an amulet the Heart represents the integrity of the wearer and so can protect against trickery or malice as well as against extremes of emotion that can cloud judgement.

In divination the Heart talks about the need to decide your priorities and weighing up options, especially where principles are at stake. Follow your heart rather than being swayed by sentiment or emotional pressure from others.

▲ *Integrity is the key.*

The Ladder

The Ladder represented the means by which the deceased could gain access to the heavens. Osiris used a ladder created by Ra to ascend into the heavens and he and Thoth or Horus would help the deceased to climb the ladder.

In early Egypt it was believed that the floor of heaven was a huge iron plate standing on four pillars at the four directions, where the blessed dead would reside with the deities. Hence, the ladder was needed to ascend to the heavens and a hieroglyphic of the steps had similar meaning (see also page 173).

Amulets or model ladders made of wood were placed in tombs right through the Middle and Late kingdoms, but you can draw your ladder on any brown stone, such as fossilized wood or brown jasper.

As an amulet the Ladder is a good symbol for any high-flown ambitions or major projects and for a major burst in optimism and confidence. It also helps to overcome restrictions or problems caused by the blinkered vision of others.

In divination the Ladder says that you should aim high and seek to fulfil your dreams, however impossible or far away fruition seems. You will find help and support from people in higher positions, perhaps unexpectedly. A good time for formal spiritual learning or seeking the advice of a spiritual person.

▲ *Aim high is the key.*

Menat

Menat, which takes the form of an overflowing jug, is the symbol of nourishment, reproduction and fertility, both human and of the land, represented by the annual flooding of the Nile. In myth this was caused by the tears of Isis at the death of Osiris and the rich silt left when the water receded was her gift to the people. Anuket was the goddess from whose womb the Nile waters flowed and she was bringer of abundance. She filled the grain houses and cared for the poor. Menat also represented the union of male and female and ensured fertility as well as nourishment in this and the afterlife.

This amulet was made in bronze or ceramics. You can draw it on any red crystal, such as carnelian or even reddish orange amber, and was carried ritually or worn as a pendant.

As an amulet it has retained its ancient meaning of attracting joy, health and abundance and with the frog amulet forms a powerful fertility icon.

In divination Menat represents the need to give freely, whether of your time or of love, and says that any input now will be richly rewarded in the future. Love and family matters are particularly auspicious, especially in terms of increased commitment.

▲   *Giving is the key.*

Nefer

Nefer signifies happiness, beauty and increased good fortune as well as harmony. It represents the ancient Egyptian oud, a lute-type instrument with between nine and twelve strings. We know that Queen Hatshepsut's daughter played one, for it was buried with her. The amulet Nefer placed on the deceased promised eternal happiness. The oud is indeed a thing of beauty. In a Cairo bazaar I was shown one inlaid with mother of pearl and with wonderful pearl images of people dancing. Ouds are still hand crafted in Egypt and are used in sacred Coptic music. The perfect form and harmony of the instrument represented fulfilment and pleasure.

Hathor, with whom Isis is closely connected, was goddess of music and dance, joy and creativity and red is her colour.

The amulet was made of gold, carnelian or other red crystal or ceramic. You can use jasper, carnelian or reddish amber for your drawing of Nefer.

As an amulet you can still use the image to attract joy and harmony as well as good fortune into your life. It also enhances inner radiance and beauty.

In divination Nefer augurs happy harmonious times and good luck, but says it is important to focus on your inner harmony, rather than trying to act as peacemaker to others. Spend time in activities that give you personal joy.

▲   *Happiness is the key.*

The Pillow

This amulet is a model of the pillow or gold headrest placed under the neck of the mummy in the coffin or among funerary goods to uplift and protect the head on the journey to the afterlife journey so that the deceased could see over the horizon. Ancient Egyptians feared that the head of the deceased might become separated or be severed by demons and the Pillow offered protection.

As well as gold, these amulets were made of haematite and this or another black crystal such as obsidian is a good choice on which to draw the symbol.

As an amulet the Pillow is very protective against all dangers and promises to lift your spirit if you are depressed or worried. Wear it or place it beneath your own pillow if you suffer from nightmares or insomnia.

In divination the Pillow promises better times ahead or that you will be uplifted by support you did not expect. If you can look beyond the immediate problems or limitations, you will become aware of success and lasting happiness ahead.

▲ *Be hopeful is the key.*

The Scarab

Sacred to Khepri, the god of the sun at dawn who was depicted as scarab-headed and was himself represented by the hieroglyph of the scarab, this amulet was a profound symbol of rebirth to the Egyptians. It was a beetle that laid its eggs in a small ball of dung to provide nourishment for the young. The Egyptians saw the beetle offspring emerging from the balls as a symbol of rebirth and transformation. Even today, you won't walk more than a few yards in any Egyptian town or large village without small boys thrusting blue ceramic lucky scarabs in your hand and demanding a dollar. The scarabs themselves live on in Egypt, though they bear little resemblance to the flesh-devouring beetles of the popular Mummy films.

The scarab's association with the sun and new life comes because it is said to roll the ball containing eggs from east to west and also because it flies when the sun is very hot. Khepri means 'he who rolls' and Khepri was likewise said to roll the ball of the sun across the sky, bringing each new day.

In a mummy, the scarab often imposed on a heart shape and given wings was placed in the heart cavity. Scarabs are found in a variety of colours and materials, including green marble, turquoise and blue faience. The green heart scarabs were inlaid with gold, but the most popular colour is sky blue. You can engrave the scarab on bright blue howzite or turquoise or alternatively rich green amazonite or malachite.

As an amulet use the Scarab in the traditional manner for protection against all ills and as a promise of new beginnings at times when you are experiencing stagnation or after loss.

In divination the Scarab says that you carry within you the seeds of new potential and talents you have either set aside or never developed. It is a time for transformation and for maximizing opportunities and beginning new enterprises. The Scarab works in single-month units, since the eggs take twenty-eight days to hatch, and improvements will usually be felt within a month.

▲ *Transformation is the key.*

Shen

Shen represents the orbit of the sun around the earth and so was a symbol of endless time. As an amulet placed upon the dead, it promised eternal life so long as the sun endured.

In funerary paintings on tomb walls, Isis and Nephthys are pictured kneeling and resting their hands on Shen, which is sacred to Ra. The amulet was painted in tombs and on coffins as well as on offering tablets. It was set close to the heart in the mummy.

Generally, as an amulet Shen was made of lapis lazuli, red jasper or carnelian. You can use any blue or red crystal on which to draw it as an amulet.

As an amulet traditionally, Shen is worn to bring long life and health and to protect the wearer from sudden unwelcome change or downturns in fortune.

In divination it represents long-term goals and relationships and is a good omen for a love match or a new job. Above all it is a reminder that the sun does rise every morning and that tomorrow really is another day of opportunity. There may never be an ideal time to act, so seize the moment.

▲ *Permanence is the key.*

Tjet or Buckle of Isis

This amulet represents the Buckle of the Girdle of Isis, and is associated with the fertilizing blood of Isis. There are numerous ancient chants that have passed from the funerary texts into popular folk tradition beginning 'The blood of Isis and the strength of Isis and the words of power of Isis' that can be woven into a protective chant to empower this amulet.

The amulet is usually red – whether carnelian, red jasper or red glass – though it can also be crafted from gold. Sometimes there was a green crystal as part of the design.

The Buckle of Isis was worn on the neck of the mummy to ensure maternal protection and rebirth in the afterlife, as Osiris was reborn through the magic of Isis. It also enabled the spirit to pass into the blessed realms and to return to the body in the tomb when he or she wished. It is also important in knot magic (see pages 31–2).

As an amulet use this as it has traditionally been worn and carried for fertility, for protection especially of women, for increasing magical power and for the renewal of lost love.

In divination the Tjet appears when you need to rely on inspiration and intuition rather than logic or conventional solutions. It says that any creative venture or gifts should be developed and that these will bear fruit before a year has passed. It also promises the renewal or restoration of what has been lost.

▲ *Creativity is the key.*

Uchat or The Eye of Horus

The Eye of Horus is a symbol of inspiration. In fact, there are two forms of it. One faces left and the other to right; the right is the sun eye and white, while the other is the moon eye and black.

Usually the sun, or white eye, was portrayed in amulet form; it is also called the eye of Ra (see pages 95–6 and 207–8). The sun eye is associated in particular with the summer solstice, when offerings were made to it and new eye amulets were empowered in the eye of the sun, at a time when it was at its brightest.

It was from this eye that Hathor drew power for her magic mirror that saw into the future on one side and on the other reflected the seeker in his or her true light (see pages 113–14).

Horus's moon eye was damaged by Set during a fight between them in the desert, but Hathor restored the sight in it with gazelle's milk.

The Eye of Horus, which is found throughout Egyptian history and indeed throughout the Near and Middle East and Europe until the nineteenth century as an antidote to the evil eye, was usually made of either lapis lazuli or blue faience, but is also found in gold and silver.

The moon eye was made of haematite, red jasper or carnelian. In death it was placed on the mummy to ensure a place in Ra's solar boat. Death masks sometimes have a crystal sun and moon eye in the eye sockets.

As an amulet the Eye of Horus has retained its traditional significance as a bringer of good fortune, health and energy and against all forms of malice.

In divination the Eye of Horus talks about looking beyond the immediate present and using your clairvoyant vision or inner eye for inspiration. As symbol of truth and integrity it warns about duplicity in others. It also says that if you do not value your own worth, neither will others.

▲   *Clear vision is the key.*

The Vulture

The Vulture hieroglyph represents the protection and power of the Divine Mother Isis and was used as protection for the deceased with the ankh for life engraved on each talon. Isis demonstrated the power of maternal protection when she cared for Horus in the marshes, guarding him against his evil uncle who would have destroyed him. Her wings were also outstretched shielding Osiris and the pharaohs.

Nekhbet was another Egyptian vulture goddess who was said to give her maternal milk to the Pharaoh. The symbol of the vulture is the hieroglyphic for Mother. Her image also was worn on the Nemes, the Pharaoh's head-dress, along with the Uraeus, the cobra serpent's head (see pages 123–4). The vulture was a symbol of Upper Egypt, while the cobra symbolized Lower Egypt.

Often made in gold, the vulture can be drawn on a yellow crystal such as citrine, or otherwise a clear crystal quartz or amethyst.

As an amulet the Vulture is protective to all who are vulnerable and fierce against those who would do harm to the wearer. It is also a good amulet for travellers, especially those in dangerous places or for air travel.

In divination the Vulture indicates you may need to spend more time than usual with family members or friends who are vulnerable. But do not forget yourself. Avoid any who criticize you or seek to diminish your self-esteem. If necessary you may need to reveal that, gentle though you are, you have talons you will use in defence of loved ones and yourself.

▲   *Protectiveness is the key.*

Wedja or Fire

Wedja means 'fire' and because fire was used by the ancient Egyptians to forge metal and smelt gold, it represents prosperity. However, the hieroglyph was based on a bow drill that was turned in a shaped piece of wood (as seen in the lower part of the hieroglyphic) to produce fire by friction, thereby generating vitality from itself rather than an external source of fuel.

Traditionally the Wedja amulet was often made of gold, but you can use any golden crystal such as tiger's eye or a rich red blood agate. Sekhmet is the lioness-headed goddess of fire, courageous and determined and answerable to no one – not even her father/consort Ra or her Memphite consort Ptah.

As an amulet Wedja has traditionally been worn to attract prosperity and had the same meaning on tomb walls. It can also create inner fire and vitality at those times when you need to make your mark, or shine socially or professionally.

In divination Wedja advises looking to yourself for strength and says that we can succeed through our own efforts, especially if others are being unhelpful or even obstructive. This is especially so in financial and career matters. Make sure others do not take credit for your ideas and effort.

▲ *Initiative is the key.*

6

FIRE AND WATER MAGIC

In Egypt today, the land is dominated by the power of the sun and by the waters of the Nile, as it has been for thousands of years. These two contrasting forces formed the central core of Egyptian magic. The sun represented order and time, as the rising and setting of the sun marked the parameters of day and night and the passing of the year (see pages 16–17). The Nile was chaos, but also provided the nutrients that is still responsible for the fertility of the surrounding land, as the desert stretches vast and arid on either side. It is barely 35 years since the creation of the Aswan Dam in Southern Egypt stopped the annual flooding of the Nile. Today, though polluted in parts, the Nile is still gloriously blue; the strips of green land around it, watered by irrigation canals, are still sown with seeds by farmers (who are followed by sheep or goats that tread the seeds into the soil) and ploughed by the large horned bullocks that stand flank high in the water cooling themselves from the blazing sun.

The glory of the sun
The solar gods were always the most important deities in Egyptian magic. This is because of the significance to the Egyptians of the hot sun, which shapes the nature of the land.

Ra in his many forms was the most important and permanent sun deity over three millennia. The rising sun was named after Khepri, the scarab god. It was also sometimes called Ra-Harakhte, or Horus on the horizon. The latter was the name given to the young Horus, and was associated with his rising from the lotus that opened at dawn (see also Nefertum on page 206). Horus was also visualized bathing in the field of reeds that lay on the edge of the dawn horizon. Its symbol was a winged sun disc. The sun at noon was Ra himself and the evening sun was the old creator god Atum, or sometimes the ageing Ra, whose secret names Isis skilfully managed to discover. There was also a legend that each morning, in the form of a primal goose, Amun the supreme god – or Geb the earth god – laid the egg of the sun.

The most memorable solar deity, the Aten (the sun disk), was supreme for a relatively short period. Yet during this time the Aten not only eclipsed all other gods but also brought monotheistic worship to Egypt. His patron on earth was King Akhenaten ('the glory of the Aten') who changed his name from the family name Amenhotep IV ('Amun/Amen is at peace'). He ruled for a relatively short time, from 1352–1336 BCE, yet his actions gained him the name of the Heretic King and his name was removed from many of his monuments after his death.

On his father's death, Akhenaten revolutionized Egyptian religion – and, by implication, Egyptian magic. Aten, the sun disc, became the one supreme creator who was both male and female. Statues of deities were destroyed, which proved problematic for the king's people, who were used to relating to human-like forms. The sun disc never had the same appeal, even though it was shown radiating light. Yet effectively Akhenaten was saying that without the sun there is no life and that we all receive our own inner radiance from the undifferentiated source. He built a splendid new capital, Akhet-Aten, near what is now el Armana, halfway between Memphis and Thebes, and the fabulous temple to Aten was adorned with religious art. His own statues were part male, part female to represent the new concept of male/female as one in the creator and there were numerous offering tables found near the temples, where ordinary people left gifts for Aten in the form of his son on earth, Akhenaten himself.

With the reign of Tutankhamun, the boy king, perhaps Akhenaten's grandson, who wisely changed his name from Tutankhaten, Amun the supreme God and the other deities were restored. The new city was abandoned as swiftly as it had been built.

The great hymn to the Aten

There have been many hymns of praise made to the sun, especially to the god Ra. But the most famous and enduring has been the hymn to Aten, created by Akhenaten himself and traditionally recited facing the sunrise.

If you do stand in the ruins of Akenahten's splendour facing east at sunrise, or in the desert where the sun rises huge over the horizon, you will need no words to understand what prompted Akhenaten to worship the sun disc. But Egyptian magic is universal because it is fundamental to human experience. You can recite your personal hymn at sunrise over a silent city, over snow fields or over a green temperate landscape. Each has beauty and represents a morning miracle, the triumph of day over night and the ordered continuation of the world.

Creating your own hymn to the sun is perhaps one of the most important magical acts, since you can recite it at different times of the year and in different places.

My favourite setting for reciting the hymn is on a clear spring morning in the grove of trees overlooking the sea near my caravan, where I spend a great deal of time working and with the family. If I have been tossing and turning all night, fretting about family matters, cash flow problems or an impossible work schedule, I make myself get up just before light and go over to the grove, scattering the first birds and the rabbits who have been nibbling my herb pots.

I open my arms to the first light and recite my hymn. Afterwards, I am either filled with energy at the prospect of another day or able to go back to sleep properly for an hour, having had my world put into cosmic perspective. For the rising sun is wondrous.

Cassandra's hymn to the sun

Greetings to you great sun as you break the bonds of the night. The birds rise in the light, the bats return to their hollows.

Young animals stir and leap with joy while their sedate mothers turn their faces to the warmth after the chill of the night.

The fishing boats come back and cast their catch on the scarlet wave-danced shore, while in the towns, the clear fresh whiteness cleanses the grey buildings and makes their windows scarlet as rubies.

The serpents of my fears, the scorpions of old sorrows and the lion demons of doubts that trouble the dark hours are fled at your golden shafts of light.

The first sun shone over the dark waters and the mound of the earth rose and life began in its millions of wondrous forms from that creative light.

I am a daughter of that light, child of Sekhmet, fierce sun lioness who protects her young with her sharp arrows and her healing radiance.

Hathor also is my mother with her ever-flowing milk, who carries the sun disc proudly and who reflects ourselves as we might be if we dare step into her light beams.

The sky is radiant, purple, scarlet, golden. Mother, Father Sun, Sekhmet, Hathor, Amun, Atum, Aten all, Re and Horus spreading your wings of pure gold.

I will step into the light and shed all fear. I am the sun and walk in hope to be reborn each morning in faith and to live on after the body has ceased to be so long as the sun itself endures. Shen, Shen, Shen, be golden and glorious eternally and make me glorious in my testing hour.

Your own hymn to the sun

There are a number of translations of the hymn to the Aten, and also to Ra, on the internet and you can download these for personal use. I have used these occasionally, but I find a personal and shorter empowerment is endowed with one's personal essence. The principle behind Egyptian magic is the creative process and few people practise it without finding themselves reciting spells, chants and hymns to the ancient deities that seem to come from the mists of time.

▲ Do not worry about verse or form. I would suggest you do rise at dawn and just speak your feelings into a tape recorder and this will give you the basis.

▲ Note down your feelings and impressions of the sun during the day until the sun disappears.

▲ If you want to work with the concept of a sun goddess, try the ancient Egyptian goddess of fire and healing, Sekhmet, or the solar Hathor with her magical mirror glinting sunlight and the cow horns on her head, between which sat the sun disc.

▲ You might like to include some of the themes from the original hymn to Aten:

  1. At dawn the sun rises and fills the world with beauty.

  2. The sun shines over all the earth, over all that it has created, and gives life to everything.

  3. How dark the earth is after sunset as fears and danger as the night return, pictured as serpents, while their creator sleeps.

  4. When the sun returns at dawn, the birds fly high from their nests, animals begin grazing, flowers and greenery open and fish leap in the rivers. The chicken bursts from its egg. All seeds of new life come from the life-giving power of the sun, infants: new plants, animals, cities and all the nations of the earth.

You can add details personal to your own way of life and your own world.

Creating a Shen space

There is also the universal aspect of the sun – the fact that it shines everywhere on earth, every day, and has done so for millennia. Its power is symbolized by the hieroglyph Shen (see page 64), which means that so long as the sun shines, earth shall endure.

You can draw the symbol in the earth or in sand as the sun rises, out of stones on grass or in chalk on a yard. Make it large enough to stand in as you recite your hymn to the sun.

The Nile

Like the sun, the Nile shapes the nature of the Egyptian world that in many aspects has remained unchanged over five or more millennia and for this reason water deities were also highly significant in Ancient Egypt. Though the Nile represented the forces of chaos and might either flood too deeply or be too shallow, in paintings and papyri it was always shown as a calm river, with the fertile land on either side of it.

The Egyptians never showed chaos, age, sickness or death except to enemies of the state, for in painting perfection they believed they created it magically.

Egyptian magic is about the necessary balance between order and chaos and a number of temple fire and water rituals were intended to assist in maintaining the cosmic order, especially at times when the Nile was due to flood. The annual flood, where the high ground was surrounded by waters, followed by the receding of the waters probably inspired the early creation myths of the first mound rising from the waters of Nu or Nun.

At these times, offerings were made to Hapy the Nile god that he would send a good flood, so that the irrigation ditches and villages would not be washed away but also that there would be sufficient depth of silt when the water levels dropped and that there would not be drought later in the year.

Hapy, god of the Nile

Out of the chaos of the Nile came fertility and so it was as important as order.

Not surprisingly there were also two hymns to Hapy of the fertile waters, praising him and promising him offerings.

There was also an early poem in praise of Khnum or Khnemu, an early creator god and guardian of the first cataract, written during the Third Dynasty by King Djoser, whose Step Pyramid formed the prototype for later construction. The King was seeking to invoke the help of Khnum to save the land from a seven-year drought. Other water deities also praised included Sobek, the crocodile god, and the fertility and protective deities the frog-headed Heket and the hippopotamus Tauret. These water deities may have evolved from the primal deities believed to have risen from the first waters in the creation myths of Hermopolis. There are also the beautiful water plants, the lotus or water lily and the papyrus.

Beautiful water goddesses existed too. Satis was regarded as Lady of the Nile Waterfalls. Her mother, Anukis, was also a water goddess and sometimes the roles of the two goddesses were reversed in Egyptian myth, so that Satis became the mother figure; at other times, the two were thought of as sisters. Both Satis and Anukis were also said to have been the daughters and consorts of Khnum. Anukis was portrayed in the form of a desert gazelle, or as a woman with a high feather head-dress. Satis was depicted as a beautiful woman; she wore the white crown of upper Egypt and had two gazelle horns on her head-dress. Both were associated with the cooling waters and the abundance of grain stores.

The hymn to Hapy

Traditional Egyptian prayers to water deities include the following common elements: the fertility of the Nile and its teeming creatures; its water plants; the way that it springs from the earth at the bidding of Osiris; the story of how its clay was used to fashion the first people; the crops that are watered by it and fill the barns; the people who have water; the cool trees; and the hardships of the dry times. The hymns ask Hapy that the hardships will never return and promise offerings to appease the god.

I made my own hymn of praise to the sacred waters when I went to visit Doctor Ragab's Pharonic Village on an island in the Nile not far from Cairo. Here Doctor Ragab has recreated three thousand years of history and boats pass through the marshes of papyrus – a plant he has brought back into natural growth after its decline in the last century. I stood shaded by trees near a lotus pond close to the temple and I watched the birds swooping over the blue water of the canal.

But there are many cool green places throughout the world that can inspire your hymn to the sacred waters – a river, a lake, a waterfall, a stream or a restored inland canal, or even the wild sea. When you recite your hymn it may be a sunny day with the light rippling on the water, or one on which the sky pours down water and you become part of the flow. You can dedicate your hymn to one or more of the Nile deities or to a more abstract spirit of the fertile flowing.

Recite your hymn as the afternoon sun moves lower.

Cassandra's hymn to Hapy

Hail to you, Hapy who over thousands of years and more have released the fertile waters to give life and growth to the land.

I greet you too fierce Sobek, wise Tauret, Heket the protectress, who keep from me danger and despair when my life floods too fast, threatening to overwhelm me.

I call on you lady of the gazelles, Satis and mother of the grain store, Anukis. Let not the parched times return the arid baking times when no inspiration comes and I am alone in the desert of howling fear. Pour your cooling waters to quench the heat that scalds and blisters.

I thank you, Hapy, also for the overflowing granaries and storehouse, the teeming shoals of fish, the white birds who drink on the shore, the bullocks diving deep to cool themselves from the plough, the green growth holding back the barren sands of the red desert land.

I drink deep of the waters of fertility and coolness and flow with you to the sea over thousands of miles from the monsoon lands far south, allowing you and your sisters and brothers to carry me where I should go, not where I seek or where others tell me I should be.

I will make offerings to the sea birds and to the polluted waters that I too may be purified and may drink always of your wisdom and bounty so long as the water flows.

The sun and the Nile – keeping the balance

Balance between fire and water so that both would manifest their creative aspects, fell under the control of Ma'at, the cosmic principle of balance. This was personified as the Goddess Ma'at, the goddess of order, truth justice and goodness in this world and the next.

The importance of the cycle of sun and flood was recognized as early as the fifth millennium BCE and the stability that it brought about may account for the advanced civilization in Egypt from early times (see also Appendix 2).

This balance was the responsibility on earth of the Pharaoh, manifestation of Horus the sky god, son of Ra. The ancient Egyptians believed that the universe – including the sky – was surrounded by water and so Ra, accompanied by Bastet, Ma'at and other deities, plus the blessed dead so chosen, were thought to sail across the waters of the sky. At night Ra sailed in the night boat through the Duat, which was associated with the waters of the womb of the sky mother Nut. In this way, water was believed to be part of the solar journey through the day and night.

In modern magic, fire and water balance rituals can be used at times when we need either change and fertility (chaos) – as represented by water – or order – as represented by the sun.

You can use the three Egyptian seasons as a focus for different kinds of ritual. There is no need to wait until the precise calendar dates (which varied slightly in any case), but you should try to spend spare moments in the days before and after these rituals working with fire in the form of an oil lamp, or a candle and water, or perfume at your altar.

Inundation – Akhet

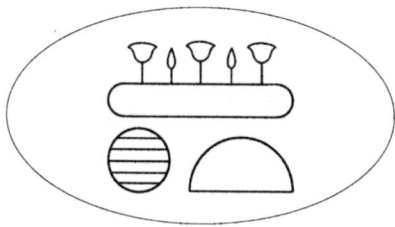

Akhet

Akhet means 'when water predominates'. At this time Sirius became associated with Isis, heralded the coming of the flood (see pages 194–5). The star goddess Sopdet (Sothis to the Greeks), who was usually depicted with a star on her head-dress or as a cow with a growing plant within her horns, was a representation of the actual star. Sirius signalled the beginning of the Egyptian New Year. Because the ancient Egyptian calendar became slightly out of step with the solar and lunar year as time went on, the Egyptians relied on the star, rather than the season, as the herald of both the New Year and the yearly flood (see pages 190–1).

Use the time of water for rituals for change, for fertility, for washing away what you no longer need in your life, for emotional matters, love and family and for taking steps into the unknown and the unpredictable. Work for your main ritual outdoors near water, the sea, a river, canal, lake or pond. If you need to work indoors, use a very large clear bowl of water.

Focal deities

Isis known to the Romans as Stella Maris, Star of the Sea,

Hapy the Nile god; portrayed as fat and male with female breasts and with a papyrus plant on his head; prayers and offerings were made to him for a good flood (see page 202).

Tauret the hippopotamus goddess.

Heket the frog fertility goddess; also prayed to for protection.

Sobek the crocodile God.

Osiris who caused the Nile to rise from the underworld and is often associated with the flood itself (see page 207).

Satis or Anukis prayed to for gentleness, to enable oneself to engage one's feelings of sympathy towards others.

A water ritual

To bring new energies into your life, you will need: water; a white flower – a lotus if you can find one (otherwise, use a water lily or another water flower); some seeds and a long branch, preferably from a tree that grows near water. If working with a bowl of water you can scale down your equipment.

▲ Work in the late afternoon. Set the tools for the ritual on a white rectangular cloth near the water edge.

▲ Draw the hieroglyph for water. This was particularly associated with the Nile flood and fertility in soft earth or sand near the water's edge:

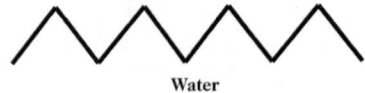

Water

▲ If there is no suitable earth you can trace the invisible hieroglyph on grass or where you are working.

▲ As you draw your water symbol, say the following line:

'Kings of the Flood, fertile Queens of the blue water, I am the fertile Nile and would flow with you.'

▲ Standing on the hieroglyph, or its visualized equivalent, face the water and take your flower between your hands. Say:

'I am the flower of the sacred waters, child of the sun. But the time of the flood is near and so I must be carried to new places, to seed new life.'

▲ Cast the flower on the waters.

▲ Next, cast your seeds on the water, saying:

'Flow, grow, swell as the water and bring the change/opportunity I desire.'

▲ Name your purpose and the fruition of that desire.

▲ Stir the water with your branch and name the focal deity/deities of the ritual, which can be entirely of your choice. If you prefer, you can leave the deities unspecified in which case you can refer to them in the way you did earlier, as kings of the flood, or fertile queens of the blue water. For example, you might say something like:

'Isis, Heket, Tauret, Hapy, carry this prayer and this ritual and accept my offerings.'

▲ Gaze into the water and half close your eyes; you may see an image of the nature of the future change.

The Growing Season – Peret

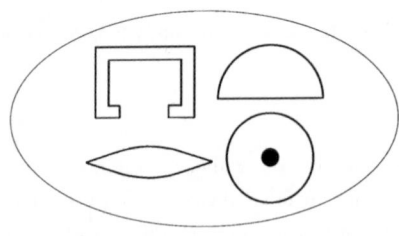

Peret

Peret means the balance of water and fire. Once the flood had receded, around October or November, the season of planting and sowing arrived, when people used sheep and goats to tread seeds into the ground. The water was still important in a means of irrigating the fields through the canal system and by drawing water using the ancient shaduf, a bucket and a pulley, devices still in use five thousand years later. But the sun was also vital in enabling the crops to grow and so this period represents the balance of water and fire, river and sun.

As with the inundation magic, you can invoke these energies whenever you need them.

Use the time of water and fire for rituals and empowerments for growth and improved fortune in any area of your life, for stability, for harmony and for balancing different needs, relationships or responsibilities.

Work in a garden, park or open green space, or on a balcony or patio with green plants.

Focal deities

Geb the earth god. He was often pictured as a red or brown prone figure with an erect phallus and vegetation growing from his body, lying beneath Nut, his wife the sky goddess, in the centre of an ocean.

Osiris in his role as god of vegetation.

Isis who in her dark form, especially with Horus on her knee suckling, was a representation of the earth mother, Christianized as the Black Madonna.

Nefertum as the young god who emerged from a lotus as it opened in the morning. In the Cairo Museum, there is a famous statue of Tutankhamun's head as a symbol of Nefertum emerging from the lotus of rebirth.

Khnum the potter god who created humans from clay is also associated with this balance, for he was said to release the waters of the Nile at the first cataract.

The Lotus head of Tutankhamun

A fire and water ritual

This ritual is designed to gain you greater balance in your life. You will need: an area of soil or a tray of soil large enough to stand in; a jug of water; some herbs such as lavender, which grows profusely in Egypt; basil, mint, parsley or thyme, which were popular herbs in Ancient Egypt (see pages 161–3); and two outdoor torches. You can buy oil-fuelled torches at garden centres and these are especially suitable for ancient Egyptian magic. Alternatively, you can use the candle type of torch. Indoors you can use a conventional gold candle or an oil lamp.

▲ Begin as the sun is setting. Light your torch to the south of the earth area and stand on the earth so you are facing the light. Set the jug of water to the north in this ritual.

▲ Using a stick, draw or trace the symbols for Water, Nefer or harmony and the sun in a row from left to right, in the centre of the earth plot. Leave spaces between them and make them large enough to walk around.

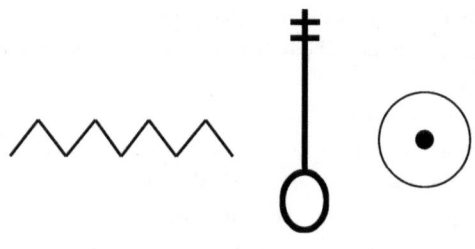

Water-nefer-sun

▲ With great care take the torch and circle the water symbol clockwise, saying:
    'As fire joins to water, so shall the land flourish. I am the land and the crops that will grow tall. Geb (or one or more of the deities named) hold my course straight and true.'

▲ Return the torch to its place and taking the jug, circle the sun hieroglyph clockwise and sprinkle a few drops of water in a circle round it as you do so. Say:
    'As water joins fire, so shall the land flourish. I am the land and the crops that will grow tall. Geb (or one or more of the deities named) hold my course straight and true.'

▲ Set the jug in its place.

▲ Taking the herbs, with a small trowel, dig a hole over the hieroglyphic Nefer for harmony and place the herbs in the ground. Say:
    'So do I plant the roots of my future harmony deep within me. I am Geb (or your focus deity) and I receive the offering of life thus planted.'

▲ Water the herbs from the jug and then pass the torch clockwise around the herbs, saying:
    'As water joins fire, so they are harmonized in the fertile soil. I am the fertile soil and the crops I have planted will grow as harmony within and from me towards others. Geb, I am Geb (or your focus deity) and I hold the course straight and true.'

▲ Tend the herbs regularly and as they grow with sun and water, so you will feel the harmony extending through every part of your being.

Harvest – Shemu

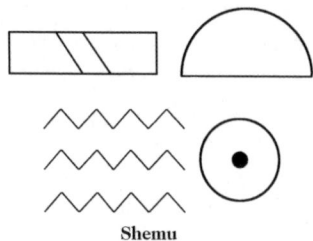

Shemu

Shemu is the dry season when fire predominates. By March or April, the river Nile was at its lowest and the canals, too, were becoming dry. But the water had done its work and in this time when fire predominated, the crops could be harvested. If the original flood had been high enough to spill over into desert lands, flowers blossomed at this time. It is said that Nephthys, who represented the desert, made love with Osiris when such a flood overwhelmed her. He was symbol of the flood and she conceived and gave birth to Anubis, jackal-headed god of mummification and the underworld and the alter ego of Horus, son of Osiris by his true wife Isis.

The desert was the chaotic element, in later dynasties associated with Set, Osiris's evil brother. However, Set retained his protective function against evil and was one of the original elder gods (see page 209) ensuring necessary change and destruction of the old and redundant elements in life. The desert had fierce sandstorms and also in times of drought might encroach on the once fertile land.

At the time of the harvest, the rebirth of Osiris was celebrated as the ripened grain and thanks were given to Isis as corn mother who used her magic to give him life. Part of the rite was a ceremonial burial of a grain Osiris, a small, flat hollow clay model of the Osirian mummy or Osiris himself which contained a compartment filled with grain. These were also placed in tombs. The Ashmolean Museum has a fine extensive collection of these.

Use the time of fire for rituals to bring success, power, the fruition of plans and hard work, for health, for justice and for abundance.

Focal deities

Min the phallic fertility god.

Osiris as the ripened crops.

Thoth whose sacred bird, the ibis, came to eat the corn in huge droves at this time. Though the ibis is rare in Egypt, flocks of white egrets can still be seen in fields beside the canals in June and July.

Isis and Osiris also central because of their strong fertility associations.

Nephthys as the desert flower.

Sekhmet goddess of fire.

A fire ritual

For this personal power ritual you will need: a dish of seeds such as sunflower, poppy, cumin or caraway; a ball of clay or dough; some dried grasses or ears of wheat and barley; red cord to tie them; four large red flowers, which can be silk or paper; a large outdoor incense stick or torch of orange; poppy; sandalwood or frankincense if possible.

▲ Work in sunlight, preferably at noon.

▲ Set a yellow cloth on grass or on a large rock where the sun, or at least the noon light, can shine on it.

▲ Set all your tools on the cloth except for the incense torch.

▲ Light the incense to the south-east of the altar.

▲ Around the cloth, set the four flowers at each of the main compass points, beginning in the south and moving clockwise. Make the area large enough to sit and stand in and to hold the incense torch. At each point say:

> 'So blooms the desert flower. So blossoms my life. So shall I reap the harvest even of desert places.'

▲ Sit facing south. Taking the clay, hollow out the shape of a man, just deep enough to contain seeds. Say:

> 'Grow, be fertile, man of clay, you who are reborn.'

▲ Set within it the seeds, saying:

> 'I have within me also the seeds of the harvest grain. I take in the power to be born anew and ever reborn in assuredness of success, but only with good intent.'

▲ Leave the figure in the centre of the altar and weave the dried grasses round it in knots.

> 'Mother Isis, I make the magical knots. I weave and bind the power only for good and the highest purpose. Fill me with power. I am the knot. I am the power.'

▲ With care carry the incense just within the four flowers, beginning in the south and moving clockwise around the four compass points, making a trail of smoke and saying:

> 'Desert flowers, blossoms of the sun, I ask the blessings of the harvest. I am the harvest and will bring abundance into my life and to others.'

▲ Return and sit facing south within the circle, allowing the sun or the light to enter and fill you with confidence. You might like to make a private invocation to one of the harvest deities or visualize the image of one or more in your mind.

▲ When you are ready, take the clay figure and, leaving the circle by the southern flower, dig a hole and bury it in silence, facing the east that it may be reborn.

▲ Next, gather the flowers, beginning with the one in the south and moving clockwise, and leave them as an offering on top of the earth where you buried the figure. If you do not have suitable earth, use a large pot with growing flowers and bury it there, still facing east.

▲ Extinguish the incense torch in a dish of sand or soil, or a plot of earth if it is available, and dispose of it in an environmentally friendly way.

▲ Use your cloth at home on your altar for a while instead of the white one and add a vase or pot of red flowers.

7

DEITIES OF
MAGIC AND HEALING

The world of the Egyptian deities reflects the natural features of sun, water, the fertile and desert lands, the stars and the moon. These were vitally important to the Egyptians in a world that remained relatively unchanged over three thousand years and, in spite of modern technology, still runs as a deep current beneath modern Egypt.

Different deities and creation myths gained and lost supremacy according to the dynasty of kings who ruled at the time, and who elevated their own personal or local deities. However, though the changes in the popularity of particular myths was not a progression, gradually a core of deities – Thoth, Horus, Isis and Osiris, Set and Nephthys – was incorporated into the mythical cycles and became widely and personally worshipped by the people irrespective of the ruler.

The Egyptian symbol or determinative to indicate a deity was Neter, which is illustrated by the hieroglyphic of an axe. This symbol dates back to the first deities in prehistoric times, who were predominantly warrior gods, and reflects the early struggles of different tribal peoples for supremacy of Egypt.

Neter

Though there were supreme creator deities, the varied deity forms allowed people to relate to different gods and goddesses for specific needs and at different times of their life. This is not difficult in magical or healing terms, any more than it is problematic to work with different archangels or saints.

The ancient Egyptian priesthood would make prayers or offerings in the king's name, since he was the appointed representative of the deities, Horus on earth; indeed, the king was regarded as a manifestation of the god himself. There was a belief from the Middle Kingdom, initiated by Queen Hatshepsut, that the supreme god played a major role in royal births. Desperate to establish her right to rule as Pharaoh, Hatshepsut claimed that the supreme god had impregnated her mother in her father's stead, and that therefore she (Hatshepsut) was of divine lineage and ruled by divine right. Subsequent pharaohs used the same myth, claiming

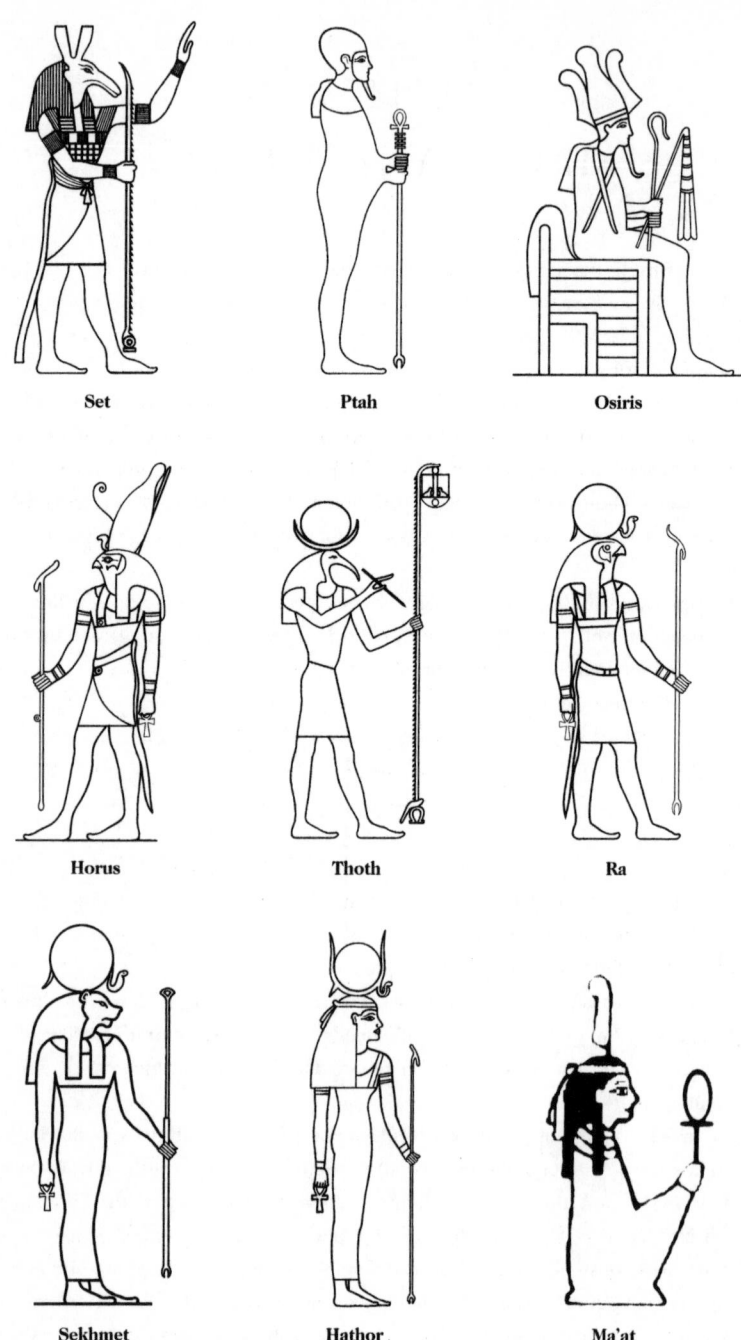

Set   Ptah   Osiris

Horus   Thoth   Ra

Sekhmet   Hathor   Ma'at

either that their mother had been impregnated by the god in a dream or by his taking over the father's body during conception.

The King was also supposed to reap the first crops and dedicate them to the deities in thanks. But, of course, he could not be everywhere, so priests and priestesses spoke with the King's voice. Put another way, in Egyptian ritual we are speaking with our own inner high king or queen voice. That is why it is so important – even if we are asking for powers or protection for ourselves – always to act with true intent and to pass on any blessings to others, even in small ways such as feeding wild birds or helping a colleague you do not like but who is struggling.

Good and evil

The battle between good and evil was a development from the polarity between order and chaos, expressed in later myths as the battle between the young god Horus and his uncle. In an early creation myth, the earth god divided Egypt into two parts. Lower or Northern Egypt belonged to Set and Upper or Southern Egypt to the god called Horus the elder, a distinct solar deity of the sun at noon associated with the falcon. He later merged with Horus the younger, son of Isis and Osiris, and became Horus when he had grown up and fought his uncle.

It may be that Set became demonized because he was the god of the losing side in the unification of Egypt around 3100 BCE. The mythological battle between good and evil, and specifically between Horus and Set, may represent an actual struggle between the peoples who worshipped the two gods during the predynastic ages. Horus was victorious and the early dynastic kings were called Horus kings. During the Second Dynasty, King Sekhemib, who worshipped Set, triumphed, restoring Set to his former glory for a while. By the Third Dynasty, the Horus kings were again supreme and the vilification of Set became more intense until he became god of storms and whirlwinds and the red barren desert, murderer of Osiris and persecutor of the infant Horus – in other words, the original archetypal wicked uncle. However, he did retain something of his original protective role and was called upon in life and after death to protect against demons.

Horus is most famous for his battles against his uncle Set. But most significantly, though he overcomes Set, he does not destroy him – thus preserving the dynamics of the cosmos, the friction that is necessary to keep the life force flowing. Indeed, though the Horus kings were triumphant, the fact that from the beginning of the third millennium kings wore the joint crown of Upper and Lower Egypt signified that they embodied the characters of both Horus and Set within themselves. Within the King, then, the balance of order and chaos was maintained.

Creation myths

I will briefly describe the main creation myths. You might like to choose one and use its imagery in rituals when you need to generate energy for a major undertaking or for a new beginning. These creation myths share core characteristics: that a mound came out from the primal waters Nu and that in early times the deities lived on earth during what was a Golden Age of peace and plenty, when Osiris taught the people the laws of civilization and agricultural techniques. During this Golden Age too, wise Thoth endowed humanity (or at least Egypt) with the gift of writing, mathematics, medicine and astronomy. In all the myths, too, magical power (heka) was instrumental in bringing about the various aspects of creation and this original generative act is repeated on a small scale in every act of magic or empowerment. The question is: who was the creator god who called forth the first sunrise?

Atum as creator god

The earliest creation myth, dating from the time of the unification of Egypt around 3100 BCE, relates that the god Atum rose out of the swirling waters of chaos. Because there was nowhere to stand he created the first mound. As the Sun-god, (later associated with the setting sun once his period of glory was eclipsed by Ra) he was also responsible for the first sunrise at Heliopolis, city of the sun, now part of Cairo. This image of the sun rising gloriously over the mound is contained in the symbol of the phoenix or benu bird.

Atum then created the twin deities Shu and Tefnut out of his bodily fluids, a way of saying that they – and the deities Shu and Tefnut in turn produced – were all aspects of Atum because they were created from his essence. Shu was god of the air and Tefnut was goddess of moisture. But Shu and Tefnut became lost in the waters (in other versions of the myth, the primal waters reared them). Atum sent his only eye, symbol of the sun, to seek them out. He replaced it with a second moon eye.

On their safe return, Tefnut gave birth to Geb, the god of the earth emerging fertile from the flood, and Nut, the sky and sky goddess. Shu, or the atmosphere, separated earth and sky. Shu was pictured upright, supporting Nut with his hands with Geb prone at his feet, forming the hills and valleys. Shu and Tefnut are sometimes represented as lion-headed.

Along the underside of the extended body of Nut, Ra – who became identified as the Sun-god from about the Fifth Dynasty onwards – would sail in his boat in the day, to be swallowed by Nut at night, creating darkness. He was then reborn through her thighs each morning. Ra is identified as the shining sun god in his disc.

Nut gave birth to four children at the same time: Osiris and Isis, who loved each other in the womb, and the shadow pair brother and sister Seth and Nephthys; the fertile and the barren pair. (However, Nephthys did have a son by Osiris.)

Osiris and Isis in turn produced Horus, thereby giving rise to the Ennead or nine major deities, who are central to this cosmology and who lived on earth to teach humanity. Some modern theories have suggested that the last five (and sometimes also Thoth as the elder god) came from Atlantis, explaining how Egyptian culture was apparently able to evolve so quickly to its state of perfection in the Old Kingdom. Another theory suggests they were extraterrestrial beings who came perhaps from Sirius B, the then unknown dwarf star of Sirius A that heralded the Flood.

Ptah as creator

From the time of the Old Kingdom, Ptah was acknowledged as divine artisan or fashioner of gods and vegetation. Today the ancient capital of Memphis, Ptah's cult centre, south of Cairo, which retained its importance throughout the three thousand years, is almost buried beneath the ever-encroaching Sahara desert.

On the surface there is little to see at this site about fifteen miles south of Cairo: a few statues, set in a green garden shaded by palm trees, a profusion of flowers with the desert beyond and remarkably few tourists.

The millennia melt away with the fumes of Cairo city, giving way to shimmering canals with green banks and crops ripe for harvest, with the sand stretching across the white haze horizon. The village outside the open-air museum at Memphis is largely unchanged also, with donkey carts laden with fruit, the old women sunning themselves in front of the houses, watching the children gambol and chase goats.

For it is said that at Memphis, the deities walked in that still, quiet green sanctuary in the desert and do so still. Here Isis and Nephthys took the body of the murdered Osiris. In this place too, Osiris entered the underworld and became the supreme judge at Memphis. The same court gave Egypt to Osiris's son Horus after his struggles with Set, though some myths set the court close to Philae in the south of the country.

The Memphis creation myth with Ptah as hero displaced the earlier myths, though all of the myths remained important in their region of origin, gradually merging together. If details seem confused or contradictory in other versions of the myths you may read, it is because the mythology has, like all good myths, evolved to meet the needs of the people and has changed in the telling and retelling.

The Memphis myth

Ptah created himself and is often associated with the Sun-god Ra.

Though Ptah was the great creator god, he created eight other lesser gods and the world with his heart, the seat of thought and his will and the lips with which he pronounced the magical words of power.

These eight gods combined characters from the earlier myths with local deities. They helped shape creation and humanity. They were: Atum as Sun-god; Nun and Naunet the primal waters; Tatjenen, a local god of Memphis who represented the earth created out of chaos; Horus, Thoth, Nefertum, the Lotus-god, son of Ptah and Sekhmet; and a serpent deity whose name is uncertain.

Most intriguing of the eight was Amun, in later myth regarded as the creator god himself who rose from the primal mound, out of the waters, and brought about the first sunrise.

The creative processes were more sophisticated than those at Heliopolis. Ptah thought creation and then magically, by his words, brought it into being. Sometimes these words were thought and spoken by Thoth making him the elder god. This is magic par excellence.

The Hermopolitan myth

Claimed by some to be the oldest creation myth, this version comes from the region of the city of Hermopolis in Middle Egypt.

Before the world began there was chaos, according to this myth, but within the chaos were four principles that emerged to bring about creation. They were pictured as eight deities in four pairs, the gods taking the form of frogs and the corresponding goddesses as snakes. It was through their coming together in a fusion of power (like the modern Big Bang theory) that the isle of flame was created and Atum was born. They were called the Ogdoad. Nun and Naunet were the male and female deities of the primal waters; Huh and Hauhet, the male and female deities of space and eternity; Kuk and Kauket, the male and female deities representing darkness; and Amon – or Amun – and Amaunet, the deities of air. But they were not immortal and after their death, they descended to the underworld. From here they were responsible for regulating the daily journey of the sun and the flowing of the Nile.

With the fusion of the gods' energy, a mound – the first earth – emerged at Hermopolis and on the mound appeared an egg from which emerged Atum or Ra, according to this version of the myth. (In later versions, Nun was Ra's father.)

Geb – or Seb – the earth god was said to have laid the primordial egg, which is why Geb has the goose as his symbol. Thoth was also implicated in incubating this primal egg.

Amun as creator

This was the last and, relatively speaking, the most recent of the creation myths. The legend grew up around Thebes, near modern Luxor, where Amun was worshipped during the period of the New Kingdom, between 1546–1085 BCE. It was necessary to incorporate the other myths into this 'supermyth' in order that all the people of Egypt would accept Amun. This made a rich but somewhat confusing story.

Amun – or Amen – is first mentioned during the Fifth Dynasty, but the first known temple to him is found much later, during the 11th Dynasty. Amun-Ra, as he was known, increased in power and – combined with the figure of Ra – became a supreme deity. All the other deities were manifestations of his power.

His rise to supremacy was in part political and during the middle of the 16th Dynasty, when the alien eastern invaders the Hyksos ruled from Memphis, Amun-Ra became the symbol of the liberated Egypt, free from invaders. The most famous of his temples were at Luxor and Karnak and Thebes became the centre of religion and the state.

Amun was married to Mut, the vulture goddess, shown as a woman wearing a vulture cap and the double crown, or with a lioness's head. They had a son, Khonsu the Moon-god, forming what is known as the Theban Triad (c.f. Osiris, Isis and Horus of the Heliopian myths). From the New Kingdom onwards, this marriage was celebrated ritually at Thebes at the annual Opet festival.

Gradually, Amun-Ra became the unknowable, secret god; no god knew his name because he represented ultimate total divinity. In this evolved form, he was invisible, like the air – the creator, yet remote from his creation.

Yet though he was unknowable he did have a statue form, dating back to his earlier phases of evolution. He was shown holding the ankh in one hand and the scimitar, symbol of power and defeat of over foreign enemies, in the other.

Amun-Ra's statue at Karnak was annually carried to Medinet habu on the west bank at Thebes, where he met his ancestor the primal snake Khem-atef. The snake represented the renewal of Amun-Ra, constantly restoring his vitality as a snake sheds its skin. In procession Amun-Ra's statue was carried inside a curtained shrine or wooden boat so that people could not see his form.

In later times Amun became a trinity. He was Ra or Re, the Sun-god who represented the ever-shining face through which each day he made himself known to humanity. Ptah was his body, the earthly manifestation, and Amun the hidden divine invisible aspect. Amun also absorbed other god forms directly through which he made himself known to humanity, for example Amun-Re-Atum, Min Amun and Amun-Re-Horakhty, joining his power to that of Horus and Ra in the rising and noonday sun.

From the Middle Kingdom, Amun-Ra was regarded as the father of each king, coming to the mother in a dream or superimposing himself on the body of her husband to conceive the child.

One fascinating image of Amun-Ra is that of the great goose calling creation into being by his cry and laying the egg of the sun, a direct assimilation of the myth of the Hermopolis 'Great Cackler', the primordial goose Geb.

Working with the creation myths

It does not matter whom you see as creator, or indeed if you regard the process in more symbolic terms as an actual sunrise over the mound that emerged from the waters when the Nile floods receded. Nevertheless, the creation story provides a powerful framework for creative rituals of all kinds, from conceiving a child or initiating a creative venture to starting all over again.

A creation ritual

You will need a deep bowl of water, a smaller empty bowl, a quantity of sand or dark earth enough to pile in the smaller bowl, a small trowel and a pure white candle.

▲ Decide on your creator deity – or, if you prefer, you can follow another tradition and work with Isis as the ancestress of the gods, as author and Egyptologist E.A. Wallis Budge maintained.

▲ Work at sunset; take the large bowl of water and set it on dark linen on the floor or a low table so that you can kneel before it.

▲ Focus on the purpose of the ritual and define this aloud, for example:

'I wish to start my own design business from home. I ask that the right circumstances may be created and the venture come forth, as the first mountain did from the waters.'

▲ Start to tell the story that you can adapt or expand. For example, you might say: 'In the beginning was the water and the water flowed, containing the possibility of life.'

▲ Take the second empty bowl and float it in the water of the first, saying something along the following lines:

> 'Then came the thoughts of the creator and wise Thoth spoke the magic words that brought the world into being. Let the thoughts of the great Ptah be given form by these my words.'

(I once heard an Egyptologist pronounce Ptah's name as 'Pitta', but I have also heard the name pronounced as 'Tah' and 'Pitach', with the 'ch' pronounced like a very soft version of the otherwise harder sound at the end of the Scottish word 'loch'.)

▲ Start to heap sand or soil into the floating empty bowl very carefully so that it does not tip over. It does not matter if sand or soil spills into the waters. Say: 'Then the first mound appeared.'

▲ Keep heaping your mound as you speak:

> 'And so the creator could stand upon the dry land. Then he called forth the light.'

▲ Carefully steadying the bowl, bury your candle in the sand and light it as you say:

> 'And so came the first sunrise of the first day. May light likewise bring into being my endeavour. I am in the light of the first morning. I am the light.'

▲ If you wish you can add the creation of other deities to give strength to specific aspects of your project. For example, if you were using the Heliopian myth, or for that matter adapting the Memphite one, you might say:

> 'And the children of the creator brought forth Geb the fertile earth and Nut, the lady of stars. May my endeavour likewise be firmly rooted in reality and progress step by step to ever-greater heights. I am the dark earth and I am the stars. Geb, Nut be in me, be me.'

▲ Add the names of as many deities as you wish, improvising and combining myths to weave your purpose.

▲ When you are ready, blow out the candle and say:

> 'And the sun entered the womb of the sky mother and darkness fell. So will my dreams lie fallow and in the morning my venture will be born with the light.'

Working with deity forms

There are so many deity forms from the ancient Egyptian world that if you refer to detailed books on the deities or use your web browser, you can find a deity for every occasion. In this chapter I have written briefly about some of the most popular deities, who spanned a number of dynasties and form a powerful focus for magical work. I have listed their main positive qualities that you can work with. At the end of the book, on pages 199–210, I have summarized the deities I describe in this book and suggested their special qualities. I have not listed the deities in alphabetical order here, but in what I consider the order of their magical importance.

Isis

If there were only one deity you could invoke in magic and for inspiration, it would have to be Isis. Her importance as Mistress of Enchantment has survived to the present time in Western magic and goddess spirituality. She was so popular throughout the Roman Empire that at one time it was thought her worship would replace that of the Christian Virgin Mary, with whom she is closely identified.

Isis is idealized as the perfect wife and mother and one to whom ordinary Egyptians could relate, tell their sorrows and make offerings at her shrines.

Isis, who was once an earth-dwelling deity, promised that they, and not just kings and nobles, would have immortality. Her buckle amulet the tjet (see pages 64 and 70) and images of her in her form of protective mother vulture were placed in the poorest of graves. She is probably the inspiration of the Black Madonna statues of mother and child that have been found all over Europe and the east from mediaeval times.

The myth of Isis and Osiris

Throughout this book I recount several myths concerning Isis. On pages 41–2 I described how she discovered Ra's secret names and so learned the secret of his magic. But the most famous myth involving Isis tells of the events that occurred after Set killed his brother Osiris to win the throne of Egypt. This was probably based in another early tribal clash, for we know that Osiris is a very ancient god, referred to by Wallis Budge as the ancestor of the gods.

Set put Osiris's body into a wooden trunk and threw it into the Nile. Isis rescued the body from the Nile at Byblos and took it to Memphis with her sister Nephthys. On pages 65–6 I described another version of this myth, in which the trunk became part of a tree and Isis had to split it with thunder and lightning.

But Set pursued them, cutting Osiris' body into 14 pieces and scattering them throughout Egypt so that he might not be resurrected, since his spirit would have no place to return. Isis, assisted by her sister and Heket the frog goddess, searched to find the pieces and each place where one was found became a sacred place to Osiris. Once they had reassembled the body, Nephthys's son the jackal-headed god Anubis bound it together, creating the first mummy. This procedure was thereafter carried out on the corpses of elevated humans so that their body might not be attacked and scattered by demons. Only Osiris's phallus could not be found and so Isis created one for him.

Isis became a sparrow hawk and with her swooping wings and magical incantations (here once again we see the might of the powerful life force of heka, or magical words), breathed life the mummy so that Osiris might awake and impregnate her. Afraid that Set might kill her son in the womb or in infancy, Isis hid in the papyrus marshes of the Nile Delta. Osiris descended into the underworld to become king and Isis gave birth to her son alone and hid him from Set. So she became an icon for every birthing mother or woman alone or in difficulty.

Once he came of age, Horus was able to fight his uncle and so Isis became the protectress of the kings – the incarnations of her son.

Unusually, Isis is portrayed in a number of ways. Sometimes she is seen as the young mother with cow horns and a solar disc between them; often she is coloured black and portrayed suckling her infant.

In earlier times, Isis was shown with a throne or plumes on her head. In statuary, she was portrayed as a more mature woman carrying a sistrum and wearing a knotted shawl (this image was prevalent throughout the Roman Empire where her cult was popular among women). As mistress of enchantment she is sometimes shown with the lunar crescent on her head beneath the sun disc or with the full moon disc alone. Astrologically she was the star Sirius and Osiris was the nearby constellation Orion (see pages 194–5).

Invoke Isis for magical energies, for all women's issues, for fertility, marriage and fidelity, mothering and protection, for moon magic on the crescent moon and the full moon and for healing. Her colour is red.

Osiris

Osiris was the teacher of humanity, appointed to rule the world by his father the earth god Geb. It was he who gave men agriculture and, as an early fertility and vegetation god, he was regarded as the embodiment of the corn. But Set was jealous and tricked his brother into getting into an ornamental trunk, which he then closed and threw into the river.

After his body was mummified, Osiris descended into the underworld, where he became the embodiment of the deceased king just as his son Horus represented the living one. For this reason Osiris is portrayed wearing the crowns of Egypt and carrying the ceremonial crook and flail.

He represents the annual growth of the corn, watered by the tears of Isis, the Nile Flood, and so ensures that the cycle of life, death and rebirth continues as the corn is cut down but sprouts again. In this, Osiris complements the ordered passage of the Sun-god.

Osiris was an important god, as it was believed he could claim a place in the heavens for all who followed him.

It was believed that in the underworld Ra nightly joined with Osiris and thus gained the power for rebirth.

Osiris can be invoked for regeneration – including the rekindling of hope and enthusiasm in a relationship or starting over after loss – for fertility of all kinds, for male rituals of all kinds, for nobility of purpose and for reaping what you sow. His colours are black and green.

Horus

Horus was once two distinct gods. Horus the Elder took the form of the falcon or the falcon-headed god, brother of Set, later identifiable with Ra; Horus the younger was a naked youth portrayed with a lock of hair over his face and his finger on his lips. Some authorities do not identify the elder Horus as a separate god from the younger Horus, but use the terms to refer to Horus when he was grown up and old enough to take on his father Osiris's role as god king of the earth.

The young Horus was sometimes regarded as being synonymous with the young Lotus-god and the rising sun that was born anew each day. So he represented all kinds of new beginnings, both in the year and in people's lives.

Welcomed at all royal festivals, Horus is sometimes depicted as a falcon wearing the double crown of Egypt or in his falcon-headed form with a crown. A falcon was engraved behind statues of kings sitting on their thrones or hovering overhead.

Invoke the young Horus for healing, for renewal and new beginnings, enthusiasm, action and courage; invoke the elder Horus for power, responsibility and nobility.

His colour is green or his wings may be shown as gold.

Thoth

Sometimes regarded as the father of the deities, self-created and present at creation, as seen in the Memphite myth, Thoth was the god of law, writing, medicine, mathematics, time and the spoken word. He also had command over all magical knowledge.

Thoth brought creation into existence by uttering the thoughts of the creator and was later called the heart and tongue of Ra (i.e. he translated thought into word and so animated the sun). He rode in the solar boat with Ra. In this capacity, he ordered the measurement of time.

As an elder god Thoth taught Isis the magical incantations to restore life to the body of Osiris. He also gave Isis the healing formula to restore young Horus to life after scorpions had stung him. (This was after she had caused an eclipse by stopping the sun boat.)

Depicted with an ibis or baboon head, or simply as these creatures, Thoth is also seen as a scribe with his magical palette, recording the words and commands of the deities and writing the laws for humankind.

Invoke Thoth for all forms of wisdom, learning and knowledge, including magical knowledge, for order in your life and in the world, for oratory and divinatory skills and for creative ventures. His colours are white and blue.

Ra

Some say Ra was the first deity to be worshipped and that his origins are lost in prehistory. The cosmic egg in some myths contained Ra, the Sun-god; his birth set time in motion. Over the centuries he became linked with the major creator deities, Ptah and as Atum-Ra and Amun-Ra. Over time his role as father of the gods became undisputed and he was said to have created himself, a fact that did not stop him entering the womb of Nut, his mother, every night.

He was portrayed as the sun at its full power and is depicted by the symbol of the sun and also in his solar boat. Ra is shown variously as a man or a hawk-headed man, crowned with the sun disc and sacred Uraeus serpent and with the usa, a dog-headed, forked rod of power.

Invoke Ra for power and for fulfilling ambitions, for self-confidence, for illumination in every aspect of your life and for making the most of time. His colours are yellow and gold.

Ma'at

Ma'at embodies cosmic balance, order and justice and is sometimes seen as the female alter ego of Thoth. She also rode in the solar boat and, like Thoth, was present on the solar barque at the first sunrise. Some myths say that Ma'at, like Thoth, was instrumental in the creation of the world by Ptah. She has been called the daughter of Ra, though she is an elder god.

In temple ritual, from the time of Thutmoses, around 1479 BCE until the Roman period in Egypt, the king or high priest offered a feather or tiny statue of Ma'at as a pledge to uphold order and justice.

In the afterlife, Ma'at weighed the hearts of the deceased against the ostrich plume feather from her head-dress to see if the heart was free from sin.

She is depicted as a slender woman with a single ostrich plume in her head-dress.

Invoke Ma'at for justice, truth, good conduct in the lives of self and others, balance and harmony. Her colour is white.

Sekhmet

One of the most powerful and ancient deities, the lion-headed solar goddess Sekhmet was both fierce avenger and protectress of the living and the dead, especially the Pharaoh. Her cult centre was at Memphis.

Statues of Sekhmet stood in the Treasure Room in the tomb of Tutankhamun. They bore a blue faience tear, indicating that Sekhmet wept for the young king. She was goddess of both war and healing and doctors practised in her name. She is sometimes called the eye of Ra warrior, her father.

In the afterlife, her protective role is predominant and in one ancient text, often placed on inscriptions of her statues, she says:

'I am the ardent heat of the fire that put a million cubits between Osiris and his enemies.'

Because of this, she also guards the blessed dead, protected by Osiris.

Known also as a lady of magic – especially magical healing and protection – her best-known statue is in a small temple in the enclosure of Amun at Karnak. When the full moon shines it casts a shaft of pure light upon the statue, making it seem as though she is alive.

Frequently, Sekhmet is pictured with the sun disc on her head and the sacred cobra, protectress of the Pharaohs, on her brow. She also takes the form of a lioness. In her lion-headed form she carries an ankh or sistrum.

Invoke her for courage, for defence, for fire magic and for healing, but never for revenge. Her colours are red and gold.

Hathor

The goddess of happiness, love, dance, music and joy, love, fertility, marriage and women and like Isis and Nut, one of the primal mother goddesses, Hathor was the sister and gentle aspect of Sekhmet.

Like Sekhmet she was the daughter or consort of Ra and she was a protector of women. She is patroness of modern businesswomen.

Hathor is depicted wearing a sun disc held between the horns of a cow.

Her protective image is found in many Egyptian tombs. Most spectacularly, she is shown as a large cow covered with lotus flowers or ankhs in the tomb of King Amenhotep III. His image is painted black, the colour of death, and he is depicted in the position of prayer under the head of the cow. By contrast, a small statue of Hathor, found in Deir el Bahar and dating back to the 18th Dynasty, portrays him in red, the colour of the living (i.e. reborn), and drinking from the teat of the cow. This shows that the goddess had adopted him.

Invoke Hathor for protection, for nurturing and all mothering issues, for marriage and committed love affairs, for harmony, fertility, inspiration, joy and for protection. Her colour is red.

Nephthys

Wife of Seth and sister of Isis and Osiris, Nephthys's role is invariably helpful and benign. She searched with her sister for Osiris's body, helped her to reassemble the body her husband had mutilated and remained a helpmate to Isis through her pregnancy and the early days of motherhood.

However, Nephthys is often most remembered for her protective role in the underworld, standing behind Osiris as the heart of the deceased is weighed. She also helped Isis in her role of assisting and protecting the dead. With Isis, Neith and Serqet, she formed the quartet of deities who protected the young Tutankhamun and other Pharaohs and nobles in death. Isis and Nephthys face each other with outstretched wings on the lids of mummies or stand at the head and foot of the mummy.

As a nature goddess, Nephthys represented sunset and both she and Isis rode on the solar boat at the first sunrise. However, as the shadow alter ego of Isis, she symbolized the darkness, silence and hidden mysteries and what was invisible. Isis was the birth goddess; Nephthys was the death goddess. Yet the death led to rebirth and so she is a symbol of hope.

Nephthys is usually portrayed as a woman with a pylon – a tower shape with a dish on the top. When she is depicted protecting the Pharaoh's body after death, she is shown with outstretched wings, like her sister Isis.

Invoke her for compassion, gentleness, reconciliation, acceptance of what cannot be changed, for soothing sorrow, for support in difficult times and for endings that lead to beginnings. Her colour is black.

8

DREAM INCUBATION
AND INTERPRETATION

To the ancient Egyptians, dreams were an important means of communication both with the deities and with personal ancestors. In sleep, both deities and deceased relations could respond to petitions and offerings by giving information about the daily world. They also interceded, it was believed, with higher cosmic powers and also warned and advised the living on future events.

In contemporary terms, dreams enable us to access a very deep level of personal wisdom and knowledge that is blocked by the conscious mind. It may also be possible to move beyond the physical world in sleep to higher planes where we can not only tap into past and future events, but also use the energies to bring about what it is we need. To the Egyptians, these creative thought processes in sleep mirrored the process Ptah and Thoth used to bring the world into being. Indeed, Thoth was one of the deities believed to give counsel in dreams. In the later Ptolemaic period, Serapis, associated with Osiris and regarded as the husband of Isis by the Romans, was the god of dreams. He was often depicted with a bull's head.

The dream of Thutmoses or Thothmes IV

The most famous predictive dream in Egyptian history was that of King Thutmoses IV, who ruled from 1400–1390 BCE. Studying it may give us clues to the process behind ancient Egyptian dream-work.

Thutmoses had his dream while he was still a prince and not directly in line to be the next king. A record of his dream can still be seen on a stela, a commemorative tablet, between the front paws of the Sphinx at Giza. The stela tells that during a hunting expedition near Giza, Thutmoses became tired and fell asleep, shaded by the Sphinx, which was half buried in the sand. In his dream, the Sphinx appeared and complained that his statue had been neglected and was rapidly disappearing into the sand. The Sphinx promised the prince that he would become king if he restored the monument to its former glory.

Though he was not heir to the throne, Thutmoses agreed and, when he was later made king, kept his promise and erected the stela to record the experience.

It could be argued that the prince was subconsciously making promises in his sleep to the deities that he would take care of the old treasures if he were allowed to hold divine office. It could also be said that since he was conscious of the importance of the past he was psychologically a good candidate to be chosen for kingship. Most significantly, the dream gave him the confidence to aim high and perhaps to display more openly qualities that marked him out as a worthy successor. Dreams in both the ancient Egyptian world and the modern world are all about potential and following one path rather than another. The wise unconscious mind, evolved self or magical inner Sphinx can hold the key in dreams.

Creating dreams and night visions

Important though spontaneous dreams are, the ancient Egyptians recognized that it was possible to create significant or psychic dreams to bring answers or solutions. One source of wisdom, especially on domestic matters was Bes, the household dwarf god.

Late in the evening before bed, would-be dreamers drew an image of Bes on their left hand, the hand that was thought to be linked to lunar and hidden knowledge.

They would then ask for Isis's blessing upon a large black dream cloth to amplify the secret dream knowledge and they would wrap their left hand in the cloth.

The dreamers would not speak until bedtime, when they would enfold themselves in the dream cloth. The cloth was a form of sensory deprivation to shut out the external world.

You can modify the original ink recipe for drawing Bes, which required ingredients – such as the blood of a white dove – that are inappropriate in the modern world. Some of the original ingredients of the magical ink, such as frankincense and myrrh, you can burn as incense in the bedroom before sleep. Substitute a glass of cranberry juice or blackcurrant juice for the original mulberry used in the ink.

Use mineral water to dilute the juice (the original ink recipe demanded rainwater). You can drink a little of the cranberry juice and water just before sleep.

Inducing a significant dream

▲ About ten minutes before bedtime, light frankincense or myrrh in the bedroom and a tiny nightlight to work by.

▲ If possible, avoid talking to anyone – whether by phone, e-mail or in person – as this will keep your mind in the conscious world.

▲ Just before bedtime, on your left palm draw an outline of Bes (see page 56) with his crown of feathers in smudge-proof dark lipstick or eyebrow pencil or use concentrated vegetable-based paint and a fine brush (test your skin for sensitivity).

▲ On a slip of white paper, use conventional black ink to write the question or request that will form the source of the dream.

▲ Taking a long, wide, dark scarf or shawl, ask Bes, Mother Isis or any personal deity or angelic form to bless the garment and enfold you in protection during your sleep travels, saying:

> 'May the seer of truth come from his/her sacred shrine this night and visit me with dreams
> of truth and gentleness. May I see only goodness as I work only with highest intent.'

▲ Enfold yourself in the scarf and read the question aloud. Fold the paper and place it under your pillow.

▲ Blow out the light and lie in the darkness, tracing the outline of Bes through the scarf and repeat the question as you drift into sleep.

▲ Keep a pen and paper by the bed so whenever you wake you can write the symbols of your dream before it fades. Draw an image of Bes at the four corners before you begin recording your dreams and say:

'*Bes, aid and make true my memory of this dream.*'

▲ Before you get up, look at the uncovered Bes on your hand and repeat the question for the final time. If you remain still the answer will come into your mind and you will see how the dream expands on the words and suggests the direction in which you should proceed.

▲ Wash your hand very carefully, thanking the deities for their wisdom.

Deities in dreams

The importance of a dream deity is, like any wise angel or guardian spirit, a way of knowing that the information comes from a higher source, whether the divinity is within us or a personified source of higher power. Though the following method can be used for absolutely any question, it is especially potent for issues of a spiritual nature.

I found this spell in a corner of the British Museum Egyptian displays that was being refurbished. It was written in demotic, a popular script in later ancient Egypt.

It said that if you light frankincense in front of the lamp and look at the lamp through the smoke, you will see a deity in the smoke. Thoth was often invoked via this process. How will you recognize the deity? Perhaps by the head-dress or animal head if you are familiar with the deities. If not, ask in your mind and you will telepathically know the deity and the strengths he or she brings.

▲ Again, prepare your sleeping place by lighting frankincense. Sleep close to the ground – for example, on cushions or a futon mattress. The reed mat traditionally recommended is hard to find and very uncomfortable.

▲ Switch off phones and faxes and try to make a time before sleep when you can be alone and undisturbed.

▲ Have a light supper and avoid stimulating television programmes. Instead, spend the evening listening to gentle music.

▲ Relaxing in a bath to which a little lotus or rose essential oil has been added is a good way of marking the boundaries between the everyday world and magic. Lotus is such a beautiful oil, it is well worth trying to get hold of it, as it was so central to Egyptian magic (see pages 132–3).

▲ Go into the place where your sleeping mat is – perhaps in your temple, as this is a special experience.

▲ Originally the following hieroglyphs were written on a strip of white linen that was folded and used as a wick for the lamp. You can more easily and safely write the symbols around the rim of the lamp before lighting, if you use one of the flat ceramic oil lamps with a floating wick. Otherwise you could engrave the hieroglyphics on a white candle with a nail or nail file.

Part of a spell

▲ Light the candle or lamp and recite the wish or question seven times.

▲ Half-close your eyes and look around the halo of the lamp or candle, visualizing a red mist and the deity form walking out of it. The deity may not be the one you expected or asked for, but will be the idealized form who can best advise you on the question.

▲ Greet the deity you see or – if the god or goddess is unknown – welcome whoever has come to help you and ask that he or she will protect you in sleep.

▲ Extinguish the lamp or candle and then go to sleep. Again, visualize yourself walking into the red mist towards the deity.

▲ As you drift into sleep, you may wish to ask the protection of Thoth or Mother Isis, asking that the answer or truth may be revealed in the dream.

In a later version of dream incubation recorded in the third century BCE and called 'dreaming true', someone with a question went to a cave that faced south and sat in the darkness gazing at the lamp or candle flame until they saw in it the face or form of a deity. The person would then sleep in the cave and in dreams the guardian god or goddess would bring the answer to the problem.

Meeting your dream guardian

You may find that while using this method an Egyptian figure appears to you instead of, or as well as, the deity and this person will regularly act as your dream guide. It may be your wise Egyptian spiritual ancestor (see pages 19–20) or a very old Egyptian priest or priestess with a kind smile.

Not everyone desires a dream guide, but if you do want one you will not be disappointed and many spontaneous dreams of old Egypt may follow over the next few months. In your dreams you may learn more about this character, for example his or her name, and if you try past life work in scrying (see pages 111–13) you may understand the connection and why he or she chose you. Such a figure is always benign and invariably helpful. Some say it is your own old wise soul that is connected to this oldest form of wisdom.

Letters to the dead and dreams

These are communications from the living to the ancestors, asking them for help and guidance through a dream. This form of communication was placed on household ancestor shrines, or in mortuary temples, or – for a major request – set in the tomb at the time of the funeral, perhaps with an amulet or image (see page 57). Psychologically and psychically, the action of writing down feelings, needs and fears and then seeking intervention from a wise ancestor who was believed as one of the Blessed Dead to have access to the deities, is a way of externalizing internal feelings and needs and then sending them out to cosmic forces for resolution.

Ancient Egyptian dream letters

These dream letters have existed right from the Old Kingdom through to Late Period Egypt. They were often not letters at all but a small pottery bowl on which the request was written around the edges in hieratic (hieroglyphic writing). Offerings would be made in the bowl to the ancestor. However there were almost certainly more conventional letters, created on linen or papyrus, spoken aloud and then burned in a lamp.

Requests might include protection for the living family against wandering kas, souls for whom offerings were not made or whose tombs were abandoned. But most asked about matters that concerned the family, such as the lack of a baby to a beloved daughter, problems about the inheritance or the need for justice. Sometimes the letter might remind the deceased of kindness done for them in life by the petitioner. On one such bowl, a dutiful son reminded his late mother how he had hunted diligently for seven quail she had wanted to eat and he warned her that if anything happened to him, there might be no one to make offerings or pour water over the shrine to refresh her ka.

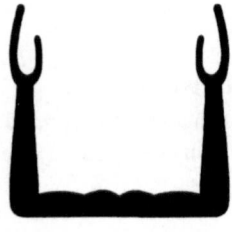

Ka

The Ka was represented by the hieroglyphic of two outstretched arms.

A Ka carved on the wall of the Pharaoh Teta's tomb at Saqqara tells another story from the ancient world. A husband reproached his wife, who had been dead for three years, and asked why she would not let him get on with his life as he had been a good husband. He blamed her for the misfortunes he had encountered since her death. In this case we know he wrote to his wife on papyrus, read the letter in her tomb and then tied it to the statue. It is not known if she came to him in dreams and reassured him.

After placing offerings in the bowl, the seeker would go home, hoping that when night came, the relation would appear in the dream with an answer. Sometimes the seeker would address the statue of the ancestor or a deity in a special prayer niche outside the temple. The messages were often remarkably homely, enquiring how the deceased was faring after moving to the West, or whether if he or she was enjoying life in the field of reeds.

The dream might also take the form of a battle in which the relation was seen doing battle with demons or with malign kas to protect the family.

One popular chant of the time ran: 'Become an akh before my eyes. Then can I see you in my dreams fighting to defend me. Then shall I make offerings to your glorious spirit.' The akh was the transfigured spirit in the afterlife who was believed to have magical powers. But the Egyptians neither sought nor wanted to see the ancestor actually materialize before them.

Dreams of the wise ancestors

In the modern world, when you make your petitions and offerings of flowers, incense or perfume on the table you have created as a memorial for your family ancestors, you are not calling forth ghosts or summoning spirits. Rather, you are invoking positive energies from the past and from higher sources that are represented by the knowledge gained after death by the wise ancestors. You may remember the kindness and compassion of a particular relation during his or her lifetime or feel kinship with someone from the distant past in your family. Or you can work with the spiritual Egyptian you remember in your private place of the ancestors.

Spontaneous dreams of relations who have died are common in all ages and places and I have collected hundreds in my own research in Western Europe, Australia, New Zealand, South Africa, the Americas, Canada and Japan.

You may decide you do not want to carry out this aspect of dream-work. If so, you can simply read the section and move on. However, in the modern world the loving energies from the past have become confused with sensational material about spooks and malevolent ghosts and I think this has meant we have cut ourselves off from a rich source of healing energies.

After my mother's death, when I was 19, I was so spooked that when she appeared to me in dreams, I went to the doctor, who prescribed sedatives for me. This stopped the dreams but delayed the healing for me.

In seeking ancestral dreams, you are seeking to make a connection with the loving energies of those who have lived before you. They exist on the dream plane that the ancient Egyptians, and many western practitioners, believe lies between life and death. Even if you find it hard to accept the actual survival of a loved one, you can symbolically tap into that reservoir of love and wise counsel that I believe never dies. If the idea seems too spooky, focus on a member of your family some generations back and use them as a symbol for accumulated wisdom – or leave this work until you feel you would benefit from it.

▲ Work during the hour before sleep.

▲ At times when it seems no one understands, it can be very helpful to go into your temple and write down all your worries and fears in black ink on white paper.

▲ Place the completed paper on the ancestor table or if you fear there may be prying eyes in a locked box hidden within your temple.

▲ Use your normal script so that all your feelings, negative and positive about a matter or concern can flow.

▲ Use a proper nib pen and when you have finished blot the paper dry and read what you have written aloud without pause and without altering it, as usually the first attempt reveals your true uncensored thoughts.

▲ If there are negative expressions, do not feel guilty You are merely offloading them as the grieving husband did on his deceased wife in what may have been a mixture of unresolved grief for her loss and guilt that he wanted to move on after many years together. From my own experience much unfinished business is resolved in dreams after we have expressed negativity about or to someone who has died.

▲ Now you are going to summarize and formalize your petition.

▲ You can follow the traditional method of using an unglazed pottery bowl and writing a few words around the rim to summarize what you are asking. Buy a number of these pottery bowls as they are relatively cheap and can be bought in bulk on markets second quality or chipped stalls. Or make your own.

▲ You can use waterproof ink, paint and a small brush or a marker pen or special ceramic paint and will become skilled in time. As you write, say the words aloud. Just use five or six words to summarize the issue.

▲ Alternatively, use a square of glass or glass bowl. You can buy special glass decorating paint and brushes in garden centres as well as craft stores.

▲ Fill the bowl with offerings that seem appropriate. These might be small crystals, flowers, incense, a favourite kind of small chocolates or flowers, or for an elderly grandfather perhaps a little of his favourite tobacco.

▲ Raise the offering bowl and say:

> '*I make these offerings willingly and ask the blessings of the highest powers of light and life. I seek only that the answers to my questions be made clear and that I be given the strength and courage to do what I must, drawing on the wisdom and love of my ancestors.*'

▲ Leave the offering and the issue. Few are so urgent that there must be an immediate resolution. You will receive the answer in a dream over the next few nights and perhaps see, hear or sense the presence of the ancestor on the dream plane. If the person does not come in a dream the time may not be right or you may see a symbol in an unusual place that answers your question.

▲ You can also use the dream letter method for contacting a deity whose counsel you desire. For example, you might write to Nut the protective sky mother with her body of stars, wise Osiris who washes away the stagnation and brings new growth or Heket, the frog fertility goddess who so well understands women's problems. You can also write a letter to your dream guardian if you have not yet met him or her and wish to hasten the meeting.

▲ Alternatively, you can write a letter to a living person from whom you are estranged – or, indeed, to whom you would like to move closer. If it is their will also you will meet on the dream plane – and then hopefully in reality in a positive way.

Dream interpretation

To the ancient Egyptians nothing was accidental or random. A dream was more than a physiological reaction to stress or too rich a meal and was of great significance. Consequently, dream interpretation was highly regarded, practised by priests, professional dream interpreters who operated, they claimed, by mandate of the deities and also wise women, intuitively skilled though they may not have had access to the official dream-works.

As early as the second millennium BCE, a dream book was created, giving the meanings of images, rituals to bring good dreams and even revealing how to send bad dreams to enemies. We have a later copy of this in the form of the Chester Beattie papyrus, now in the British Museum, which was found in Thebes in Upper Egypt and dates from about 1350 BCE.

Dreams were regarded as good or badly aspected, although different dream papyri and different interpreters did mean that the same symbol could provide contrasting and sometimes conflicting meanings. To the ancient Egyptians there were three kinds of dreams. The first were revelations about unknown aspects of known events, when deities or other wise figures such as the ancestors gave advice or warnings. Healing dreams, in which a remedy was revealed, came under this category, as did those that showed where a lost or stolen object was hidden. It was also believed that in dreams people could see the afterlife and many of the visions described in the texts of the Dead (see pages 118–19) were received in sleep.

The second kind of dreams were pious or sacred dreams. In this kind of dream, a deity demanded that a particular offering or service must be performed in order that a blessing might be received or a disaster averted. The dream of Thutmoses IV falls into this category.

The third kind, often wrapped in deep symbolism, were the prophecies. I shall discuss these in greater detail in the next chapter.

None of these concepts is strange to modern psychology and psychic research. We know that the mind is like an iceberg – that we can access knowledge in dreams that is not available to the conscious mind and thereby trigger our own innate healing powers (more of this on page 153). One of the most interesting aspects of dream interpretation in Ancient Egypt is the concept that we dream the opposite of what we hope or fear, in the present or – in the case of predictive dream – in the future. So, for example, if you dreamed of a great feast and of a full granary, you were thought to be afraid of being short of money and resources. Freud and more recent dream analysts have recognized these compensatory or denial dreams. King Kheti introduced the concept rather earlier in the book he wrote for his son Merikare around the beginning of the second millennium BCE.

Overcoming nightmares

Nightmares or those dreams recognized as bad omens – for example, a man making love to his wife in broad daylight, which indicated his secret failings would soon be exposed to the world – could, it was written in the old dream books, be prevented or banished through ritual or protective amulets. For example, to banish night demons (which bad dreams thought to be) – especially around the bedrooms of pregnant women and children – images of Bes wearing a fierce expression and brandishing knives would be placed at the bedside and the magic boomerang wand flicked outwards as though being thrown.

Specially engraved headrests made of stone or wood were placed at the bed head to protect the sleeper from harm. Formulas would also be chanted after a dream predicted misfortune. Isis was regarded as a special protectress against the consequences of bad dreams. In one remedy, the dreamer on waking would eat freshly baked bread and green herbs made soft with the special barley beer that was the nourishment of deities and humans alike. Isis would be entreated at first light with such words as: 'Isis, my mother, enfold me and take what I see far from my home and my land.'

Adapting the old ways

To drive away nightmares, try engraving an image of Bes wearing a fierce expression and holding knives on a protective crystal, such as amber or amethyst, and keeping it next to your bed. Alternatively, fix an image of Bes, or one of Thoth in his blue protective baboon form, at the head and foot of the bed.

Children need gentler protection, perhaps an image of the winged Isis and Nephthys at the head and foot of the bed. Another option might be to hang a protective wand above the bed showing Thoth as a beautiful ibis, the winged Isis, Heket as a smiling frog, Tauret in her more benign hippopotamus form and the falcon-headed Horus at the rising sun (see pages 13–14 for making one). You can tell gentle stories about the Egyptian guardian deities and waft the room with gentle lavender or rose oil before bedtime.

Before going to bed, and again on waking, you and your child can also create protective chants like the one about Isis and yourself. Alternatively, you could drink water in which a clear quartz crystal, an orange carnelian or sparkling citrine has been soaked for eight hours, to drive away any lingering fears with the dawn light.

Dream temples

These served several purposes. They provided the setting for dream incubation to receive answers to questions, to stimulate healing remedies or actual healing in dreams and they offered interpretation by skilled priests and priestesses of the dreams received in the dream temple. The very best dream interpreters would encourage the dreamer to apply the images to his or her own life and so to make wise decisions, based on the impressions and feelings, not just the images, left by the dream.

Dream temples were especially powerful because of the collective energies built up by the many dreamers visiting them and also because they were built in places of beauty where spiritual energies were high. Seekers of dreams were required to be pure of mind and body and so they carried out various cleansing rituals. For this reason the temples were usually close to water. We know that as well as dream temples for Thoth, Serapis the god of dreams, and Isis, there were also dream temples for Amun-Ra and Imhotep, the scribe and architect who created the Djoser Step Pyramid in 2650 BCE at Saqqara and was elevated to divine status because of his wisdom. Memphis and Thebes had important dream centres.

Even relatively ordinary people could gain access to them and, before sleeping in the dream halls, might make offerings to statues of the presiding deities; perhaps in making prayers to them they might lay the foundations for the dream.

Many of these temples were open to the stars and as the moon shone on the water or the statues, it is not surprising that the dreamers felt they were in a magical land. Those who came to temples dedicated to Isis were often drawn there because they had already seen her in a dream and she had told them to come. She was very special to women and young girls.

In later times, Imhotep was associated with Aesculepios, the Greek god of healing dreams. The Greeks in Egypt created dream and healing temples to Imhotep at Philae and Memphis.

Creating your own Egyptian dream book

On moonlight nights you may occasionally wish to sleep on your mattress in your temple, burning lotus or rose oils before sleep and sitting in lamp or candlelight, allowing thoughts to come and go. At such times even if you do not structure dreams by focusing on specific questions, your dreams will be rich and vivid and your dream guide may take you back to the old places.

▲ If you have a special dream spontaneously, or one you incubate at any time, record the symbols as soon as you wake.

▲ In the evening, sit quietly either in the open air or in your temple, holding a moonstone, an amber crystal or a clear crystal sphere and light your lamp or candles so that the crystal dances with light.

▲ Let your crystal speak to your heart and let the words flow through you. You can either tape record the words or write them down as soon as they have ceased flowing in your mind. You may have woven a story about the sun and the Nile, the deities, or a temple by moonlight next to a lake that represents the primal waters of Nu.

▲ Begin an A to Z section in your book of Egypt. Note down not just dream significance but the meanings of specifically Egyptian imagery, a marsh of swaying tall green papyrus reeds, a lotus unfolding in the sun, a crocodile sunning himself who turns into a god. In the next chapter you will work with different forms of divination and you will discover that the imagery seen during divination is identical to dream imagery.

▲ Use pictures from the internet, books and videos. Go to museums and look at the lovely old Egyptian statues there. At the back of this book I have listed museums in many parts of the world that house Egyptian artefacts, but you can also get virtual museums online.

▲ Above all, take steps to familiarize yourself with features that are common to Egypt. Walk in sunshine on sand or on marshland if you can; work with clay; play with the sand-box on your altar table as you did when you were a child. Seek out the ibis, the heron, Egyptian geese in bird parks and watch falcons or other birds of prey in flight. Gradually, the world of Egyptian imagery will penetrate your consciousness and prove a rich vehicle for your dreams.

9

ORACLES, OMENS AND DIVINATION

Ancient Egypt was the source of oracular wisdom throughout the Classical world. Popular legend describes how two black doves flew from Thebes, one of the main ancient Egyptian oracular centres. The first dove settled in Dodona in the grove of oaks sacred to Zeus, the father of the Greek gods and, speaking in a human voice, declared it the place where an oracle would be established. The second dove flew to Libya, to another site sacred to Zeus in the form of Amun/Ammon, and established a second oracle there.

In fact, the two doves were priestesses kidnapped from the oracle at Thebes. Though it is mainly priests who were associated with the oracular centres in Egypt, we know that an oracular priestess tradition existed there also. As in other cultures, this may be older than the priestly tradition, possibly dating from Neolithic worship of the Mother Goddess. Indeed, the mythical seven daughters of Hathor, who were goddesses of Fate and visited newborn children to assign their fortune, were probably an ancient hereditary order of seven oracular priestesses at one of Hathor's temples.

The oracle in Egypt

The word 'oracle' can be confusing in this context, as it refers not only to the predictions or prophecies that were made, but also to the priests or priestesses conveying the message and the temple where the prophecies were given.

In Egypt, the oracle was regarded by both the great and the humble as an important part of decision-making. The priesthood was able to control a weak king by informing him of the will of the gods through oracles. During the New Kingdom, the priests of Amun-Ra increasingly used oracles to dictate the way they said the god wished the Pharaoh to rule. Indeed, in the 21st Dynasty the priests of Amun seized control of Egypt, and reigned in the deity's name.

But even in times of a strong king, the oracles influenced state and personal matters, choosing the heir to the throne, giving legal judgements and determining the best time and place to plant crops or to site a temple.

Priestly oracles

These are, in a sense, the most conventional oracles, and the most easily understood in the modern world. A priest or priestess in a higher state of consciousness or semi-trance would act as a trance medium, speaking in the voice of the deity. It was believed that the wisdom entered the priest's heart from the deity and was translated through his tongue, a re-enactment again of the first creation.

In the earlier Egyptian period, the priest might appear wearing a mask or head-dress representing the deity, thus symbolically assuming the persona of the god and so speaking with full authority. An Egyptologist I met in the reconstructed temple complex at Dr Ragab's Pharonic village explained that to ordinary people the appearance of a masked and robed figure would strike wonder and terror in their hearts as they believed that the deity was indeed manifest before them.

Later the priests used holes in the temple walls to convey answers to petitioners outside the sacred inner precincts and in some cases the holes were behind or within a huge statue so that the statue seemed to speak in answer.

We should not dismiss this as trickery, since it was believed that the ka of the deities did live within their statues and that the priests acted merely as the mouthpieces. What is more, the mystery of the experience served to distance it from the everyday world, thereby enabling the petitioner to make a spiritual link with the deity oracle, so that he or she might continue to receive wisdom in the hours and days afterwards, both in dreams and waking visions.

The oracle of the Apis bull

The most famous Egyptian oracle was that of the Apis bull. The bull of Apis was no ordinary animal, but was regarded as a physical manifestation of the creator god Ptah and its soul was identified with the ka of Osiris. The ka of Osiris remained within the wonderful bull form and when one bull died, it passed into the successor creature.

According to the Greek historian Herodotus, who provided a great deal of information on Ancient Egypt, an Apis bull who was always black was chosen for its distinctive markings, including a white triangle on its forehead, another white mark in the shape of a winged vulture across its shoulders and a piece of flesh in the shape of a scarab under its tongue.

The bull resided within Ptah's sacred dwelling at Memphis in a specially constructed temple that contained two sacred bull pens as well as an exercise courtyard. People were able to ask questions that the bull would answer by moving into one or other pen in the outside area. More fortunate petitioners were allowed to offer him food and if he refused it the venture about which they asked was considered to be inauspicious.

How might this form of oracle have a valid basis? To the ancient Egyptians – and indeed to a number of modern philosophers, such as Jung – no action is random or accidental, least of all that of a divine bull. Therefore, a petitioner would deliberate on an issue and then assign one of the two possible areas as the positive response in his own mind. Put another way, the questioner's unconscious wisdom knew the right course but was unable to convey this to the conscious mind except through an outward sign.

But the oracle of the bull was only the first part of the process. The experience opened a doorway that involved the deeper wisdom of the seeker, triggered by the experience. Either during or after the event the bull might appear in a vision, perhaps while the seeker was travelling home in the shimmering heat or in dreams as he slept in a tent in the cool desert with shimmering stars under a huge, mesmeric moon. The original seemingly stark 'yes' or 'no' message was expanded in the seeker's mind and explained on the dream or daydreaming plane.

Oracular processions

Unlike the vocal Greek and Roman oracles, who might deliver long – albeit cryptic – messages, oracular wisdom in Egypt remained simple and straightforward, a trigger for the inner psychic powers of the petitioner.

Oracular deity statues would be carried on the shoulders of priests in procession at festivals. The priests carried the statue in a wooden boat, symbolizing the solar boat or barque travelling though the heavens.

A petitioner might ask a question of the deity who paused in front of him and by the movement of the deity as the priests paused, an answer would be given. The statue might seem to nod in approval or turn away to indicate the venture should not go ahead. Sometimes two options were written on pottery shards and the deity would indicate the favoured choice by stopping in front of it. It was believed that the deity directed the movements of the priests carrying the statue, so that the statue served the function of a giant cosmic choice pendulum.

The priests bearing such a heavy weight over a long route in blazing heat would – with the music and the sistrum ringing, the whirling of dancers and the noise of the crowd – slip into a trance-like state whereby they did not consciously choose a particular option or move the statue deliberately. The questioners too would be in a highly spiritually charged state, having been in contact with the spirit of the deity, and this would almost certainly lead to personal visions and the deity's voice in their head. This private expansion or mitigation of a basic yes/no verdict explains how the apparently random movements of a bull or statue could give answers that helped to form the lives of kings and ordinary people alike.

While any god carried in procession could offer wisdom, certain deities in particular were regarded as sources of oracles: Amun-Ra, Horus, Isis, Hathor and Set in lands and in times where he was revered.

Oracular wisdom from the deities

If you have a favourite deity – or, while working with this book, if you find one or two god or goddess forms that seem to resonate with you – it is possible to adapt the following method as a means of accessing oracular wisdom.

I have a number of small Egyptian statues in black stone and bronze, but I tend to work with the lioness-headed statue of Sekhmet, goddess of fire, especially at those times when I seem to lurch from crisis to crisis – not usually of my making.

However, you can work equally well with a picture of a deity or a full-sized statue in a museum. If the need is urgent and you have no physical focus, write the chosen deity's name and visualize him or her standing directing the pendulum swing.

▲ You will need a crystal pendulum or a pendant on a chain – anything that has a stable weight at one end and can swing freely – a statue or picture on which to focus (or the deity name written on paper) and a pen and notebook. The pendulum acts like the movements of the priests, prompted by unconscious knowledge manifest as a muscular response that causes the pendulum to react in a certain way in answer to a question.

▲ The question you ask should consist of two options that can be distinguished as a 'yes' or 'no' swing – for example: go/stay, speak/be silent, act/wait. If you are alone, you can speak aloud.

▲ The active/yes choice corresponds with the positive response from the pendulum, usually a clockwise circling. If in doubt you can discover the positive and negative responses of a pendulum by thinking first of a happy event then a sad one and seeing how the pendulum responds. Finish by thinking of another happy event to create good vibes.

▲ Try to find a time when you can be quiet and peaceful.

▲ Hold the pendulum in your power hand – the one you write with – and face the focal deity or deity name.

▲ Ask your question and, holding the pendulum between you and the statue (or visualized deity), wait until the pendulum responds.

▲ If it remains still, allow another question to come from within you spontaneously. Trust your unconscious mind, however unrelated what you are asking seems.

▲ Without analysing the result, focus on the deity form (or visualized deity) and let words and images come either into your mind or aloud about the issue and all your emotions and concerns, just as you did when writing the letter to the ancestors.

▲ Wait again. You may hear a voice within your mind, clear and quite distinctive, or the deity may continue to speak through your own inner voice. You may recall snatches of poetry, or old songs.

▲ The answer may, however, come in symbols and you may also see images of golden, sunny places, ancient temples or the cool, blue Nile.

▲ When the flow ceases, write down any key words or symbols to remind yourself of the most important points and then go for a walk and allow the whole experience to come together.

Scrying in Ancient Egypt

Scrying is the process of looking into a reflective surface, such as water, to see images either within the substance itself or in your mind's vision, stimulated by the movement of the light on the surface. In Ancient Egypt, scrying formed an important method of private divination and is still practised by some family elders who do not see the wise voice within as conflicting with their religious beliefs. When I was in Egypt, I learned from a family of Bedouin origin the relatively more recent art of coffee reading, using the thick, syrupy coffee that has been around from about the sixth century BCE. I also discovered a very ancient form of casting stones on sand. I have described this on pages 115–17 as it has been handed down from ancient Egyptian times, especially among wandering tribes. If you find any of the methods described below difficult, this is because your conscious mind is acting a monitor. Relax, and then stare at the water, close your eyes open them, blink and name the first image that comes into your mind. You can repeat this for subsequent images. In time you will not need to do this.

Oil lamp scrying

This is a very easy and effective method of scrying as long as you are very careful with the bubbling oil. It is certainly not a method to use around pets or children. And remember: never try to put out oil that is burning too fiercely with water. You must cut off the air supply with a metal lid. A safer alternative is the modern electric-powered lava lamp which follows exactly the same principles – although again, you should exercise caution, as it can be very hot to the touch.

You can obtain flat Egyptian-style oil ceramic lamps with a floating wick and a heatproof lip for carrying in gift and household stores and museum shops, as well as by mail order on the internet.

Though olive or palm oil was traditionally used, you may prefer a scented lamp oil. I like to work with darker coloured oils. If you use unfragranced oil, burn frankincense, myrrh or sandalwood incense, all divinatory fragrances, to help you to move beyond the everyday world.

▲ Work in the early morning, as the sun is rising.

▲ Set the lamp on a low table so you do not have to get too near the hot oil.

▲ Place the lamp on the east side of the table and sit on the west side facing east across the lamp, so the first light illuminates the oil.

▲ Light the lamp and formulate an area of your life in which you would welcome guidance.

▲ Chant in a soft voice several times:

   'Lamp light, lamp bright, show to me what is to be.'

▲ As the oil begins to bubble, half close your eyes and allow scenes to build up and flow one into the other to make a story. Until recently, I have worked by connecting a series of single images formed by the bubbling oil, but the story method in which you are the hero or heroine seems much more fruitful, especially for life path decisions.

Oil and water scrying

Another method used by ancient Egyptians was to float drops of cold oil on the surface of a bowl of water. You can occasionally still see this method in tourist bazaars, on stalls where scented oils are for sale. Because the oil is constantly moving, this is a very effective and easy method if you find hot oil scrying unproductive. I prefer this method to using hot oil, as you can create a series of images very slowly and it is very good for showing the way ahead or for untangling dilemmas.

▲ Use one of the dark coloured oils, as this contrasts with water in a clear glass or ceramic bowl. The very dark virgin olive oils are traditional too and give strong physical images. I have also experimented with a smoked glass bowl and used a yellow olive oil on the surface of the shadowy water.

▲ This method seems to work better in the hour before sunset, a traditional time for scrying, but you will need to sit in the east, facing west across the bowl. Remain silent.

▲ As the shadows deepen, place a pure white or beeswax candle at the back of the bowl to cast light on the oil.

▲ Allow the shadows to form part of the imagining process.

▲ When you are ready, drip the oil drop by drop, either through an eyedropper or by using a bottle of fragrance or essential oil, allowing it to swirl and form images.

▲ If you are sparing with the oil and pause between drops to allow the oil to swirl, you will build up a series of images, each evolving from the first.

▲ Afterwards you may find it easier to draw the images randomly on a page in your Book of Egypt and then to study the page by candlelight, allowing your deep mind to make the connections. Together the images will give insight into an aspect of your life, leading you gently into the future so that you can make wise decisions.

Water and ink scrying

Ink scrying remained popular in the Middle East right through the Middle Ages. One version involved tipping ink into the palm of the hand and reading the formations created by the lines and grooves. However, that is a very messy method. If you buy black ink cartridges, the kind you use in pens, in a plastic tube you can use them much as you did the oils. This scrying method is good for specific issues or choices concerning family and your immediate circle.

▲ Fill a glass bowl with water. Again, work at sunset and sit east of the bowl, facing west.

▲ Prick the narrow end of the ink cartridge. Alternatively, use waterproof ink and a thin brush. Drop by drop, put the ink very gently on the surface and as it swirls name images. You should get three or four images before the water clouds.

▲ If you wish, you can then light candles around the black water and gaze into that for further clarification.

Hathor mirror magic

Hathor was the Ancient Egyptian sky goddess of joy, love, music and dance and protector of women. In the ancient world she promised good husbands and wives to all who asked her. Hathor was allowed to see through the sacred eye of her father/consort Ra. In this way, she had knowledge of everything on the earth, in the sea and in the heavens and the thoughts as well as the deeds of humankind. Hathor also carried a shield that could reflect back all things in their true light.

From this shield she fashioned the first magic mirror. One side was endowed with the power of Ra's eye so that the seeker could see everything, no matter how distant in miles or how far into the future. The other side showed the gazer in his or her true light and only a brave or pure person could look at themselves without flinching.

Hathor mirrors were originally made of polished silver or bronze with an image of Hathor on the handle, but you can work with a conventional single-sided mirror with a handle. Years ago dressing table sets with embossed handled mirrors were very common; these can still be picked up cheaply from garage sales and are absolutely perfect. You may also find a Hathor metal mirror in a museum shop. There are a number of online museum shops and it is well worth seeking one out for pride of place in your temple.

Of course, you can use any round mirror and some practitioners of Hathor magic prefer to use a swivel mirror on a stand. You can also adapt a highly polished plain silver or pewter tray.

Beginning mirror divination

As well as being a potent means of bringing to the surface issues concerning personal identity and potential areas of development, mirror divination is – as it was in Ancient Egypt – effective for discovering the identity of a future partner, and for answering questions about love, fidelity, marriage and permanent love relationships, fertility, family concerns and for discovering the location of an item or animal that is lost or the truth about a matter that is hidden from you.

▲ Work during the hour before sunset.

▲ To distance yourself from the everyday world for this special form of scrying, have a bath beforehand in water containing rose petals, rose essential oil or bath essence. Roses are sacred to Hathor.

▲ When dressed, you can if you wish circle round your eyes with turquoise eye shadow, believed in Ancient Egypt to increase the power of the inner clairvoyant eye and ward off all harm. Both men and women used this method.

▲ Circle the mirror with tiny turquoise crystals, Hathor's own stone of power. Alternatively, use golden jewellery, the sacred metal of Hathor, perhaps in the form of small gold earrings. You can also use imitation gold or golden coins in the circle, but try to have one piece of genuine gold, however small, in the circle.

▲ Hold the mirror or swivel a table mirror so that if possible the last light is reflected in it.

▲ You can also light red candles, Hathor's colour, so this light also catches the mirror reflections. In more modern magic, orange and pink have also become her colours.

▲ Light rose incense on either side of the mirror.

▲ Tilt the mirror angle so that you do not see your own face reflected, unless you are seeking to discover yourself in your true light.

▲ Ask a question of Hathor and wait for the images to form – either within the mirror or in your mind's eye. Both are equally valid and with practice you can cast the images from your psyche into the mirror.

▲ To do this, visualize the image in a tunnel of light passing from the centre of your brow, the location of the psychic third eye, so that the pictures re-form within the glass.

▲ Alternatively, begin by visualizing the image you saw in your mind on the surface of your magic mirror, then gradually see it receding deeper within the mirror and becoming three-dimensional.

▲ Either way, you may see single images or whole scenes.

▲ As before, if you experience difficulty, close your eyes, open them, blink and look at the mirror, naming whatever image you perceive in your mind.

▲ Once you have an image, either look away or close your eyes again, open them and blink.

▲ Continue until you have evoked five or six consecutive images.

Interpreting mirror images

I find that drawing the images and then sitting quietly and gazing at them in candlelight, will allow the unconscious mind to make sense of them.

It may also be that sounds, impressions or fragrances formed part of your mirror-scrying experience. All the psychic senses are linked and the more you work on the spiritual plane, the more readily your other psychic sense become part of what will eventually be a multi-sensory psychic experience. Whenever you come across a new symbol, add it to the Book of Egypt. You will also find that the more you work, the more new meanings you will add to existing symbols. In time, a major image may fill a whole page.

More formal mirror scrying

From the early mirror work evolved a series of rules for mirror scrying that has survived into modern magic. However, you may prefer not to use these rules if they conflict with your more spontaneous interpretations.

▲ An image moving away says that an event or person is either moving away from the scryer's world or that a past issue or relationship may still be exerting undue influence on the scryer.

▲ Images appearing on the left of the mirror suggest actual physical occurrences that either have influenced or may influence the everyday world in the near future.

▲ Images appearing in the centre or to the right tend to be symbolic.

▲ Pictures near the top of the mirror are important and need prompt attention.

▲ Those in the corners or at the bottom are less prominent or urgent.

▲ The relative size of the images can indicate their importance.

You can also use the same method with the clear crystal sphere that you use for healing (see page 168).

Stone and sand divination

A number of divination methods involving sand have passed from Egypt and Africa to westernized magic. It is difficult to know which are truly 'authentic', in that they were practised in Ancient Egypt in roughly their present form.

The relative fluidity of soft sand does make it an excellent medium for divination, whether you are sitting under a tree in a desert place or working with a sand box on your temple altar or with a larger one in your garden or on a balcony surrounded by potted plants. Children's park sandpits in the early morning are an excellent area for sand work.

If you spend time allowing your fingers to run through sand with your eyes closed, all kinds of wonderful images and impressions will be released.

A reliably authentic method was described to me that is still practised by Bedouin wise women. I have followed this up in my research and believe it is well worth trying. Sand reading is remarkably good for bringing to the surface any hidden aspects of your life, or events or opportunities that are as yet hidden and have not moved on to the horizon.

All you need are seven small smooth stones – six white and one red – and an enclosed area of sand, which can be a circle of two metres or so wide, marked off by sand walls or a large rectangular or square sandbox of similar dimensions. You will also need a long, thin dry stick – if possible, from a sun tree such as palm, orange, lemon, bay, ash, laurel or any fruit- or nut-bearing tree. If you are using a tray, make sure the sand comes to the top of the rim. When your stones are not in use, keep them in a drawstring bag. You can carry out a mini-version with seven small crystals, if you keep sand as your earth element on the altar.

▲ Work alone where and when you will not be disturbed.

▲ This time, do not ask any question or focus on anything specific. You may, however, find it helpful to have a portable tape recorder handy to record your words.

▲ If possible, work in natural sunlight so that a shimmer appears on the sand.

▲ If working on a beach, in a large sandpit or desert, mark the approximate limits of your divinatory area.

▲ Kneel or sit so you are above the sand.

▲ Close your eyes and allow your hands to run through the sand, forming it into ridges and hills, softly calling as a continuous chant:

> *'Nephthys, lady of the desert, flower of barren places, speak this hour the truth I need, not crave to hear. Mistress of the hidden places, reveal what is shrouded in the mists of what will be, that I may see in sand your message.'*

▲ When you are ready, open your eyes and gaze at the sandscape again without consciously focusing on any issues. Switch on your recorder as the shimmering sand hills may evoke images or impressions.

▲ Hold the seven stones between your cupped hands. Then close your hands, shake the stones and cast them downwards, so that they make a formation in the sand.

▲ Using the red stone as the marker, note how the stones are clustered. The one containing the red stone – or, if it is alone, the area of the red stone – defines the hidden issue. If the stones are scattered, there are a number of factors that will need to come together and once you discover what they are from the divination, you can devise ways of hastening the integration.

▲ The greater the number of stones close to the marker stone, the more major and imminent the event or change.

▲ If there are two or three distinct groups of stones, the future step forward may come slowly, through smaller stages.

▲ Now close your eyes, open them again and stare at the main group of stones – or the red stone if alone – set among the contours of the sand heaps. Speak what it is you see and feel into the recorder, projecting yourself into the desert scene and making each of the stones part of the backdrop.

▲ Go through all the other groups in the same way. Finally, close your eyes, open them again, stare at the whole scene in the sandbox and let the words come.

▲ Only one stage remains. Taking the stick in your power hand and, with your eyes closed, allow it to draw a large shape enclosing the stones. Allow the stick to move in and out, creating its own pathways. As you do so, repeat once more as a continuous chant:

> *'Nephthys, lady of the desert, flower of barren places, speak this hour the truth I need, not crave to hear. Mistress of the hidden places, reveal what is shrouded in the mists of what will be, that I may see in sand your message.'*

▲ When you are finished, open your eyes and – staring hard at the sand – say:

> *'Let me see in sand your message.'*

▲ Without a pause, name what shape or animal you have drawn and – again, without stopping to think – name its significance in your future life.

▲ Replace the stones in the bag and erase the sand images so the sand is smooth again.

▲ In the evening, light orange, lotus or cedar oil, or incense. Replay the tape in your temple by the light of a single oil lamp or night light, and let the ideas fall into place. If you have an altar sand box, run your fingers through it as you speak.

▲ Draw up an action plan in your mind to make future positive events come into your life when the time is right.

- 10 -
ANIMAL MAGIC

Today as in the past, animals are an integral part of the Egyptian landscape. Goats wander about on unmade tracks opposite stylish stone houses with lush gardens behind high walls; donkey carts challenge the motorized traffic on the freeways of the larger towns. Newly planted seeds are trodden in by sheep and cattle graze on strips of green beside the Nile beneath apartment blocks, or pull the plough in their slow, unbroken rhythm. Godlike cats with pointed ears guard their young in nests beneath worn monuments in green public gardens; clouds of white birds peck at the harvest. Herons, scarlet-winged at dawn, swoop over the marshes or cluster round oases like gossiping women and huge bats with wingspans like those of seagulls whirr around the palms trees in modern hotel complexes.

While many working domestic creatures have shared the harshness of the lives of the human workers over the millennia, family pets were cosseted in Ancient Egypt. Wealthy owners would mummify them and take them for burial in one of the sacred animal cemeteries. They might even be buried in wealthy owners' tombs. Paintings on tomb walls anticipated the reunion of pet and owner in the afterlife and depicted food that would be magically activated for the creatures when they rose from the dead.

Sacred animals
The most important ancient Egyptian animal associations were, however, those to do with the creatures sacred to a particular deity. These would be kept in large numbers at a temple and well cared for. But their lives might be short, for when a pilgrim wanted a mummified animal to offer to the deity, the creature would be killed and prepared so that a petitioner's prayers might be answered. Indeed, Bast's sacred cats were routinely killed at only ten months of age in order to be mummified as offerings.

The magic of animals
To understand the sometimes contradictory role of animals in Ancient Egypt, it is necessary to differentiate between the idealized creatures that were revered as representatives of a deity and the individual members of the same species that might be hunted for food, hides or ivory and sometimes maltreated.

The ancient Egyptians believed that after death a spirit could assume the form of animals or birds and temporarily return to this world. A number of chapters in the Book of the Dead gave formulae whereby the deceased's ka could transform itself into a hawk of gold, a heron, a swallow or a serpent.

For example, in the Wallis Budge translation of the Book of the Dead, the following formula was given in the papyrus of the scribe Ani so that his deceased spirit might recite them and assume the form of a swallow at will. The Osiris Ani, whose word is truth, saith:

I am a swallow, I am a swallow. Hail, O ye gods whose odour is sweet – I am like Horus – let
me pass on and deliver my message – although my body lieth a mummy in the tomb.'

It was assumed that the deities could also assume bird or animal forms, sometimes choosing one particular sacred animal. One example is the bull of Apis, which lived a pampered existence (see page 109) as a manifestation of Ptah on earth. When this creature died, another would become the shelter of the god. But all the sacred creatures were representative of that totem deity. Therefore, the body of a creature that had contained or represented divinity could not be allowed to corrupt in case the deity came back to seek it.

Some sacred animal and bird mummies received special treatment and it may be that this particular creature was one that had demonstrated special signs of being possessed by the divinity.

They were buried in bronze or even gold boxes on which was an image of the animal. In the case of the cat, the box would be adorned with jewellery such as the ankh, a scarab and gold earrings. Alternatively, the image of the totem deity might appear on the coffin

Power animals and their deities

These sacred animals and birds embodied the most positive characteristics of their ruling gods and goddesses. Each Egyptian town and region – called a Nome – had its own local sacred animal, centred on the place where the related deity was most venerated. It is hard to imagine the huge scale of this veneration, but archaeologists have excavated vast acres of cat cemeteries at Bubastis, Bast's cult centre on the Nile Delta, where an estimated four million mummified cats were buried. Close to the step pyramid of King Djoser at Saqqara, were the huge complexes of sacred falcons of Horus and the baboons and ibises of Thoth, which were kept in large flocks within a complex of buildings west of the pyramid. Here the ibis mummies alone ran into millions and it is certain that the offering of sacred animals by pilgrims in return for favours from the deity was one of the most important ways ordinary people connected with the deities.

Over time, these mummified creatures became associated with magical powers themselves, a belief that has lasted into the 21st century. Just as I was completing this book, I read in a newspaper that the Egyptian police had arrested a Syrian who had acquired 7,000 reptile mummies that he intended to grind up and use to make aphrodisiacs.

So central to worship were the animal symbols of power that many deities – though not all – were portrayed either in animal form or with an animal head. These images have translated well into modern life. For example, the powerful lion-headed solar goddess Sekhmet still acts as an icon of courage for women.

Animals and deity worship

Animal associations were a good way for ordinary people to understand the different characteristics of the deities – whether through a creature they feared but admired, such as the desert lion, or one that was famed for nurturing mothering qualities, such as the cow imagery employed in the worship of Hathor, for example.

Of course, no one actually worshipped Hathor as a cow. The connection was more metaphorical, implying that just as a cow provided milk for its calf and for humans so Hathor would eternally suckle humankind (see also page 202) in death as well as life.

We do not know how far back these animal icons date, but in many early societies the animal totem was central. In those indigenous cultures where spirituality has not changed over many thousands of years, the shaman or magician priest healer still wears bird or animal masks and feathers, as did the Palaeolithic magician priests.

Animal totems of power are still a part of spiritual worship for Native North Americans, Australian Aboriginals, Maoris and sub-Saharan Africans.

What is remarkable – and perhaps unique – to Ancient Egypt is that the animal icons developed relatively rapidly into a complex and highly sophisticated system of spirituality. One recent theory has suggested that the visitors from another galaxy who some argue brought civilization to pre-dynastic Egypt did appear in partial animal forms. Other, more down-to-earth theorists believe that because in creation myths animals were made from the primal material from which humankind came in a more evolved form, they mirror or reflect the untainted forms of particularly valuable human qualities and strengths. Indeed, the original group of eight (or 'ogdoad') deities of Hermopolis were depicted as frogs and serpents.

Animal cults

While sacred animals were always central to the ancient Egyptians, animal temple cults developed into their most popular and widespread form during the Late and Ptolemaic periods, between 664 and 30 BCE.

As well as mummified creatures, many thousands of bronze or faience animal figurines have also been found buried at the cult centres, while numerous others have been found as protective amulets in human graves. These amulets of sacred animals were carried or worn to place the wearer under a particular god's protection and to endow them with the desired qualities that were shared by the deity and the creature. Amulets bought at a cult centre were considered especially magical.

Animals and the afterlife

It was to exact revenge against enemies that a spirit might turn into a crocodile or serpent and return temporarily to the world. So the living feared that they might be under attack not just from a real snake, but the spirit of an old enemy.

As Budge tells us, the dead were believed to have spells that enabled them to transform themselves into one of these ravening creatures, declaring themselves the crocodile god in person, who seizes his prey and lives among the fierce earthly crocodiles, waiting to exact revenge. This form of incantation survived right through the period of mediaeval magic.

For this reason, some of the fiercest animal deities were used as protectors in the afterlife to keep the spirits of the deceased safe from the demons and snares that must be overcome in order to reach the Field of Reeds, as well as protecting the living from predatory creatures – both normal and paranormal.

In the antechamber of Tutankhamun's tomb there were three funerary or ritual beds, and on each of the bed-posts there were representations of protective animals to ward off danger. These beds were used during the three main stages of the mummification process.

One had an image of the goddess Ammet, the great devourer of souls who failed to become one of the Blessed Dead. She is represented by the head of a hippo, the tail of a crocodile, and the paws of a feline; her teeth are made of ivory and her tongue is stained red. Her role was to drive off all harm from the young king in the afterlife.

The second bed had twin cow heads, on each of which the horns flanked a solar disc. The bodies become the heavenly vault, covered with symmetrical spotted fur. The cow represents Hathor and Nut, queen of the sky. A golden head of Hathor also stood guarding the antechamber of the tomb.

The third bed features twin lion heads, in honour of Sekhmet.

Animal power in the ancient world

Below you will find a list of animals that were regarded as especially holy in the Egyptian world. It is still possible to work directly with these sacred animals that were central to Ancient Egypt. Some are still common, living wild or domesticated in a number of regions of the world, but many others can be found in conservation parks. The internet is a good source of images, while there are plenty of wildlife videos available that will also help you to connect with a particular creature. Animals that symbolize or transmit their particular strengths or positive characteristics to humans are sometimes known as 'power creatures'.

▲ Read through the following animal suggestions and choose two or three that seem to fit in with your personality and your current needs. Of these, select one species that is empowering and one that is protective. Collect information about these creatures, both from the ancient Egyptian world and from more recent times.

▲ Buy a picture or statue of the chosen animals or the animal-headed deity or create one from clay to make your altar a focus for animal work.

▲ Spend time in the soft early morning light and at twilight, times when animals are particularly active. If you have chosen a night creature, sit quietly outdoors away from street lights. Allow the creature to speak to you (see pages 130–1 for details on how to take on the animal powers).

▲ Draw the power creatures on stones or crystals or buy tiny charms so that you can carry one or more of your power creatures with you when you need the strengths.

Making an animal oracle

You can also make a set of white cards, about the size of playing cards, and on each one glue or draw the image of a different creature. Laminate the cards to make them more durable. When you need guidance, or in the morning of what promises to be a potentially challenging day, shuffle the pack and place the cards face down in a circle without looking at the images. Select one, turn it over and it will indicate the special protection or power you will need. This may be different from the strengths of your usual power creature. Trace the image with your index finger on the palm of your power hand and when you need the strength you can visualize the image during the day and feel the power rising up your arm into your body. If a creature appears regularly to you, you may need to add it to your collection of personal power creatures.

As the deity connections are so central to animal magic, I have sometimes repeated the core qualities of the relevant deity in the examples below.

Baboon

The baboon was associated with Ra, the sun god. The Hamadryas, a dog-headed baboon, was said to greet the sun at sunrise and sunset. Images of these baboons in groups of four appear in temples to Ra. Twelve of them appear painted on the burial chamber wall of the tomb of Tutankhamun, marking the twelve months of the year.

The blue baboon was a manifestation of Thoth, god of wisdom and writing whose word was said to cause the energy to initiate creation.

Occasionally, Khonsu the moon god was also depicted with a baboon head. The baboon was a lunar symbol.

Hapy, the son of Horus, who guarded the canopic jar that held the small intestines of a deceased person, also had the head of a baboon. This was a common image on the lid of canopic jars.

Sometimes Thoth was depicted in baboon form, sitting on top of the centre of the scales of judgement in the underworld. His presence was believed to ensure that the judgement of the heart of the deceased would be a wise one.

Work with the energy of the baboon, or any large monkey, to give you wisdom, knowledge, skill in writing or painting, or lunar power. Sunrise and sunset are particularly good times for this.

Bull

I have already written about the Apis bull cult of Memphis. However, there were also bull cult centres, linked with sun gods, for example that of the Mnevis bull at Heliopolis.

The bull cult is probably the oldest of all animal cults and may have derived from an ancient Neolithic tradition that the mother goddess gave birth to her son in the form of a bull. Indeed, the Pharaoh was often called the bull of his mother, referring to Hathor (see Cow below).

While the Apis bull was the spirit of Ptah, the Mnevis bull was the spirit of Atum-Ra.

At certain periods in ancient Egyptian history the flesh of the deceased sacred bull was eaten by the Pharaoh to endow him with the power of the divine creatures. The mother of each sacred bull was also kept in luxury and – as a manifestation of Hathor – was given an elaborate burial. Eventually the zodiacal sign of Taurus (see page 188) evolved from the sacred bull.

Bulls represented the power of the Pharaoh to crush enemies – an image seen from the Pre-dynastic period onwards – and also his virility.

Work with the energies of the bull for male power and for virility and to give strength to both sexes to overcome any obstacles or opposition.

Cat

The cat represents probably the most famous Egyptian animal connection. All cats – not just those of the sacred Bastet temple – were revered as manifestations of Bastet. In practical terms cats were essential to the Egyptians to protect the grain from rats and mice – both of which were prolific breeders in hot lands – and from cobras and other snakes, so they became a protective symbol. In her fiercest form Bastet protected the solar boat each night by driving off the serpent Apep as his tentacles grasped the boat. Sometimes Ra was referred to as the Great Cat and the tomcat was considered a manifestation of him. But the cat is primarily a female image. Many temples had their Bastet image, at which offerings of milk were made.

Bastet, the cat-headed form of the goddess, was originally a desert cat. She was often portrayed suckling kittens in her cat form and symbolized fertility and lunar magic as well as her protective function. The moon connection arose from the way the cat's eyes glittered at night.

There were huge cat cemeteries at Bubastis, Giza and Abydos, as well as at Dendara in Upper Egypt. Both temple and family cats were mummified and buried with rats, mice and even milk to sustain them in the afterlife.

Linked also with music and dancing, and in her cat-headed form pictured holding the sistrum, Bastet was considered in a number of myths to be daughter of the sun god Ra or Re and consequently was the spiritual mother of all the Pharaohs and their divine protector. She also gave protection against disease and vermin.

Use the energies of the cat for all forms of domestic protection, for nurturing fertility, for lunar energies, for happiness, love and female sexuality and for protection against disease.

Cobra

The cobra, or Uraeus, is one of the symbols of a creature who, because dangerous, could also protect against danger and she was invoked in healing spells against snakebite.

The Uraeus was one of the two main power symbols of the Pharaoh. The other was the vulture and both were worn on the Pharaoh's head-dress. The erect cobra was also a symbol of Ra's flaming eye, worn on his forehead to destroy enemies by fire, a power transferred to the Pharaoh.

But the origin of the cobra goes back into prehistory, for serpents are among the oldest symbols of the mother goddess. In Egypt she was Wadjet or Uadjet, the cobra goddess of the prehistoric kingdom of Buto, a goddess of the underworld, justice and truth. Her symbol became that of Lower Egypt.

The two strands of cobra lore were combined, but it is the female imagery that has remained important in her role as protectress of the Pharaoh in life and death and as guardian of all who ask for her care.

The cobra, a sacred creature but one capable of bringing death, was pictured as winged and crowned, rising to strike, in ancient Egyptian art. Wings denoted protectiveness in the images of the goddesses of Ancient Egypt. Sometimes Uadjet is also shown as a snake with a human face.

The cobra guarded the infant Horus in the reeds while his mother Isis was looking for the body of her husband; as she was associated with the heat of the sun, the cobra was called Lady of Heaven.

Another important cobra goddess was Renenet, a fertility goddess who was sometimes depicted as nursing children and as protector of the Pharaoh.

Use the energies of the cobra for all forms of protection, especially against spite and human venom, for reclaiming power and for the fierce defence of those we love who are under attack.

Cow

Hathor was represented as a cow, or as a goddess with cow horns between which sat a sun disc – a reflection of her solar and lunar links. She was called the 'Mother of All', as was Isis, another divine cow icon. (Note that although Isis is portrayed with horns and a solar disc, she is never actually portrayed as a cow.) Hathor was particularly associated with the rising sun.

The goddess Nut, in the form of a heavenly cow, was mother of the deities. She was the mother of Ra and birthed him each morning.

As mothers of the Pharaoh, Hathor and Isis were fertility and life-giving symbols. Hathor continued this role in the afterlife – many wealthy tombs contained a golden cow to suckle the owners when they were reborn.

Use the energies of the cow for fertility, for being nurtured by and nurturing others, for renewal and for protection and for all matters concerning mothers and children of any age.

Crocodile

The crocodile is another protective icon, because of the inherent fierceness of the species. It would preserve those who made offerings or who wore crocodile amulets to guard against many dangers and predators in life and in the afterworld. The crocodile was also a form taken by spirits to enable them to return to the world and take revenge on enemies. Magical crocodiles, fashioned in wax or clay, were also created to attack living enemies (see pages 43–4).

The most important crocodile deity was Sobek, or Sebek, who was portrayed as a human with the head of a crocodile, or as a crocodile seated on a sacred shrine. Because crocodiles appeared in great numbers during a strong flood, they became linked to the subsequent rich harvest and so crocodiles became fertility icons. Crocodile amulets were frequently worn by childless men, or by those with only daughters who wished to conceive strong male heirs.

The phallic connotations of the crocodile's shape meant that men in particular made offerings to Sobek. At Sobek's temples there were lakes that represented the original waters of Nu in which the sacred crocodiles live. Over the years archaeologists have uncovered a large number of mummified crocodiles; crocodile eggs were also buried as fertility offerings.

Set was also symbolized by the crocodile.

Use crocodile energies for protection against physical dangers, mental aggressiveness and psychic attack, for sharp thinking and the will to go after what you really want, for fertility and especially for male potency.

Falcon/Hawk

One of the most common empowering and protective symbols, the falcon or hawk was the bird of Horus, and so of the living Pharaoh.

On statues the falcon or hawk is often perched behind the throne of the Pharaoh, enfolding the king in its protective wings or hovering over his head. It is also frequently found spreading its wings protectively behind the head of the king's statues.

The hawk is a bird associated with the sun, as it was believed hawks could fly close to the sun and gaze at its rays without being burned or blinded. Many other kinds of birds of prey were associated with Horus and were offered as mummified birds in his shrines, especially the one in Saqqara.

The spirit was often depicted as a falcon with a human head. There were several bird-related spells in the ancient papyri of the dead, including one to become a hawk of gold.

The falcon was also sacred to Menthu, god of war, who carried a sickle sword and the ankh and had a solar disc and two feathers on his head. Menthu protected his father Ra from enemies and likewise guarded the Pharaoh in battle and during the course of dangerous sports, such as hunting.

The son of Horus, Qebehsenuef, had the head of a falcon. He guarded the funerary canopic jar that contained the deceased's large intestines.

Use the energies of the falcon to focus on what you need, to aim high, for clarity of vision, swiftness of purpose, courage and action.

Frog

A female symbol associated with the Nile, the pre-dynastic frog goddess Heket was often shown as a frog-headed woman or as a frog seated on a lotus, symbol of new life.

Because frogs were so numerous, especially during the Nile floods, and because of the rapid transformation from spawn to tadpole to frog in a seemingly endless cycle, they were regarded as symbols of fertility and transformation. Indeed, Heket presided over conception, pregnancy and childbirth and metal images of frogs would be cast into the Nile waters by women who wished to conceive.

The fact that frogs were seen in the rich mud left by the Nile made them, like the crocodile, a symbol of abundance and prosperity. The hieroglyphic of the frog was the symbol for 100,000, or indeed any large number.

Use the energies of the frog for wealth, abundance of any kind, fertility and renewal of hope and opportunity after a stagnant or difficult period. It's especially good for all matters of female conception, pregnancy and labour.

Goose

The goose is a powerful symbol because of its association with laying the cosmic egg on the first mound, from which the sun or the sun god emerged. Two creator deities are linked with the goose, neither of which – in spite of the egg association – is female.

Amun was called the 'Great Cackler', as was the earth god, Geb or Seb. Geb wore a goose or goose-feather head-dress and in some early legends was said to lay the sun as an egg every day. According to some myths, the first sound was the cackle of the goose as it laid the egg and this sound was believed to have stimulated the creative processes. Because of this, the goose was prized in ancient Egyptian households and sacred geese lived on special lakes at temples of Amun.

Many mummified geese and goose eggs have been found near Amun's temples; they were offerings to ask for fertility. Egg-shaped stones and crystals were prized as fertility amulets and as symbols of the life force. The goose was also an important symbol of rebirth and so mummified goose eggs were placed in human tombs to bring about rebirth

Use goose energies for all new beginnings, to launch ventures, to bring what is hidden or undeveloped to the attention of others and for regeneration in all aspects of life.

Heron

The heron is identified with the benu bird, the original mythical phoenix that featured in some versions of the Heliopian creation legend. The benu heron perched on the first mound and represented the first sunrise.

I did not understand this concept until I saw a white heron suddenly soar up and across the scarlet sunrise, over the marshes near my home on the Isle of Wight. While I was in a papyrus maker's shop in Egypt, I was talking about this over a cola with a designer; he showed me a reproduction of the benu sitting on top of the original mound with the sun rising behind it.

He told me the following words from one of the incantations to the dead, which he said he found inspiring when he was feeling stagnant: 'I flew into life from the waters on the first sunrise. I have spread my seeds like the green growing papyrus. I am the seeds of the gods and they are in me. I am the sun that rises. I rise anew each day.'

When I researched further, I discovered that in ancient times the benu was considered to represent the spirit of Ra and Osiris. In the original Heliopian legend it represented the spirit of Atum, the creator and solar deity whose identity was merged later with Ra.

Because the herons return with the floods they are regarded as creatures of rebirth; they also fly from the water at dawn. The benu is said to be consumed by flames every five hundred years and the young bird rises, carrying the ashes of its parent that it buries beneath the sacred mound. The risen bird is associated with Osiris. Another version says it flies from Arabia carrying the egg of the young and as the young bird is born it burns up in the sunrise.

Use the energies of the tall flying sunrise heron for faith and hope in tomorrow, for power and for rebuilding anew, for ascending spiritually and for the destruction of what is redundant in your life.

Hippopotamus

There was great ambivalence towards the hippopotamus. Taweret, Tauret or Thoueris was the benign goddess of childbirth and protection of households. She was shown as a pregnant hippopotamus, with human breasts and arms and the back and tail of a crocodile, or with a crocodile on her back as a reminder that she was fierce in protection of those under her care.

The hippopotamus is a very good mother and this devotion made her a natural symbol of protection for all mothers, babies and children. She was one of the earliest goddesses, and may have been associated with the primal waters; as I mentioned earlier, blue faience hippopotami models decorated with lotus flowers were an ancient amulet of protection.

Her image was placed on household shrines, rather than in temples, and was given offerings; it was also drawn on protective wands and her amulets were held by women during childbirth. However, the male of the species was not so well regarded and was linked to Set, who turned into a fierce male hippopotamus while battling with young Horus. The herds did a lot of damage to crops and so the males were regularly hunted.

Use the energies of the female hippopotamus for protection of your home and family, for all matters concerning fertility, pregnancy and childbirth and for compassion. Use the power of the male sparingly, for a sudden thrust of power to fight against injustice and to forage for survival.

Ibis

The sacred ibis is almost extinct in Egypt today but was one of the most common birds there five thousand years ago. Sacred to Thoth – deity of wisdom, magic, writing and speech – the bird is sometimes surmounted by a full lunar disc between horns. Thoth is also shown with the head of an ibis. Its beak represented the crescent moon and the black-and-white ibis represented the dark and light halves of the moon.

The ibis was regarded as a protective bird, as it ate the eggs of crocodiles and killed snakes, and so the ancient Egyptians symbolically gave it a protective function, especially to all those who were involved in learning, teaching or the magical arts. After the cat the ibis was the most popular mummified offering and was particularly popular with pilgrims seeking answers to questions or help with making decisions.

Use the energies of the ibis for wisdom, for magic, when you need to learn or write, for understanding mysteries, for grace of action and word and for protection against predators – emotional as well as physical – in your life.

Jackal/Dog

One of the most fearsome yet protective creatures was the jackal, a predatory wild dog that came from the desert in search of prey and which consumed the bodies of those that had died in the desert, both animal and human. Jackals were often seen around the tombs in the Valley of the Kings and Queens and their nocturnal howling was thought to signify their protection of the deceased. Some jackals were tamed and became fierce guard dogs. So who better to guard against hostile forces – in this world and the next – than Anubis, the black jackal-headed god?

Anubis, the alter ego of Horus, guided the deceased through the underworld, having embalmed and prepared their bodies as he did for his murdered father Osiris. In fact, as deity of twilight, he was said to have absorbed his dead father.

Black-and-gold statues of Anubis as a jackal were set to guard the tombs of kings and queens, and the rich generally, from grave robbers. Sacred jackals were kept at Anubis shrines.

Tuamutef, the jackal-headed son of Horus, protected the canopic jar in which the lungs of the deceased were kept.

A more popular magical tradition, which has recently been revived and rather sensationalized in the film Return Of The Mummy, records that a jackal Anubis hunted down the unrighteous and that the jackal-headed warriors of Anubis were magically sent against powerful enemies.

Use the energies of the jackal to cast a protective boundary around your home, especially if you live in a city, for inspiring loyalty in others, for outfacing threats and for removing whatever is no longer needed in your life.

Lions

In Ancient Egypt, lions – like bulls – were symbols of kingship and the sun; the charging lion represented the power and courage of the emperor to lead and overcome all enemies. Indeed, pairs of lions represented and guarded the eastern and western horizon, a tradition sometimes also reflected in the positioning of pairs or rows of sphinxes.

In the warmest summers lions would come from the East and from western deserts to drink at the Nile and this coincided with the beginning of the period of the rising of the constellation later called Leo.

Shu and Tefnut, two of the original Egyptian deities, are represented as lions. Shu, who was associated with the sun, was regarded as defender of the sun and the air. Tefnut, his consort, was defender of the moon and the waters and in her leonine aspect was known as the Lady of the Flame.

Most famous is lion-headed Sekhmet (see page 208) who is said to be a fate goddess as well as a protector of the young and the vulnerable (as the lioness is popularly considered to be an attentive mother). However, she is also the destroyer of evil in her lioness form. Representing the full heat of the sun, she blazes in the underworld, driving away darkness. Representations of recumbent lions were placed as guards to protect temples and formed the base of the King's throne.

The body of the sphinx was that of a lion; its face was usually that of a Pharaoh – for example, the face of King Khafre adorns the sphinx that guards the pyramid at Giza. The sphinx was also the solar guardian of the horizon. You will be able to understand this aspect of the sphinx's significance if you visit Cairo and find yourself a suitably lofty vantage point from which you can see the sphinx standing against the horizon formed by the great pyramid of Khefu and the pyramid of Khafre. Before the area became built up, travellers approaching Giza would realize, as was the original intention, that the head of the sphinx combined with the two pyramids either side behind it formed the hieroglyphic for 'horizon', which depicts the sun rising between two mountains.

Use the energies of the lion for courage, power, leadership, authority, maturity, nobility of spirit, for the widening horizons of all kinds, for protection and also for vigilance in making sure you are not deceived.

Ram

One of the most exciting power creatures, the Ram – which later gave rise to the astrological sign Aries – is symbol of male potency. Symbol of the great Amun-Ra, its horns are both protective and combative.

The Creosphinxes, guardians of Amun's temple at Karnak, formed an avenue of ram-headed sphinxes each with a lion's body, representing the creator god himself. It was thought Amun would only let those who were pure pass, as the Temple of Karnak symbolized heaven.

Khnum, or Khnemu, was the ram-headed god who created men on his pottery wheel and was Lord of the First Cataract of the Nile (see page 204). With his wife Heket the frog goddess, he assisted at every birth. Sacred rams were killed and mummified at his sacred temples in Upper Egypt, where he was worshipped as a potency symbol. Khnum was prayed to in the hope that he would allow a rich Nile flood, which would make the surrounding lands fertile.

Use the energies of the ram for potency and creativity, for meeting challenges, for bringing abundance into your life by your own actions, for sexuality and the release of inhibitions, for demanding high standards from yourself and others and for defending the weak.

Scorpion

Some of the very early Egyptian kings took on the title of Scorpion King as a sign of their mastery over enemies. (There are two kinds of scorpion in Egypt: the dark, relatively harmless species and the pale, poisonous kind.)

The most famous scorpion icon is Serqet, or Selkit, the scorpion goddess. She was sometimes depicted as a woman with the head of a scorpion, and sometimes as a scorpion with the head of a woman.

Serqet was one of the four protective death goddesses (see pages 204 and 208). She also fought against the enemies of Ra, her father, and served as the protectress of Pharaohs in life and death – against natural as well as humanly created disasters.

Seven scorpions protected Isis while she was searching for Osiris's body, but she could not have power over them until she learned their secret names. While she was away, hostile scorpions stung Horus and even the scorpion goddess could not save him. Only the intervention of the higher deity Thoth saved the young Horus and as a result of the wisdom Thoth imparted to Isis she became mistress of scorpions. Mothers whose infants had been stung by scorpions would invoke either Isis (see page 155) or Horus .

Use the power of the scorpion very sparingly and only with the highest intent, as it is a double-edged sword. Use it swiftly when you or loved ones are under attack or are weakened by illness and to ward off crises such as money problems or dangers while travelling.

Shrew mouse

I was very puzzled when I first saw a mummified shrew mouse in the Ashmolean Museum in Oxford, as it did not seem to represent a power creature at all; it resembles a very small mole or underground vole. Then I discovered that the shrew mouse was used as an ingredient in ancient love spells. But more significantly, the shrew was sacred to Horus in his hidden night aspect of a night creature – the alter ego of the hawk of light. For this reason statues of shrews were covered with solar symbols and pictured vertically carrying a solar disc. This aspect of the shrew's symbolism may also explain their connection with secret love and passion.

A large number of mummified shrews have been excavated near Thebes and their underground (or 'night') aspect also links them with the resurrected Osiris, who was reborn as the green corn.

Use your shrew mouse energies for night magic, for keeping secrets, for love that must be hidden, for kindling or rekindling passion, for unconscious powers of intuition and for seeking wisdom from the past, especially through divination.

Absorbing the energy of power creatures

In your reading and exploration of the world of Ancient Egypt in museums and on the internet, you may discover other power animals that – whether or not they are connected with deities – have strengths you admire or need. You can add these to the list I have provided.

To make the psychic connection with your chosen power animals, begin by composing your own ritual to become a creature of power or protection.

First let us look at a brief extract from a spell to become a hawk of gold that I found in a very old copy of a book, translated by E.A. Wallis Budge, of the Papyrus of the Scribe Ani, which had been intended to serve as the scribe's guide through the afterlife (see also page 57).

'I have risen up like the golden hawk which cometh from his egg. I fly, I alight like a hawk with the wings of mother-of-emerald of the South, with the head of the Benu, and Ra who hath entered into me.'

Spend a few minutes writing spells to symbolically become your chosen creatures, describing their characteristics, their habitat and the qualities you most seek in your life. Record the incantations in your Book of Egypt. They may be very detailed or they may take up just two or three lines. Try to capture the colour that the animal would perceive, the sense of its movement, its breathing – in short, the view of the world from the animal's perspective.

▲ Learn the chants so that you can recite them in your mind at any time, in any place and thereby assume the power of your creature.

▲ Begin by focusing on your favourite animal or bird. Picture it in a habitat you have seen it in, either in real life or in a video or photograph.

▲ Close your eyes and as you visualize the animal or bird, recite the words out loud or in your mind so that the words and pictures fuse. Add the fragrances the creature would smell, feel the air or the water around it. Become the creature as you recite the words over and over.

▲ Now fall silent and in your mind's eye see the creature coming so close to you that the boundaries between you blur and you share one physical form.

▲ You are now within the creature's space. You can see through their eyes, hear through their ears, breathe in their rhythm. The creature may be moving fast or at rest, hunting or hiding.

▲ Feel the ground beneath you and the throb of the energies you seek making your heartbeat and your mind pulsate.

▲ When you feel filled with the strength of the power creature, thank your host and allow the boundaries to begin to re-emerge as your animal very gently recedes.

▲ Mentally turn away, recreating the separate boundaries between you and the creature once more and gently withdraw your own essence back into your body.

▲ Practise this with one or two other creatures and over the weeks experiment with the different energies, creating chants and visualizing the creature in its natural habitat.

▲ In time, you can summon up the qualities of your power creature simply by reciting your original spell in your mind.

▲ Whenever you can, top up the energies by visiting the creature, perhaps in a conservation park or by watching a wildlife video containing the animal.

▲ You may dream of your power creature in deity form or see the god or goddess in meditation or quiet reverie. Accept any messages with thanks and in time one may become your special guardian.

▲ Note down the experiences in your Book of Egypt.

As you are asking favours of these powers from the animal world, it might be fitting if you could give thanks by doing something to help endangered species or badly treated animals and birds, either in your own country or abroad.

11

PERFUMES, OIL AND INCENSE

Egypt is the home of perfume and for thousands of years fragrance magic played a central role in rituals both for the living and for the deceased.

Flowers grew in the fertile areas of the Nile, nurtured by the hot sun and the cool waters. Their fragrances were available for magic and healing even to ordinary families. Flowers were used in processions, as offerings to the deities and ancestors and to guests at festivities. Today, even small modern apartments in Egyptian cities are adorned with vases of flowers.

As the waters receded after the annual flooding of the Nile, blue, red and white lotuses would shimmer on the shallow waters, filling the air with what was said to be the perfumes of the deities.

Though Egypt had perfumes of her own, such as the native lotus and the papyrus flower – used, it was said, by both gods and mortals – exotic perfumes and incenses were one of the major imports throughout the three thousand years of Pharonic history. Many came from the fabulous and fabled land of Punt, probably a region in north-eastern Africa in modern Somalia. A large number of them are still used in modern magic, including frankincense, myrrh, sandalwood, cedar and cinnamon. Some were imported as trees or plants into Egypt and now grow there.

When the British Egyptologist Howard Carter opened the tomb of Tutankhamun in the Valley of the Kings on 26 November 1922, he was surprised to find the air still filled with scents that had survived for three thousand years since the young king's burial around 1322 BCE. In the antechamber were two huge wreaths of the blue lotus, hibiscus and narcissus, which although desiccated were still recognizable.

Sacred fragrances

It was said that the spirit or essence of the plant contained magical healing powers given by the deities. This spirit was transferred into oil, perfume essence (which was oil based and contained no alcohol, unlike many modern perfumes) or incense and was released when the fragrances were used. Because the fragrances came from the gods, the ancient Egyptians believed that mortals might become more perfect by absorbing the scent. Moreover, every perfume was considered to be blessed and to contain a divine essence; it was thought to provide god-like powers, enabling the user to achieve his or her desires.

Temples were famed for their perfumeries; the art of perfume making was at its most sophisticated by the middle of the second millennium BCE. For example, at Hathor's temple at Dendara and at Edfu, some of the secret formulae for perfume manufacture are inscribed in hieroglyphics on the inner walls. However, priests passed on the most sacred ingredients and proportions orally; some modern perfumers still claim descent from this tradition.

The magic of the lotus

Recently, in London, I met a young Egyptian woman named Serena. (This is not her real name, but she works for a traditional Egyptian organization that officially frowns on even the most innocent folk magical practices.) She told me that when she was getting ready to go out with her boyfriend, she would take out a tiny glass bottle filled with lotus perfume, made only once every six years to an ancient formula. Serena anoints her forehead, her brow, her throat and her wrists with a single drop of the fragrance and recites the following words (she learned them from her mother, whose own mother had taught them to her when she was to be married):

> *'I am the pure lotus that comes forth from the light. I am the lotus of the shining one that comes forth from the fields of everlasting light.'*

This ritual, she said, gave her great power in love.

I was curious to find out more.

The words of the ritual, I discovered, were an adaptation of the spell to become a lotus from the funerary book *Coming Forth By Day* (also known as the *Book of the Dead*), which dates from the end of the Second Intermediate period, in around 1550 BCE. (The book initially took the form of about two hundred spells of formulae.) The spell described the sun child and lotus god Nefertum, son of the creator god Ptah and the lioness goddess Sekhmet or Mut, the original mother goddess; these three deities formed the holy trinity at Memphis. Cairo Museum holds the original exquisite – and still beautifully coloured – statue of the lotus god, found in the entrance to the tomb of Tutankhamun. It depicts the boy king as Nefertum rising from the first lotus. The blue lotus – which is actually a form of water lily – opens at dawn and so came to symbolize the first sunrise and to be identified with Nefertum the sun child, who is often portrayed sucking his thumb. (The equally fragrant white lotus opens in the evening.) The ancient Egyptians regarded Nefertum as the god of perfume; sometimes he is portrayed with a lion head.

In Cairo, I found a perfume shop where this rare lotus perfume was also made and I was totally overwhelmed by the psychic effects of the fragrance on me. Suddenly it seemed to me that I was in a past world, in one of the old tombs at a funeral. I was myself very old and knew that I would soon be buried myself. The occasion was the burial of my husband; we had been together for many years and the lotus was our flower. I was not afraid and was glad his spirit would be waiting for mine in the Field of Reeds. I was filled with a sense of overwhelming peace as light flooded from the flowers in the darkened tomb and I promised to bring lotus every day to his offerings temple. The air was filled with the scent of a hundred lotus flowers and a huge wreath of both the blue and the white lotus was placed in the antechamber. (I later saw the same arrangement in a reproduction of Tutankhamun's tomb in Dorchester, England.) In the momentary vision, there was an increased awareness of colour and sound as images flooded my mind.

The perfumer was not surprised by the powerful effects of what he called the first fragrance of creation. He explained how thousands of years ago, people had used such fragrances to connect themselves with the higher wisdom of what they then regarded as the deities, as well as to bring and to preserve love throughout life. In this heightened state of awareness they might receive healing as well as increased psychic potential. The perfumer also imparted a great deal of wisdom about the spiritual history of other ancient fragrances and helped me to fill in the missing pieces in my research into the old world of perfume magic.

Perfume magic

Perfumes, especially ancient Egyptian fragrances, do seem to offer an effective route to experiencing – in a light hypnotic trance or dream state – the world of Ancient Egypt. Like Maria, whose experiences I described in the Introduction, people from all over the world do admit to feeling connections with Ancient Egypt. Indeed, some feel that they once lived there in another life. This strong sense of connection may first be triggered in a museum of Egyptian artifacts, or while reading about Egypt or looking at pictures. If the person actually visits Egypt – or indeed any similar hot land – they may well find that what seem to be memories frequently come flooding back to them. Because the fragrances I discuss in this book are traditionally associated with exotic hot places, you may find that they trigger a similar reaction in you. From my own experiences in this area, I would suggest that our minds access some sort of memory from the cosmic pool of collective memories – which can be reached by almost everyone in psychic work – of places in which these kind of fragrances originated.

Some people do go to a regression therapist to discover more. But if you prefer a more personal self-initiated process, try using one of the ancient Egyptian fragrances listed in this chapter as an almost instant and very pleasurable route to past worlds. You can use any form of the fragrance, such as cologne, but perfume magic does tend to work best with a concentrated essence or essential oil.

Indeed, inhaling perfume is one of the fastest and safest methods to access other dimensions, whether you believe it is possible to mind travel to your own personal past lives or to tap into the cosmic memory banks of human experience in a heightened state of psychic awareness.

Experiment with different scents. Lotus, I have discovered, seems especially potent for arousing detailed past life experiences from Ancient Egypt, while the papyrus flower essence is effective for invoking domestic scenes from the Egyptian world.

According to my research, the ancient Egyptian fragrances listed below often induce dreams and daytime visions in certain areas of experience, though you may find differently:

Cedar – for images of starlit skies seen from flat rooftops or from the desert; for visions of alchemists and magicians conjuring up spells from vats of fragrant oils, gleaming metals and gems.

Frankincense – for scenes of shimmering sunny days and the heat of noon; for images of bazaars, deserts and nomads with rich tents and blazing ritual fires.

Jasmine – for visions of robed priestesses calling down the power of the Lady Isis on the full moon; for secret love trysts or women's mysteries; for brilliant moonlit nights by lakes and the Nile; for fragrant gardens and perfume makers.

Lavender – for scenes of fields of blue and purple flowers and flying white birds; for images of healing temples; for scenes of the Nile flood and the coming of the frogs, the crocodiles and the hippopotami.

Lotus – for specific past lives in Ancient Egypt; for visions of pyramids, beautiful shaded gardens, ancient temples and daily rituals at dawn and evening; for visualizations of gods and goddesses.

Myrrh – for scenes at old tombs; for visiting the enclosed secret sanctums in temples; for scrying by lamplight or with oils on water; for learning ancient secrets from amulet makers.

Papyrus flower – for visions of the green papyrus marshes; for Isis and the infant Horus hiding in them; for scenes of people planting the seeds and working the land and for arousing the coolness of evening; for images of Sirius rising and people preparing to move to higher land for safety from the flood.

Rose – for arousing love scenes; for family life; for worship at the temples of Hathor and shadowy images through magic mirrors; for birthing scenes and for families sitting outside homes in narrow courtyards.

Sandalwood – for scenes of processions along the river and visions of priests carrying statues through avenues of sphinxes; for lions coming from the desert in the summer heat to drink the Nile waters; for pharaohs going out to hunt and to fight; for exotic palaces and for expeditions bringing back sacred oils and incenses by boat and on donkey trains.

Inducing fragrant visions

If possible, use perfume in a glass bottle with a stopper or dropper. You can often buy these bottles cheaply from garage sales as well as from gift stores. The perfume need not be one of the above. Sometimes a favourite fragrance has the power to carry you to your chosen destination because it has happy – and therefore powerful – emotional associations for you. Smelling a fragrance is an excellent way to activate psychic powers. Alternatively, use an essential oil in one of the above fragrances. Essential oils are very strong and can adversely affect people with chronic conditions and some are not suitable in pregnancy. They should always be well diluted in carrier oil and never used near eyes, mouth or genitals.

▲ Work in your bedroom just before you go to sleep.

▲ Light a night light in a safe place in your bedroom and sit on the bed facing it.

▲ In the semi-darkness, inhale the fragrance slowly three or four times.

▲ Imagine yourself in a beautiful flower-filled garden by the Nile, near an oasis or in a palace garden.

▲ Close your eyes and allow pictures to form in your mind. Flow with the sensation.

▲ When you are ready, sprinkle a drop or two of fragrance on your pillow, blow out the light and step through the flowers into the world of dreams.

▲ Your ancient Egyptian visions may continue in sleep (this process is also a cure for insomnia and can stop you from having nightmares).

▲ Experiment with different fragrances and note down your experiences in your Book of Egypt. You may discover that a particular figure features regularly – perhaps yourself in a past world, or a representation of some aspect of yourself that resonates with ancient Egyptian life.

▲ Have a pen and paper by the bed so as soon as you wake you can write down every detail of your visions. You will find answers to issues in your present world laid out quite clearly in this dream world.

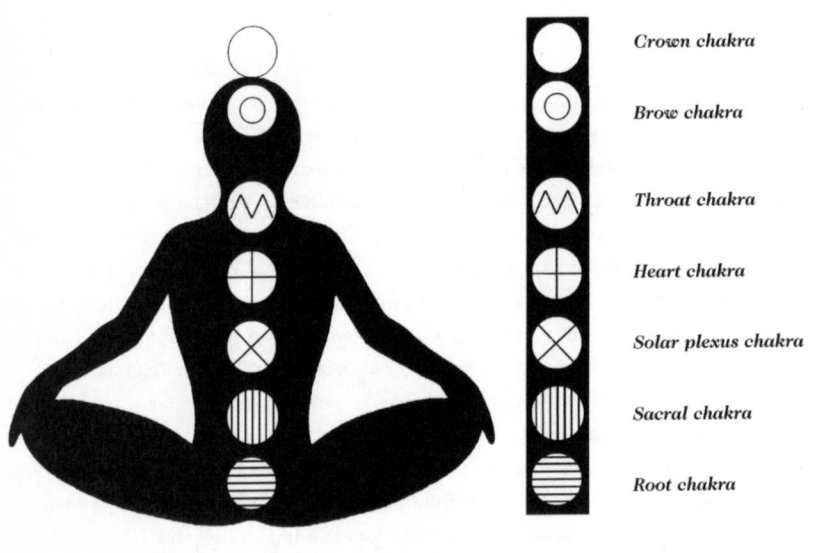

Chakras

Chakra fragrance, magic and healing

Through my studies into ancient Egyptian life I discovered that each of the psychic energy points – or chakras – of the body has its own fragrance. By using these fragrances, it is possible to awaken the psychic energy points of the body and experience not only increased psychic awareness and harmony, but also to connect with the world of old Egypt and see visions of the past. Lotus also increases inner radiance and serenity and for this reason it was used by women to become as a goddess in love.

I was shown by the perfume seller, whose family home I was fortunate enough to visit, the connection between ancient Egyptian fragrances and the chakra system. I also received insights into the potency of specific fragrances for healing as well as for increasing psychic awareness through chakra fragrances.

The chakras of the body are usually associated with India. In fact, my new friend assured me, they come from a much older African tradition that developed to a high level of sophistication in Ancient Egypt, though much of this knowledge is still orally transmitted.

Indeed, it is hypothesized that awareness of the chakras – the vortexes of psychic energy through which the life force is channelled in the human body, mind and spirit – came first out of Africa and reached India and the Far East with the early migration of tribes.

Chakras control the flow of energies to and from the aura – the rainbow-coloured energy field surrounding the human body, animals, plants and even crystals. The aura acts as a receiver and transmitter for influences from the cosmos, from the planet earth and from those with whom we interact and is the first area to reflect the effects of these interactions upon our health and harmony. A bright luminous rainbow aura indicates that the chakras are likewise operating at peak efficiency.

If an energy centre becomes blocked or overactive then it ceases to regulate the flow of positive energies through the system and a person can feel tired, irritable or unreasonably angry at trivia, according to which chakra is malfunctioning.

By working with the highest or 'crown' energy centre, situated in the centre of the top of the head, the whole body can be spiritually cleansed, healed and energized.

Choosing the right fragrances

The effect of perfumes, oils and incenses is almost instantaneous and by inhaling, anointing oneself or burning one of the appropriate chakra fragrances (see below for identification guide), it is possible to feel better and happier and to relate to others more easily.

The use of perfumes for different needs is based on traditions extending back thousands of years. I have adapted my fragrance list slightly from those that were suggested to me in Egypt, because the original fragrances are totally beautiful but very expensive and the blends can be difficult to find outside Egypt. However, similar effects can be achieved with perfumes and oils that are more easily obtainable in other countries. If you do ever get the chance to buy any of the real Egyptian essences, I would urge you to do so – they are superb and even a drop or two demonstrates instantaneously how fragrance can lift the consciousness.

While the wealthy placed barrels of rich perfumes and their ingredients in the tombs of relations, many more ordinary people used cheaper or home-made versions of perfumes. Some may perhaps have had a single precious bottle of the pure lotus essence, said to be the fragrance of the deities, which they eked out drop by drop or gave as part of the wedding dowry.

I will describe very briefly the seven major energy points and their functions; at the end of this book you will find suggestions for suitable further reading on this subject. In addition, I have suggested fragrances that can be used on each of the chakra points, although you can also burn the incense or the related essential oil to release and empower each energy centre.

I have focused both on the magical and healing significance of each fragrance. I found lotus essential oil in the British Museum shop, but it can be obtained from one of the many stores that sell a wide range of aromatherapy products, Papyrus flower is more difficult to obtain but you can get it on the internet via mail order from Egypt and from specialist aromatherapy outlets in other countries. Payment is generally made in US dollars for Egyptian products.

Perhaps significantly, in Sanskrit chakras are known as *padmas*, or 'lotuses', and the chakra points are visualized as whirling lotus petals in Hindu spirituality.

Using the fragrances

I will describe the chakra energies in ascending order, but you can approach the chakras either way – either upwards from the root chakra (via the perineum) or through the crown of the head. Because these are psychic power centres, not physical ones, they can vary subtly from body to body. Hold the palm of your power hand over the areas shown in the image above. When you reach a chakra point, you may sense a swirling like holding your hand over an emptying plug hole in a bath.

When you cleanse and empower a chakra for a particular region of the body, healing automatically takes place in that area. However, the spiritual and psychic powers that the chakras awaken, and which make you more aware of what is hidden beyond the material world, are equally important. As you work with fragrance magic more regularly, you will find it easier to tune into your innate intuitive and clairvoyant powers, because the scent opens the psychic pathways within us. In Ancient Egypt, this link through perfume was regarded as connecting the user with the deities themselves and understanding their will.

If you are using essential oils for anointing the chakra points, except for lavender and rose, dilute the oils in almond or pure olive oil, the traditional Egyptian diluting oils, in the ratio of five drops of essential oil to 30ml of carrier oil.

It is well worth building up a collection of the seven chakra perfumes, oils and incenses. Cheaper versions of fragrances, for example rose water rather than roses themselves, are also effective. If your skin is sensitive or you are pregnant or chronically ill, use lavender and rose water alternately on the chakra points, as these are very mild, but psychically powerful.

▲ The fastest-acting and most potent method is to inhale each chakra perfume, fragrance or oil in turn, beginning either from the root chakra and working upwards or starting with the crown chakra and working downwards to cleanse and empower each chakra. You can also inhale a single fragrance to cleanse or empower a specific chakra.

▲ Alternatively, anoint the body or specific chakras with a single drop of the fragrance oils at the specific energy centres, on to the skin, being very careful if you have a very sensitive skin and around delicate areas. Some oils should be avoided during pregnancy. If you have a chronic medical condition, especially an allergy, skin problem or breathing difficulties consult a pharmacist first.

▲ You can add a few drops of the individual oils or fragrances to a bath or use fragranced bath foam to stimulate and cleanse a particular chakra.

▲ You can also burn specific oil or incense or add a few drops of essential oil to water and spray the room in which you are sleeping or working with the mixture.

▲ Rose and lavender are very mild and can be substituted for any chakra fragrance. The crown chakra fragrances can be used for whole body cleansing and empowerment and these are good all-purpose healers. Lotus is a very gentle and magical fragrance.

The root chakra

This is the chakra of the planet earth and it draws its beautiful deep red light upwards from the earth through the feet and through the perineum when we sit on the ground. Both these are points at which the root chakra can be accessed and healed.

The minor chakras in the soles of the feet are also ruled by, and connect directly to, the root. The root rules the legs, feet and skeleton including the teeth and the large intestine.

Imbalances can be reflected as pain and tension in any of these areas, for example as constipation or irritable bowel symptoms, a general lack of energy and an inability to relax even when exhausted. On a psychological level, unreasonable anger or paralyzing fear brought about by a trivial cause can be a symptom of a blockage.

The colour of the root chakra is red.

The centre of each foot is a good place to anoint, or at the pulse points at the side close to the ankle. Use cedar perfume or cedarwood (though not during pregnancy), avocado, apricot, cinnamon, mimosa or mint. Do not anoint with cinnamon essential oil, even after it has been well diluted, as it can burn the skin.

Root chakra fragrances are excellent if you are new to psychic work, as they open psychic senses, especially 'clairsentience', which enables you to pick up psychic impressions from the past in old places and to become more aware of your natural protective instincts.

Hathor is the root chakra deity.

The sacral chakra

This is the chakra of the moon and is seated in the sacrum and lower abdomen. The sacral chakra focuses on all aspects of physical comfort or satisfaction. It controls the blood, all bodily fluids and hormones, the reproductive system, the kidneys, the circulation and the bladder and is especially sensitive to the stress and imbalance created when we fall out of harmony with our natural cycles. Blockages can show themselves as fluid retention, menstrual or menopausal problems, mood swings, impotence in men and an inability to relax in sex for women. The latter can manifest itself, in both sexes, as an overemphasis on sexual performance and a tendency to flit from one partner to another to find satisfaction.

Disorders involving physical indulgence to seek emotional satisfaction can also result from blockages, especially those obsessions that relate to food or are otherwise orally related.

The colour of the sacral chakra is orange or silver.

The fragrances appropriate to this chakra are jasmine, hibiscus, myrrh (though not in pregnancy), musk and ylang-ylang. Anoint above the genitals or around the womb on the lower abdomen with a single drop, being sure to dilute the oils well in the ratio of three drops of essential oil to 30 ml of carrier oil. Avoid myrrh oil for anointing, as it can be an irritant to sensitive parts.

Sacral chakra fragrances are good for increasing your intuitive awareness. They can also boost your psychometric abilities and your psychic touch, helping you to pick up information about people's lives and their future by holding objects belonging to them.

Isis is the goddess of the sacral chakra.

The solar plexus chakra

This is the chakra of fire and it is situated above the navel, around the stomach area. Its function is to galvanize personal power and individuality and to integrate different aspects of our lives and our selves.

The body parts to which the solar plexus chakra relates include the digestive system, the liver, the spleen, the gall bladder, the stomach and small intestine and the metabolism.

Digestive disorders and hyperactivity can result from imbalances or blockages of this chakra.

On a psychological level, a host of problems can result from the inefficient working of this chakra, such as lack of self-confidence, obsessional behaviour, over-sensitivity and a tendency to become overly emotional, a habit of finding fault with others and an inability to empathize.

The colour of the solar plexus chakra is yellow.

Many fire fragrances tend to be very powerful physically so if anointing use them with care. Use frankincense, camomile, cinnamon, orange blossom, carnation, honeysuckle or marigold. (Frankincense can be an irritant, so dilute it well.) Do not go in sunlight after using orange essential oil and – again – dilute the oil well. Do not anoint with cinnamon (see above).

Sacral chakra fragrances are powerful for increasing magical potential for spell casting, for resisting negative psychic and psychological pressures and for healing.

Sekhmet is the goddess of the solar plexus chakra.

The heart chakra

This is the chakra of the winds and is situated in the centre of the chest, radiating over heart, lungs, breasts and also hands and arms.

Use the minor chakras in the centre of the palms of the hands that are ruled by this chakra for anointing yourself with fragrance.

Compassion and transformation of our everyday lives through connection with our still centre of being results from a clear heart chakra. Constant coughs, breathing difficulties and allergies can be the result of a blockage or an imbalance in the chakra, as can oversensitivity to the problems of others which leave us anxious but unable to offer real help.

The heart chakra is believed to be the place where the soul resides. The heart was very important to ancient Egyptians, since they believed that the intelligence and the will were situated in the heart as well. Therefore, according to ancient Egyptian thought, when our heart chakra is open we are more able to be aware of our spiritual nature and potential.

The colour of the heart chakra is green.

Heart chakra fragrances are good for seeing or sensing the presence of wise ancestors and for past life work; use rose, geranium, hyacinth, lilac or lily of the valley. The heart chakra is also a source of healing power, especially when amplified by crystals, herbs and other natural forces. However, as you work with this chakra you may find that you are also able to channel the pure life force from the cosmos. This higher healing energy is channelled from the universe, via the higher crown, brow and throat chakras, circulates through the heart chakra (see diagram) and out through the fingers.

Bastet is the deity of the heart chakra.

The throat chakra

This is the chakra of purity and sound and is situated close to the Adam's apple in the centre of the neck. As well as the throat and speech organs, the throat chakra controls the mouth, the neck and shoulders and the passages that run up to the ears. Blockages of this chakra can manifest themselves as sore throats, swollen glands in the neck, mouth ulcers and ear problems. On a psychological level, confusion and incoherence result if the chakra is not working efficiently.

The colour of the throat chakra is sky blue.

Throat chakra fragrances are good for oracular wisdom, more advanced dream work, out-of-body travel and 'clairaudience' – psychic hearing in which you hear voices from other dimensions. Use lavender, lilies, magnolia, narcissus and violet.

Nut the sky goddess is the deity of the throat chakra.

The brow chakra

The brow chakra is the chakra of light and is situated just above the bridge of the nose in the centre of the brow. It controls the eyes, ears, and both hemispheres of the brain and radiates into the brain's central cavity.

Blockages here can result in blurred vision without reason, headaches and migraines and blocked sinuses as well as earache. On a psychological level, insomnia or nightmares can result from blockages of this chakra.

Its colour is purple, or – in the Egyptian system – turquoise or deep blue.

Brow chakra fragrances are good for accessing knowledge from the universal memory bank through meditation, divination or scrying, for clairvoyance or psychic seeing into the future or over great distances and scrying for images in a lamp or with oil and water. Use papyrus flower if you can obtain it. If not, try lemon balm, sandalwood, juniper (though not during pregnancy), lemongrass (dilute both juniper and lemongrass well in olive or almond oil as it is a skin irritant and do not use it for anointing) and thyme (again, not during pregnancy).

The brow chakra deity is Horus.

The crown chakra

The crown chakra is the chakra of unity and bliss. It is situated at the top of the head in the centre, where the three main bones of the skull fuse at the anterior fontanel. It extends beyond the crown and some locate the centre about three finger-breadths above the top of the head. It rules the brain, body and psyche.

This chakra connects the highest or most evolved part of the self, wherein resides our personal core of divinity. This ultimately connects to the source of divinity itself, which is reflected in the many deities of the Egyptian world.

Blockages here can result in headaches and migraines, inefficient functioning of the immune system and a tendency towards forgetfulness and minor accidents. On a psychological level, blockages manifest themselves as a sense of alienation from the world.

The colour of the crown chakra is white.

Crown chakra fragrances are good for all forms of star magic, for mystical experiences and direct channelling from Egyptian deity forms and the merging of mind, body and spirit. Use lotus if at all possible, or frankincense (in which case use one of the other fragrances for the solar plexus), amber, camomile, neroli, sage (though not during pregnancy) or chrysanthemum.

The lotus is a flower of love, especially committed love and married love in the highest, most spiritual sense as the uniting of two people as one soul.

The crown chakra deity is Nefertum, the young lotus god of fragrance and the first light.

A ritual to harmonize the chakras with fragrance

▲ Work at sunset and if necessary light a single candle in your altar room.

▲ Prepare the seven chakra fragrances so that you can anoint yourself with a single drop on each chakra point. If you are using essential oils, make sure that you have diluted a small quantity of each in almond or olive oil. If possible, use tiny coloured glass bottles with droppers for each fragrance so you can use each dropper to anoint a chakra. If not, put the fragrances or oils in tiny dishes and use different fingers to apply each. Use the fingers first of your power hand, then of the other hand, beginning with the finger next to the thumb, but miss out the thumbs.

▲ Have a bath or shower in entirely plain water and towel yourself dry. Wrap yourself in a loose robe or dressing gown that unfastens down the front. Then you can decide if you wish to work without clothes or in the robe.

▲ Begin with the lotus or the chosen crown essence or oil you are using and face the altar.

▲ Speak slowly and quietly; the later chants are adaptations of the original one. You can use the words I provide here for any fragrance belonging to a particular chakra – just change the fragrance name, as each chant refers to the qualities of the chakra:

> *'I am the pure lotus that comes forth from the light. I am the lotus of the shining one that comes forth from the fields of everlasting light. Greetings, Nefertum, Child of the Dawn.'*

▲ As you speak, anoint the centre of your hairline with a single drop of lotus – or your chosen fragrance – and visualize pure drops of white light flowing within your body, spiralling round each energy centre and passing down interconnecting psychic energy channels – known as nadirs – like entwined snakes.

▲ Next, take the papyrus flower, or another brow fragrance, and say:

> *'I am the pure papyrus flower that comes forth from the light. I am the flower of the shining one that comes forth from the fields of everlasting light. Greetings, Horus with your all-seeing eye.'*

▲ As you speak, anoint the centre of your brow with a single drop of papyrus flower, just between and above your eyes, and visualize turquoise or purple light mingling with the white and spiralling up and down the body.

▲ Next, take the lavender, or your chosen throat fragrance, and say:

> *'I am the pure lavender flower that comes forth from the light. I am the flower of the shining one that comes forth from the fields of everlasting light. Greetings Sky Mother, star woman Nut.'*

▲ As you speak, anoint the centre of your throat with a single drop of your chosen fragrance and visualize blue light spiralling to merge with the purple and white light.

▲ Take the rose or an alternative heart fragrance and repeat the chant, substituting the name of your chosen fragrance where appropriate. Recite the line: *'Greetings Bastet, joyous one, protectress of the grain.'*

▲ Anoint first the palm of your power hand followed by the palm of your other hand. If you prefer, you can anoint over your heart instead of the palms as both palms and heart are chakra entry points. Any blockages will clear and you will feel full of energy and harmony.

▲ Next, take the frankincense – or your preferred solar plexus fragrance – and repeat the chant, adapting it for the new fragrance. End with:

> *'Greetings Sekhmet, Lady of Fire.'*

▲ Anoint the centre of your stomach a few centimetres above the navel with the chosen fragrance and visualize the golden sunlight causing the inner light flow to bubble and sparkle.

▲ Then, take the jasmine or another sacral fragrance and again adapt the chant. End with:

> *'Greetings Mother Isis, Lady of the Moon and of enchantment.'*

▲ Anoint just above your genitals (for a man) or in the centre of the lower abdomen (for a woman) and allow the warm orange energy to create a sense of abundance within you.

▲ Finally, take the cedar, or your preferred root fragrance, and repeat the chant. End with:

> *'Greetings Hathor, Queen of Harmony and guardian of women seeking love.'*

This also makes a beautiful love ritual. A couple take turns to anoint each other's chakras and change the words above so that one person begins, 'You are the lotus', and anoints his or her partner and then the other person repeats the words and the action. Alternatively, you can use this ritual privately before consummating a relationship for the first time.

Fragrance love magic

The ancient Egyptians believed that fragrances were so powerful that they could bind the will of others. Unsurprisingly therefore, flowers were an important part of love magic in Ancient Egypt. Each deity was associated with a fragrance, but it was the female deities – Hathor with her roses and Isis with her lilies – who were invoked most often by people in love.

Egyptian love poetry often refers to the potency of fragrance. Some poems were recorded in a document called the Papyrus of Turin from the 19th Dynasty, which began around 1292 BCE. (It was originally known as the Erotic Papyrus of Turin.) Unusually, this papyrus featured images of sexual intercourse as well as love poetry. A translation of some of its verses was collected in a book called *Ancient Egyptian Poetry and Prose* by Adolf Erman, translated into English by Aylward M. Blackman in 1955 and published by Dover Press. This edition is currently out of print, though you can sometimes find copies of out of print books on line or in a second-hand book store. My favourite lines are:

'I am to thee like a garden,
which I have planted with flowers
and with all manner of sweet smelling herbs,
my heart is satisfied with joy –
because we walk together.'

Many early love spells in Ancient Egypt also involved flowers and by empowering them in ritual it was believed the fragrance would call the loved one.

To attract a reluctant lover, the maiden would fill a dish of lotus oil and entreat Hathor the love goddess to suffuse it with the sun power of her father/consort Ra. She would then mix dried fish – a fertility symbol – into the oil and add crushed rose petals, gathered before dawn, praying over the oil on each of the seven nights before the full moon that Hathor would grant a good husband.

On the night of the full moon the girl would embalm the fish with the moon herb myrrh, for it had now endowed its essence in the oil. She then buried the fish beneath a rose bush and smeared the oil on her forehead to bring the loved one (who, hopefully, was not allergic to fish).

You can leave out the fish if you want to try this and substitute rose or marigold petals.

Fire and fragrance love spell

The following is another of Serena's collection of love rituals from her homeland. Like a number of modern Egyptian love spells, the words seem to be a popularized folk version of some of the very ancient love poems. Men as well as women can use the spell.

▲ Create a bowl of dried hibiscus flowers – sacred to Bastet in some traditions – dried lilies – sacred to Isis – and dried rose petals for Hathor.

▲ Crush and mix them with large cinnamon chips or powdered cinnamon for passion, working in silence and picturing a known or unknown lover's face.

▲ Slowly cast the mix on to an open fire, for example a small bonfire, saying:

'The flowers burn, like my love for you. The perfume rises as my heart rises in joy at your footsteps. It rises to the skies. Come to me, I call you in the flowers and flame again, my heart.'

In theory, you can use any fragrant dried flowers and lavender is good for a first love. If you cannot make a fire, crush the flower very finely and burn a small quantity in a candle set on a metal tray or in a deep metal pot filled with sand.

Recite the words, then bury the rest under a sycamore tree or any tree in leaf and repeat the words.

Incense magic

The traditional and widely quoted incense or censing prayer comes from the Coffin Texts, number 269. To date, more than a thousand coffin texts have been found. They come from the earlier royal funerary texts, known as the 'pyramid texts', which were originally written on tomb walls. The later coffin texts, which include a detailed guide to the afterlife, were written inside the bottoms of wooden coffins dating from the Middle Kingdom, from around 2055 BCE. I saw the incense prayer in Cairo displayed next to a vast array of exotic incenses and some of the most ornate gold censers I have ever seen outside a church:

'The fire is laid, the fire shines;
The incense is laid on the fire, the incense shines.
Your perfume comes to me, O incense;
May my perfume come to you, O incense.
Your perfume comes to me, you gods;
May my perfume come to you, you gods.
May I be with you, you gods;
May you be with me, you gods.
May I live with you, you gods;
May you live with me, you gods.
I love you, you gods;
May you love me, you gods.'

As I explained on page 11, incense burning was central to temple rituals of purification, in processions, at celebrations, at private rituals and while scrying. Most precious of offerings, incense was burned to send prayers and praise to the deities, both by priests in the inner sanctum or naos of the god in the temple and at homely household altars. It might be burned to honour the ancestors or when asking Hathor, Isis, Bes or Tauret for blessings. Lighting incense is an almost instant way of separating ritual or contemplation from the everyday world.

Above all, as in the temples, incense is a potent and instant way of purifying an area, whether it is your temple, room, your home or your workplace (waft incense over a map of your office rather than bringing it to work and risking setting off the smoke alarms). It will also purify the psychic energy field or aura that forms an ellipse around your body but is most clearly seen psychically around the head.

If you want to see your aura, look into your magic mirror so that you are framed in soft sunlight. Stare hard at your reflection, close your eyes, open them, blink and look again and you will see perhaps two or three predominant rainbow colours. If your aura is either very pale or clouded with dark streaks, incense is a good way of cleansing and strengthening it (see the next chapter for herbal healing magic).

Burning incense

There are two kinds of incense you can use in ritual. The easiest is the combustible kind that comes in the form of incense sticks or cones. Light the incense and allow it to flame, then gently blow it so that the tip glows red. You can buy large incense sticks, for use in gardens, that are solid and easy to hold. Incense sticks are easier to use than loose incense and have the added advantage that unlike loose incense the fragrance of the unlit stick is the same you will smell when you light it. Occasionally, loose incense can smell lovely as a powder, but can be quite sharp when burned on charcoal. Sticks are easy to carry during a ritual in a deep container, or in your hand if there is a sufficiently firm and long enough handle to hold on to, and to waft around a room or (with care) a person.

You can also put an incense cone in a censer, a metal container with holes so the smoke wafts around. Incense sticks and cones are widely available in most of the traditional ancient Egyptian fragrances (see below). But for formal ritual, or whenever you have a few minutes to spare before magical work, choose a non-combustible form. This incense is made from any plant material and is sometimes combined with essential oil to enhance the fragrance. One essential ingredient in true incense is the addition of a gum resin such as frankincense, but in practice you can burn pure flowers and wood chips directly on charcoal. You can buy most of the traditional ancient Egyptian incenses ready-made in granular or powder form and some as blends from New Age stores and aromatherapy outlets or shops selling ethnic goods.

I bought a whole selection of dried flowers and incense at a stall in Cairo, including a block of powdered myrrh, some frankincense, hibiscus flowers, saffron and some huge cinnamon and cedar wood chips. They cost a fraction of the price I pay in the UK and it was lovely to see all the barrels of herbs and spices on display and to smell the different fragrances before buying.

Tools for incense burning

For incense magic you will need:

▲ A container for the burning incense. I have recently bought a small silver censer, an incense dish with a lid with holes and a chain, a miniature version of the kind carried by priests. These are depicted on a number of tomb walls. However, you can use a flat ceramic fireproof dish with a heatproof lip to hold it safely.

▲ Some small individual charcoal blocks or discs to fit inside the censer on which to burn

the incense.
▲ Some long metal tongs for holding the charcoal while you light it. Barbecue tongs are excellent for the task.
▲ A selection of ancient Egyptian fragrances and dark, closed storage jars to help keep them fragrant.
▲ A small spoon; the kind used for sugar, which is smaller even than a teaspoon, is excellent. You can pick these up in junk shops and at garage sales.

Incense burning

▲ Whether you are lighting incense for part of a ritual or to purify your temple room or as a ritual in itself, begin by selecting the appropriate fragrance. If you are pregnant or suffer from any lung condition or allergy, it may be best to avoid incense and no one should spend prolonged periods even with fragrant smoke.
▲ Holding the charcoal block between tongs, light it with a thin taper lit from a flame and hold the taper to the charcoal until it momentarily sparks. If it proves stubborn, light it in a second place, but do not touch it with your fingers. Your charcoal may look as if it has not lit, but it becomes extremely hot even before the colour shows.
▲ Set it with the tongs into the open bottom dish of the censer. In a minute or two, you will see the red glowing through and slowly spreading through the block and after about five minutes, the block will turn white.
▲ At this point, sprinkle or scoop a little of the incense into the centre until it begins to smoke and then very slowly add a little more – too much will put out the charcoal. Ask for the blessings you seek or need.
▲ Put on the lid and swing your censer so that clouds of smoke appear. You can walk around a room or around your altar, or circle the censer in front of you, wafting the smoke with the other hand so it spreads to the aura, the psychic energy field around your head and body (about an outstretched arm span all round).
▲ When the smoke dies down, add a little more incense, making this a part of the ritual and repeating your petition.
▲ You can mix more than one incense fragrance if you have a dual need or two or three related needs.
▲ Remember to give thanks by recalling blessings you have received in your life and by offering some form of service, however small, to others or to the planet.
▲ You might like to chant your own version of one of the numerous ancient Egyptian rites, which basically say in more or less elaborate form something like:

> *'I am the incense, I am the incense. I rise to the skies. Horus carries me on swift wings and soars to the sun. I rise to Ra as pure incense and I become as the sun. I ask wise Nut – (make your petition at this point)*. I am the incense and I take my place with the deities. I am pure smoke. I am sky Horus, Nut and the benu bird that saw the first sunrise on the mound at the morning of the world.'*

INCENSE	MAGIC QUALITIES
Basil	Basil is a herb of love and fidelity and also attracts abundance and prosperity. It is good in all cleansing and anti-pollution rituals. Deity: Horus
Cedar/cedarwood	Cedar removes redundant influences and negative thoughts, bringing both cleansing and healing. Cedar is a herb of purification and protection, guarding the home and working against all negative influences and against dark thoughts. Deity: Osiris
Camomile	A sun incense, camomile brings kindness and gentleness to homes and families and is good for petitions concerning children. It brings a gradual increase in money, affection, friendship and family unity. It is also very protective and as a bonus helps insomnia. Deity: Bastet
Cinnamon	Cinnamon is a bringer of money and success. It is also a herb of love and passion. Cinnamon also rules all matters to do with healing. It is potent in increasing psychic awareness and also offers protection. Deity: Sekhmet
Cypress	Cypress brings consolation after sorrow or loss and helps one to let go of grief and to move forward. It brings wisdom, understanding and compassion towards the distress of self and others. It is a herb of healing and protection. Deity: Anubis

INCENSE	MAGIC QUALITIES
Frankincense	Regarded as the most noble of incenses, frankincense is used in ceremonies and formal celebrations bringing healing and power. It offers confidence to aim high, attracting abundance of all kinds, money, success and male potency. It also grants access to higher dimensions through psychic work and aids astral projection and past life work. Deity: Ra
Gum Arabic (Acacia)	Good for dreams, meditation, psychic protection and development, this is a powerful protector against physical and psychic harm. It is good as an incense mixture with sandalwood, frankincense or myrrh for all forms of psychic development, stimulating prophetic dreams. It also brings money and platonic love. Deity: Serapis
Hibiscus	Hibiscus is good for joy, for harmony, for beauty and radiance and for scrying and all divination. Deity: Bastet
Hyssop	Known as the 'holy herb' throughout the Middle East, and often mixed with other fragrances, hyssop is good for special occasions, such as making a love commitment, for healing and for all forms of protection, especially from psychic attack. Deity: Osiris

INCENSE	MAGIC QUALITIES
Jasmine	Jasmine is potent for all moon magic, especially on the crescent and the night of the full moon. It induces prophetic dreams and is used for many aspects of psychic development, especially astral projection. Jasmine is a herb of love and gives loving feelings a spiritual dimension. Deity: Isis
Juniper	Juniper is very protective, keeping people, animals and property safe from theft, vandalism and psychic attacks as well as from illness. It is a natural purifier for the home against past negative influences and future misfortune and for house moves. It also increases male potency. Deity: Bes
Lavender	Lavender can be burned for almost any purpose, for health and all forms of healing but especially for soothing quarrels and for kindness and affection. Lavender is the herb of love, and it attracts gentle and kind lovers – especially for women. It is also good for making wishes. Deity: Hathor
Lemongrass	Lemongrass will clear away negative emotions among family, friends or at work, past resentment and feuds from the past that no longer serve any purpose. It also removes painful memories and helps an individual to leave behind destructive relationships. Lemongrass also enhances psychic awareness. Deity: Horus
Lilac	Lilac brings joy and harmony to all domestic matters, cleansing all negativity and anxiety. It is especially good for marking smoke boundaries to keep away all malevolence and in houses in which paranormal activity is disturbing. Lilac also helps with the acceptance of the frailty of oneself and of others. Deity: Tauret

INCENSE	MAGIC QUALITIES
Lily	Lily is a natural purifier, breaking negative influences in love and lessening the hold of addictions and obsessions. It is also sacred to the Mother Goddess and so is used as incense in all goddess magic and for all mothering issues. Deity: Isis
Lily of the Valley	Lily of the valley is a flower of gentle optimism, bringing light and hope even into seemingly impossible situations. It also sharpens mental faculties and improves the memory. Deity: Bastet
Lotus	Lotus, the flower of the gods, represents new beginnings, hope, higher spiritual energies, healing, love and marriage. Deity: Nefertum
Mimosa	Mimosa is an incense of the night, for secrets and secret love. It brings love and friendship, especially for older people. Mimosa calms anxiety and over-sensitivity to criticism and brings harmony and happiness, melting away opposition and hostility. It is good for past life recall. Deity: Nephthys
Myrrh	Myrrh is one of the oldest protective and purification incenses, and is associated with the healing of mind and spirit as well as body. It is a good herb to burn for protection. Myrrh promotes higher states of consciousness and so is good for all spiritual work, especially for recalling past lives. Deity: Osiris
Orange Blossom/Neroli	This is a symbol of marriage, committed relationships, fidelity and fertility. It increases self-esteem and self-love and encourages optimism. It prevents mood swings, crises of confidence and panic attacks. Orange blossom/Neroli also restores trust after betrayal. Deity: Hathor

INCENSE	MAGIC QUALITIES
Poppy	Poppy is good for divination and scrying, for fertility, for making oneself less visible in dangerous situations, reversing bad luck and taking away grief and mental anguish. Deity: Nephthys
Rose	Like lavender, rose is a natural healer and restorer of well-being on the physical, emotional and spiritual planes. Since time immemorial, roses have been used in love rituals, to bring dreams of a future lover, to attract love and to preserve it. Rose is potent for past life recall, gentle love, attraction, dreams of love and reconciliation. Deity: Hathor
Sandalwood	Sandalwood is a ceremonial incense and so its prime focus is in increasing spiritual awareness, offering a path to make contact with the higher self and the deity forms. It is potent for all psychic and divinatory work, including astral projection and past life recall. It also heightens meditative abilities. Sandalwood is a herb that increases passion. Deity: Amun or Ptah
Thyme	Thyme is another powerful divinatory incense, stimulating prophetic dreams, astral projection and past life work. It is a health bringer, improving memory, mental abilities and gives courage and strength. Deity: Thoth

12

HEALING MAGIC

Just as magic and religion were closely intertwined, so were magic and healing. Though the ancient Egyptian priest doctors were skilled physicians and surgeons, ritual was an important tool of healing. The idea of doctors making wax images, or invoking the deities to overcome the demons or wandering kas that caused a patient's illness, may seem fanciful. However, modern research in America would seem to support the principle of magical healing. About 30 years ago, Dr Herbert Benson, a Harvard Medical School professor and founder of the Mind/Body Medical Institute at Deaconess Hospital in Boston, began to research the health benefits of transcendental meditation. He subsequently broadened the scope of his research to consider the question of how a change of thinking could bring health benefits to those suffering from stress-related illnesses. Prayer was found to be the most efficacious method of bringing about a positive outcome. 'By repeating prayers, words or sounds and passively disregarding other thoughts,' Dr Benson noted, 'many people are able to trigger a specific set of physiological changes. Invoking prayers or mantras over and over can lower the rate of breathing and brain wave activity, sometimes healing what ails you and averting the need for invasive surgery or expensive medicine.'

Moreover, it would seem that prayer and ritual carried out by outsiders can actually cause a positive change in an individual's aura energies and trigger innate healing powers. An American doctor, Randolph Byrd, carried out an experiment in which two hundred patients admitted to San Francisco State Hospital with heart attacks were allocated to a group of Christians who said daily prayers on their behalf. A further 200 similarly afflicted patients, for whom prayers were not said, were used as a control group. Significantly fewer of those who had prayers said on their behalf suffered a stroke or further heart attack while in hospital or died. The patients did not know they were being prayed for.

The same principle applies to the ancient Egyptian priest or priestess healer who, in a ritual, set a sick person in the role of the young child god Horus who had been stung by the scorpions. The healer then took on the role of Isis, threatening the deities using the words of Horus's mother Isis – that if the child was not cured, she would bring darkness to the earth. At this point all lamps would be extinguished, because in the myth Isis stopped the passage of the sun (she was a lunar deity in one of her roles) and caused a lunar eclipse.

Thoth (another healer wearing a mask) would then speak the words of healing and re-light the lamps. Such a dramatic connection with the energies of the original myth told and retold many times could act as the catalyst for the patient's own immune system to be activated by association with Horus's energies. The air would also be fused with the healing energies and, as with the power of prayer, healing powers would be transmitted into the person to be healed. Combined with skilled intervention, the prognosis would be good.

The deities and healing

The ancient Egyptians believed that the deities themselves suffered from illnesses and pain, such as headaches, and so linked their own healing work with that of the healing deities who would cure the gods. Remedies might be attributed to the deities. For example, in the Papyrus Ebers, a medical treatise recorded around 1500 BCE (although the information is probably much older), it is related that Ra had a bad headache. (Other papyri describe Thoth and Horus suffering similar pain.) Isis mixed equal amounts of coriander, poppy, wormwood and juniper in equal proportions as a poultice for Ra's head. This became a popular headache cure – partly because it was attributed to Isis. (It is now known that wormwood can have toxic effects, so it is only generally used by experienced herbalists.)

But the application of natural remedies together with positive affirmations and visualization can work wonders. I find that a rose quartz or amethyst dipped in water and applied to my temples – along with a recitation of the following affirmations – does make a real difference, especially if I am busy. This ritual is a mixture of various myths and elements of my own creation. I believe that it is important to create Egyptian ritual in order to allow the wisdom to continue to grow in the modern world. It is also – probably because it is so linked with the original creation myths – the most inventive form of magic. In Egypt you find dozens of spells, all different, which come from the same verse of one of the ancient papyri.

Ritual to cure a headache when you cannot rest

Repeat the following:

'My head,' said Ra, 'the light too bright. I must dim the sun and sleep a while.'
Isis said: 'There is no time. Your boat must sail till Lady Nut enfolds you in her cloak of stars.'
Ra said: 'The light too bright, the heat it sears me. I, Lord of Light, I seek the dark.'
Lady Nut said: 'Take then this star new risen that I have dipped for thee in the cool waters of the celestial Nile and press it to your temple.'

(At this point, hold your crystal on the pressure points of your own temples and visualize the jagged pain flowing out into the gentle starlight.)

Ra: 'The pain is eased, the sun will onward pass and fill the world with glory. The crops will glow with light and time shall not be broken. I thank thee mothers both for this thy remedy.'

Plunge the crystal into a bowl of still mineral water and repeat the ritual three times.

Try to walk in the fresh air or at least spend two or three minutes with your hands over your eyes, flowing into darkness.

Use the crystal water to splash on your temples and wrists during the day.

For children's headaches, the ritual seems to work better than tablets and they can join in with the words.

Healing deities

Sekhmet - The protective role of the goddess Sekhmet, both in life and in the afterworld, is well known. Next to her statue at a travelling Egyptian treasures exhibition in the south of England, I found the following words from an old funerary text:

'I am the ardent heat of the fire that put a million cubits between Osiris and his enemies. I drive them away and keep them far from the dwelling place.' (See also page 96)

The words I have also heard used by a goddess-worshipping group in Los Angeles, as an invocation in an opening a ritual to Sekhmet.

Sekhmet's cult centre was Memphis, but she had temples in Luxor and Karnak in the Temples of Amun and was the icon of a guild of healers and physicians. She was believed to bring plagues and illnesses to the unrighteous and so, when there was any large-scale epidemic, rituals were held and offerings were made to appease her that the innocent might not likewise suffer.

But Sekhmet was regarded both as a bringer of illness and as a major source of healing power. Her priest(ess) physicians would call her in ritual to destroy illnesses, especially those caused by malign spirits. Her time was the fierce noonday heat, the period of the day when her power could be most effectively invoked. Sekhmet was known as Lady of Life.

Invoke Sekhmet to cure fevers, viral infections and all infectious illness, from the common cold to childhood rashes, for burns and scalds, for skin allergies and for all acute conditions needing surgery.

Isis - Isis was a healing goddess and was appealed to in popular magic by ordinary people as well as by physicians. Because of this, her remedies entered into the folk tradition and she was especially associated with the illness of mothers and children.

For example, Isis would be invoked when a patient had a burn, which would be treated with a mixture including milk from the lactating mother of a male child, to create the link with Isis and her son. The spell quoted in the Papyrus Ebers says:

'Thy son Horus is burnt in the desert. There is no water.'

The goddess replies: 'I have water in my mouth. I have come to extinguish the fire.'

Invoke Isis for all women's medical problems, for menstruation, pregnancy, childbirth and new mothers, the menopause, for childhood ailments, headaches and for burns.

Khonsu - This moon child deity of Thebes was often pictured in mummified form, but with a side-lock. The son of Amun and Mother Goddess Mut, he is often seen with the crescent moon on his head. He was guardian against diseases and was sometimes seen with the young solar god Horus, his alter ego, standing on crocodiles in his healing capacity.

Invoke Khonsu for hormonal and fluid imbalances in men and women, against any bladder, bowel or stomach disorders or infections, to guard against mood swings, anxiety attacks and depression, and to keep disease from the home.

Imhotep/Imenhotep - Imhotep was a deified scribe, who created the step pyramid at Saqqara and was made the god of healing; his healing temple was built near Memphis. People came here to sleep and receive healing in dreams.

In time, Imhotep became known as the son of Ptah and Nut and was pictured as a youth wearing a skullcap and carrying a scroll.

His worship during the Ptolemaic period became combined with that of Thoth. Mummified ibises bearing the name of Imhotep were brought to the temple, as were clay models of parts of the body where there was pain or disease. He was also identified with the Greek healer god Aesclepius, in whose honour healing dream temples were built under both the Greeks and the Romans.

Imhotep was famed for answering prayers and for performing healing miracles. It is told that a woman called Taimhotep and her husband, a high priest of Ptah, prayed at Imhotep's temple near Memphis because they were barren. Imhotep came to Taimhotep in a dream and promised that if his sanctuary in North Saqqara was restored to its former glory, their prayer would be granted. This was done and a child was born on Imhotep's next festival day. The tablet recording this event during the reign of Cleopatra is in the British Museum.

Invoke Imhotep for both spiritual healing, especially in sleep, and also to help before conventional medical or surgical intervention is due.

Pregnancy and childbirth

Ritual was an important part of childbirth in Ancient Egypt although gynaecological knowledge was relatively advanced. Again, this is a psychologically and psychically sound principle. If a woman believed that protective goddesses were attending and assisting with the birth, then she was more likely to relax and flow with contractions rather than fight them. (I speak as a mother of five who gave birth the technological way.)

There were a variety of ancient Egyptian pregnancy and childbirth spells, many of which were written down on papyrus. The Papyrus Leyden – which dates from the beginning of the Christian era – is one of the most important sources of the potions, spells and incantations that were used in Ancient Egypt. (It was discovered at Thebes in the mid-19th century and assembled out of fragments from Leyden and London.) Some were influenced by Greek magic, though others were much older. According to this document, during labour a woman might be told by an attendant:

> *'I am Hathor come to give birth for thee.'*
> *'Hathor will lay her hand on thee with an amulet of healing.'*

Then a gentle touch across the brow and the gift of a tiny statue of Hathor when the mother appeared to be tiring could transmit soothing and sustaining energies.

The labour was often likened to Isis giving birth in the papyrus marshes. Isis was assisted by Nephthys, her sister, supporting her from behind and the scorpion goddess Serqet delivering. With this help, according to the Westcar Papyrus, 'the infant rushed forth from Isis, his limbs strong'. (The Westcar Papyrus dates back to approximately 1800–1700 BCE and is named after Henry Westcar, who bought it during a trip to Egypt in 1824–25. It describes displays of magic that supposedly took place before members of royalty, although the events it describes were estimated to have happened about a millennium before the document's creation.)

Images were also used to aid labour. A clay figure of the dwarf Bes would be placed on the mother's forehead or figures of Bes and Tauret holding protective knives would be set on either side of the mother and her newly delivered child.

The magical wand – of the type I described on pages 13–14, decorated with images of Bes, Tauret and fierce creatures such as crocodiles to ward off harm – were placed on the stomach of the mother as she was pushing the baby out. About 150 of these wands have been found, all dating from the Middle Kingdom and Second Intermediate Period.

If labour proved difficult, a wax ibis would be burned on the fire to call on the aid of Thoth.

Red knots, too, one for each of the daughters of Hathor who would assign the fate of the new infant, were tied in a cord before the beginning of labour. They would be untied gradually to help the passage of the child and the opening of the womb. Similar knot rituals were common in a number of cultures.

A ritual to release blockages

You can use this ritual to relieve any internal blockages, such as gall stones, knotted pain such as rheumatism or arthritis, back and neck pain, to relieve general pain, bowel, bladder and menstrual discomfort and emotional blockages that can prevent us moving on to a new phase.

▲ Stand in an open space in the afternoon facing south, a direction sacred to Isis. Visualize Isis standing in front of you with wings and a crescent moon disc on its side in her head-dress, a solar disc between her horns. Behind you is the winged Nephthys with her tall tower-like pylon head-dress. To the left is Serqet with a scorpion head-dress and to the right, Hathor with her solar disc and cow horns.

▲ In the centre, set a candle with a sharp knife on a nail and on the candle etch an ibis – like a small, squat heron – or any bird with a curved beak. It need only be a rough representation.

▲ Take a red cord and tie just four knots in it, one for each of the helper goddesses. Turn and face each deity as you tie her knot and recite the following lines:

(Facing south.) 'Before me, Isis, Lady of Enchantment, I bind your healing spells within this knot of one.' (Facing north.) 'Behind me Nephthys, Lady of the Shadowy Places, I bind your compassion within this knot of two.'

(Facing south.) 'At my left hand, Serqet, Lady of the Quicksilver Scorpions, I bind your power to help, not harm, within this knot of three.'

(Facing south.) 'And last but ever foremost, at my right hand Hathor, Lady of Gold. Hathor, I bind your nurturing within this knot of four. I greet you all. Be midwives unto me and deliver me, I ask, from what troubles me so grievously.' (At this point, name the blockage that is causing you distress.)

ANCIENT EGYPTIAN MAGIC

▲ Light the candle and say:
> *'Wise Thoth, who healed Horus in the marshes from the death sting, release your healing powers as this wax melts and carry in its flow what troubles me so grievously.' (At this point name your area of blockage again.) 'Wax flow, pains go, give to me tranquillity.'*

▲ Still facing south, untie the first knot and say:
> *'Knot unbind, thus unwind what troubles me so grievously.' (At this point name your area of blockage again.) 'Isis, Lady of Enchantment, bring release, I ask and it shall be.'*

▲ Turn to face behind you and untie the second knot, saying:
> *'Knot unbind, thus unwind what troubles me, so grievously.' (At this point name your area of blockage again.) 'Nephthys, Lady of the Shadowy Places, bring release, I ask and it shall be.'*

▲ Turn south again and then to your left and untie the third knot; saying:
> *'Knot unbind, thus unwind what troubles me so grievously.' (At this point name your area of blockage again.) 'Serqet, Lady of the Quicksilver Scorpions, bring release, I ask and it shall be.'*

▲ Finally, turning again to the south, face the right and untie the final knot, saying:
> *'Knot unbind, thus unwind what troubles me so grievously. (At this point name your area of blockage again.) Hathor, Lady of Gold, bring release, I ask and it shall be.'*

▲ Take the cord and singe its end in the candle flame, saying:
> *'Thoth, aid the wise goddesses and melt away what troubles me so grievously.'*

▲ Coil the cord to make a circle round the candle, so that it does not catch light and sit watching the light fading slowly from the sky and feel the knots within you unravelling, the blockages melting and the energies flowing once more.

▲ When the candle is burned through dispose of it and the cord.

Magical healing of bites and stings

Most famous of the many spells and rituals were those centred on the stelae, the tablets showing young Horus trampling on crocodiles. At the base of each stela was a bowl that caught the water that was ritually poured over the figure of Horus. These cippi as they were called date from around 300 BCE. Horus is naked and has a side-lock of hair to indicate that he was a child. In each hand he holds fierce creatures such as crocodiles, scorpions and even lions.

Though originally intended to cure snake and scorpion stings, the power extended to any injury or accident, skin problems, wounds, burns and allergies. The invalid drank or bathed with the water that had flowed over the stela, to absorb the magical power. Sometimes Horus was given the face of Bes. Healing formulae were engraved on the back and sides of the tablet. The following formula, which was found on the back of a Horus stela on which the god had the face of Bes, is typical:

> *'Horus, you protect me against the wild creatures of the desert,*
> *the crocodiles of the river,*

the snakes and scorpions,
the insects that sting fiercely with their tail,
and reptiles waiting in their holes to strike.'

The water could also be used for protection. As the water was poured, protective words were recited. For example: 'May his heel be bronze and the ball of his foot be ivory' referring to Horus. Then as the water was drunk, the person would declare: 'I am that Horus.'

Often such chants were recited either four or seven times. The implication was that the scorpions and snakes could not bite a bronze and ivory foot.

A Horus ritual to heal wounds

You can use this method for healing not only allergies, skin problems and wounds but also inner stings and wounds – hurt feelings that may have been inflicted by other people. There are human scorpions in the workplace and critical relations in many people's lives. Alternatively, you may carry wounds from childhood coldness or a cold or cruel lover that have never fully healed.

You can pour water over a statue of Horus or another of your favourite deities or an animal representation of them, for example a bird of prey for Horus. The statue need only be small. I have a bronze falcon-headed Horus statuette that stands perfectly in a deep ceramic bowl. Alternatively, you can find a small round rock with a flat base and draw your Horus on it and then stand it in a strong bowl on the ground. The ritual is lovely outdoors under trees in the early morning light. I sometimes work in the grove of trees opposite my caravan in the country where there is a small, disused stone trough that I can use as an altar.

▲ Stand the statue or stone in the bottom of a shallow dish so that the water can collect in it.

▲ Use a small jug of still mineral water and as you pour the water over the statue, name the illness or the pain – physical or mental (you can heal mental anguish) – and say seven times the formula quoted above.

▲ Sprinkle a little of the water on your brow and your wrists and if it is not too painful, close to the area of pain or discomfort. If it is an inner sorrow, anoint the centre of your forehead with the water.

▲ Visualize Horus and a flock of falcons driving away your hurt.

▲ Pour the rest of the water on growing plants.

▲ If you face spite or hostility at work or with neighbours or family members or know you must enter a dangerous or difficult situation, recite this line seven times after the basic chant and while you pour the water:

  'May my heel be bronze and the ball of my foot ivory.'

▲ This time, after you have anointed yourself, filter the rest of the water into a small glass bottle and sprinkle a few drops around any room where there may be hostile visitors or keep some on your workspace in a bowl with dark obsidian protective crystals. Run your fingers through it and touch your brow with the water when you feel under attack.

▲ If you are in a lonely or dark place, take a tiny phial of the water from your bag and sprinkle it round you.

▲ In all these situations, recite the words of the ritual seven times in your mind when your personal scorpion threatens to strike.

Healing herbs

I have already listed magical incenses and perfumes. In this section, some of the same fragrances in their pure herb form will be used.

As we have seen, the ancient Egyptians believed that plants were made from the first material of creation and so possessed a healing essence or spirit. When the herb was cut and empowered magically, or applied as a poultice, or drunk as an infusion or tea, the healing spirit passed into the user.

I have focused on the magical rather than the medical use of the most common ancient Egyptian healing herbs so that you can use the essential healing spirit of the herbs without having to worry about quantities and safe medical practices that would require the advice of a good herbalist or pharmacist.

I have found from my own healing work that empowering herbs and then giving or sending them to someone who is ill or distressed transmits the healing essence from the auric psychic energy field of the herbs into that of the patient. This often seems to trigger a positive response from the patient or distressed person.

Of course, you would not treat an acute illness, or a child with worrying symptoms, by magic. However, after consulting a physician you might use magical means to work on increasing the person's self-healing powers, while using conventional or prescribed herbal medicines as well, as the ancient Egyptians did.

Some illnesses cannot be cured and it is important to alleviate suffering, not least emotional suffering. Ancient Egyptian doctors recognized that some illnesses were beyond the scope of medicine and magic and in the modern world we can be unrealistic in our expectations that modern medicine – or for that matter modern magic – can cure all. If you are dealing with someone who is terminally ill, you might prefer to substitute prayers to whoever is your – or the patient's – personal deity form or ask Mother Isis and her sister Nephthys to aid a gentle passing. We all see divinity in our own way, but the essence of the healing wishes is the same.

Making healing sachets

▲ Choose a herb from the list below – or two or three if you wish. Though they are ancient Egyptian herbs they are very common throughout the world.

▲ Either buy the dried herb or cut the growing plant or bark.

▲ Chop it finely and then, with a mortar and pestle (widely available in homeware stores) or a bowl and wooden spoon, pound the herbs while chanting words of power related to the purpose of the herbs, whether a specific illness (see list below) or an emotional or spiritual need. For example, if you wanted to relieve the restlessness of a child who was finding it difficult to sleep, you might choose camomile. As you pounded the herb, or got the child to help, you might recite the name of the herb, the related deity and the purpose, for example: 'Camomile, camomile, herb of Nefertum, bring Susie sleep and good dreams.'

▲ In contrast to western magical empowerment, you should keep up a slow, steady quiet rhythmic chanting. When you can see in your mind's vision the aura of the plant – either a green glow or, in the case of camomile, a gentle golden glow – speak more slowly and quietly until the words flow into silence. Druidic healing works along very similar lines. There is a theory that refugees from Atlantis spread their advanced knowledge to both Ancient Egypt and Celtic lands, suggesting a link between the ancient Egyptians and the Celtic priesthood.

▲ Place the blessed herbs in a tiny purse or sachet made from a piece of cloth tied with four knots for the four protective healing goddesses – Isis, Nephthys, Serqet and Hathor – and give or send the purse to whoever needs the healing, not forgetting yourself.

▲ If there are small children around set the sachet high, as any herbs can be toxic if eaten by a small child.

▲ You can also empower pots or bunches of fresh herbs by placing them on a table in front of a lighted candle until burns through, and chanting until you see light around the plant.

▲ Alternatively, if it would not be appropriate to send or give herbs, light a candle and burn a leaf or two of the relevant herb in the flame, stating your purpose for the herb.

Herbs to avoid in pregnancy

I have included herbs you may find elsewhere as well as ones I have used in the book. The prohibitions apply to internal use, baths, massage and prolonged inhalation of the herb in incense form. Similar prohibitions apply to essential oils.

Avoid: acacia, aloe vera, angelica, autumn crocus, barberry, basil, caraway, cayenne, cedarwood, clary sage, fennel, feverfew, golden seal, hyssop, juniper, male fern, mandrake, marjoram, myrrh, parsley, penny royal, poke root, rosemary, rue, sage, southernwood, tansy, tarragon, thuja, thyme, wintergreen, wormwood and yarrow.

Other conditions, such as heart problems, raised blood pressure, diabetes and weak kidneys, make it unwise to use some herbs internally or to handle them. So check with a herbalist, or a good reference book, if you intend to use them medicinally or handle them for prolonged periods.

Herbs of Ancient Egypt

Acacia Acacia nilotica Acacia is familiar to most of us as Gum Arabic, a resinous incense. As a pure herb, the wood is used for all forms of magical healing, especially for rising above spite and pettiness and attaining self-love. The flowers are used to relieve skin problems, while the leaves are useful for treating coughs and also wounds.

Spiritually, acacia soothes and relaxes and also enables you to heal yourself in dreams and meditative states. It is sacred to Serapis and Thoth.

Caraway *Carum carvi* Caraway seeds, which are dark brown, long and thin, are sweet and spicy, a mixture of liquorice and pepper. They help digestion and also stimulate the intestinal walls, easing spasms and flatulence and stimulating both menstruation and maternal milk.

They are potent against coughs and also good for abdominal pains and bruises. Caraway is also an aphrodisiac.

Spiritually, caraway is protective against all sources of negativity, and enhances memory. It is sacred to Isis.

Camomile *Chamaemelum nobile* Camomile is a sun herb and was grown along the banks of the Nile. The flowers were used in funerary wreaths and were found in the stomach of Rameses II. The most gentle and soothing of herbs, camomile is sometimes called the children's herb. It can be used for healing all babies' and children's ills and sorrow. It also soothes adult anxiety and stress, relieving insomnia, nightmares, gastritis, hyperactivity in children, eye and throat problems, migraines, colic and stomach troubles – again, especially in children – and also respiratory problems.

Spiritually, camomile increases abundance, aids mediation and higher states of awareness, attracts gentle love and is very protective. It is sacred to Bastet.

Coriander *Coriandrum sativum* Coriander was presented as an offering to the deities and has been discovered in a number of royal tombs. It brings and maintains good health.

Coriander is used to relieve all forms of colic pain and stomach upsets, in children as well as adults, to relieve headaches and for all digestive and abdominal disorders. It is an aphrodisiac.

Spiritually, coriander ensures clarity of thought and creativity and relieves a troubled mind by promoting optimism. Traditionally, pregnant women ate coriander to ensure their unborn children were quick-witted and creative in life. Coriander is sacred to Thoth.

Fenugreek *Trigonella foenumgraecum* One of the most ancient of herbs, fenugreek increases health and strength and helps with respiratory and digestive disorders, especially those connected with the liver and pancreas. Its antiseptic properties cleanse and heal wounds.

Spiritually, fenugreek increases abundance in every aspect of life over a period of time and is a purifying herb, especially if used in a number of consecutive rituals. It is sacred to Horus.

Garlic *Allium sativa* Garlic is a medicine chest in every clove, and was given to the builders of the pyramids in Ancient Egypt to boost their strength and keep illness at bay. It is a natural antibiotic that does not interfere with the body's own natural bacterial flora in the digestive tract, but kills harmful organisms. Garlic is powerful against viruses and bacteria and is a good remedy for colds, bronchitis, coughs and flu; however it is best known for improving circulation and lowering high blood pressure and blood cholesterol levels.

Garlic also keeps away hostile influences, both earthly and paranormal. It is sacred to Anubis.

Juniper *Juniperis communis* Juniper berries were used to alleviate headaches and are a natural antiseptic and an excellent diuretic. They are good for all urinary infections, especially cystitis, and for water retention problems. Juniper is used also for digestive and gastrointestinal inflammations, for arthritis and rheumatism. It can heal infected gums and coughs, colds and catarrh and also increases male potency.

Spiritually, juniper is a psychic cleaner and increases psychic awareness; it also helps to guard against accidents, theft and illness. It is sacred to Khonsu.

Sweet Marjoram *Majorana hortensis* or *Origanum marjorana* Marjoram is cleansing and anti-viral, relieving stress, depression, recurring headaches and anxieties and countering signs and fears of ageing. It improves circulation in the hands and feet and prevents illnesses developing.

Spiritually, marjoram brings protection, love, happiness, health and money and is powerful in divination. It is sacred to Osiris.

Peppermint *Mentha piperita* Peppermint is one of the best remedies for travel sickness and all forms of nausea, vomiting and stomach disorders. It is also good for painful menstruation. It relieves coughs and colds and sore throats and, used in concentration, is an energizer.

Spiritually, peppermint is a purifier, driving away all negativity and illness. It is also good for inducing prophetic dreams. Peppermint is sacred to Sekhmet.

Rosemary *Rosmarinus officinalis* Rosemary is used for bringing health and maintaining it, for relieving headaches and depression, to aid digestion, to relieve muscle pains and to aid the liver and the gall bladder. It improves circulation, increases energy levels, improves memory, focuses thoughts and is an aphrodisiac.

Spiritually, rosemary is a herb of protection, driving away bad dreams and attracting love. Sprigs of rosemary were found in Egyptian mummies, meaning that it was regarded as a herb of immortality and rejuvenation. Rosemary also aids divination and oracular wisdom. It is sacred to Hathor.

Thyme *Thymus praecox* Thyme is a powerful antiseptic and a good lotion for wounds. It soothes digestive disorders and helps sore throats and infections, tooth decay and gum disease, coughs and colds. It also improves memory and metal acuity.

Spiritually, thyme is primarily a divinatory herb, said to aid recall of the past and allow glimpses into the future, a cleaner of negativity and bringer of courage and spiritual strength. It keeps away bad dreams and may bring happy, prophetic ones.

Thyme is sacred to Thoth.

Healing crystals and metals

The Papyrus Ebers lists the healing properties of many gems and crystals. They included lapis lazuli – for eye salves – haematite, an iron oxide for stopping and preventing haemorrhages, emeralds to cure dysentery and rubies for liver and spleen diseases and to improve circulation. Lapis lazuli was also used to bring protection. The ancient Egyptians feared the evil eye and Egyptian women used protective eye shadow made from powdered lapis lazuli. Lapis amulets were made of the Eye of Horus for the same purpose.

Metals too were highly prized – especially gold, associated with Ra and with Hathor, who was called the Lady of Gold. The skin of the deities was said to be pure gold. For this reason pharaohs were placed in gold coffins; Tutankhamun was given a mask of solid gold to indicate his divine status in the afterlife. Modern goldsmiths claim descent from an unbroken tradition and still craft wonderful golden jewellery to endow power and protection on the wearers. Many amulets were and still are made of gold (see page 36) because they contained the power of the sun and the solar deities. Silver, sacred to Isis and Khonsu, was more rare in Egypt and was regarded as the bones of the gods. Copper – which, like gold, was a metal of Hathor – was famed for its healing powers and was made into rings and bracelets for this purpose, as it is today for easing joint pains and stiffness. The bones of Set were believed to be made of iron, which made it a protective metal against evil.

The healing power of crystals

Precious and semi-precious gems were used by the wealthy for healing – for example, golden topaz to symbolize the sun and to bring energy and fertility and banish fears. However, what we would call ordinary crystals were equally prized and not only by the poor. Pharaohs could have encrusted themselves and their coffins with priceless rubies and emeralds if they wished and yet the Egyptians considered coloured glass as a wondrous creation, involving magical processes that elevated the creators and wearers to the status of creative deities, for they were emulating nature in producing gem-like products.

The gold mask of Tutankhamun was adorned with lapis lazuli, carnelian, quartz, obsidian, turquoise and coloured glass, with eyes made of obsidian and clear glass. The breastplate has rows of lapis lazuli, quartz, amazonite, and coloured glass attached to the shoulders. But no diamonds – though they were used to cut stone from about 400 BCE – rubies or emeralds.

It may be that Egyptians believed that in the afterlife the semi-precious and crystalline forms they used even on the most elaborate coffins and as amulets would be transformed magically into gems more precious than any in the world.

What was important was the colour of a gem. For example, a red crystal heart was a symbol of the ba spirit and to the living was a protective amulet that ensured the health of the all-important heart, in which resided the intelligence and the essential person, as well as the emotions. Red crystals also symbolized the fertilizing and life-giving blood of Isis.

Blue faience, a glazed turquoise-like ceramic painted blue, was also used a great deal, because it was believed that in the creation of faience, power and fertility were transferred to the finished product, like glass through the use of fire and water Blue was the colour of the sky and the solar deities.

Crystal, especially calcite or alabaster, was used for dishes, cups and ritual objects to pass gentle healing power into the food, drink or offerings. Deep blue glass bottles held sacred oils.

Using healing crystals

Though gems and crystals were crushed into powders or used as ointments, other psychic methods were used to absorb their innate healing powers, which have survived into the modern day. I have suggested some of these in the following pages.

Crystal quartz seems to have been preferred to diamonds in magic and healing and quartz crystal balls were used medicinally to concentrate the rays of the sun upon a diseased or painful area of the body or in the direction of some internal organ. The following are some of the crystals that were used by the ancient Egyptians for healing and for power and protection, for magic and healing were synonymous in crystal work as in other spheres. The ones I have listed are easily obtainable and relatively inexpensive.

However, you can substitute any crystal of the same colour and if you have a special precious or semi-precious gem use that instead of the crystal of the same colour. On the whole, the crystals used belonged to the six main colours in the Egyptian world: red, blue, green, yellow, black and white.

Bloodstone (Heliotrope)

Type: Chalcedony
Colour: Opaque, mottled green and red.
This is primarily a stone of courage. The association with blood has continued through the ages and bloodstone is used in modern spiritual healing practice, as in Ancient Egypt, to stop nosebleeds and cuts, to help with menstrual cramps, to improve circulation and to enhance easier childbirth and fertility.

Bloodstone is sacred to Sekhmet.

Carnelian

Type: Chalcedony
Colours: Yellow, orange and red, occasionally brown. Translucent.
Carnelian is a crystal that defines and strengthens the identity of the wearer, bringing courage, confidence and self-esteem. It brings fertility and abundance to all aspects of life and keeps away envy and spite in others.

Carnelian warms and cleanses the blood and kidneys, stimulates appetite, sexuality, physical energy and helps the reproductive system. Carnelian is good with food-related problems, especially where a question of identity and self-esteem is involved.

Carnelian is sacred to Horus.

Citrine

Type: Quartz
Colour: Clear sparkling yellow.
In the ancient world, citrine referred to a whole series of sun stones, from golden beryl to zircon. Topaz has similar properties to what we call citrine today.

Citrine clears physical and metal energy blockages in the body. It encourages mental and emotional clarity, improving long- and short-term memory, strengthening willpower and inspiring optimism and self-confidence.

Citrine reduces anxiety and depression, relieves digestive problems and stomach tension, eases disorders relating to the spleen, gall bladder and liver, bladder and bowel and acts against food allergies and food-related illnesses.

Quartz is sacred to Ra.

Haematite

Type: Related to iron ore
Colour: Silver-grey metallic brilliance.
Haematite is a powerful fire and protective stone also related to the earth. It focuses indecision, aids concentration and improves memory.

The ancient Egyptians used haematite to soothe hysteria and worries. Strongly linked to the physical body, it is good for the spleen and the blood, aids in childbirth and acts as a shield against physical and emotional hostility. It is effective for overcoming jet lag, stress and the unwanted side-effects of anaesthetics as it was in the ancient one for overcoming stings and serpents. It also aids astral projection and past life work.

Haematite is sacred to Serqet.

Jasper

Type: Quartz
Colours: Opaque; may be multi-coloured or a single colours; yellow, orange, brown, green; also sometimes found as petrified wood.
One of the most popular ancient Egyptian stones, for amulets and as adornment for both the living and the deceased, jasper is a stone of strength and resistance against all forms of malevolence, especially in green and red.

Black

Black jasper is protective against all negativity and especially the user's own repressed feelings. It is good for absorbing anger.

Black jasper is sacred to Osiris.

Green

Green jasper protects against jealousy, increases empathy with others' difficulties and soothes bad dreams.

Good for all healing, especially general tissue regeneration, for the lungs and the absorption of minerals from food and herbs and for gradual recovery from illness.

Green jasper is sacred to Osiris.

Red

A defence against hostility, red jasper it was also worn as an amulet over the stomach to aid digestion and to prevent internal bleeding.

Red jasper is sacred to Isis.

Yellow

Yellow jasper guards against jealousy, spite and malice in others and brings acceptance of others and life as they really are. It is good for relieving problems in the digestion, stomach, intestines, liver and spleen.

Yellow jasper is sacred to Horus.

Lapis Lazuli (Lazurite)

Colours: Opaque rich medium to dark blue with flecks of iron pyrites (fool's gold).

The modern sapphire was also called lapis lazuli in the ancient world and is interchangeable with lapis.

Lapis was the most favoured blue stone of the Egyptians and its name meant joy. Its name, khshdj, was later given to the colour blue.

Known as the 'Eye of Wisdom', the stone of the deities, lapis lazuli was associated with the eye of Ra and also the sun eye of Horus and with the rising sun. It is both empowering and protective.

Because of its association with the wisdom of higher powers, lapis lazuli is considered the stone of leadership, of nobility, inspiring words and wise judgement. It is also a powerful means of bringing innate psychic awareness and clairvoyance to the fore.

In Egypt, lapis lazuli was first used in a powdered form for eye make-up and was believed to improve both eyesight and inner vision. Powdered lapis was also rubbed into the crown of the head to relieve headaches and to bring wisdom. It relieves problems with the nervous system, bone disorders, speech and hearing difficulties, the lymph glands, insomnia and inflammation and pain, particularly headaches.

Lapis lazuli is sacred to Ra, Amun and Nut.

Malachite

Type: Copper Carbonate Opaque

Colour: Green with black stripes.

Another very popular healing stone in Ancient Egypt, malachite also shares the name of the colour green in Egyptian – wadj.

A life-giver, purifier and energizer, malachite was placed in the mouth of a mummy to restore life and was also worn inside a king's head-dress to enhance wisdom and concentration. It replaces negativity with positive energies and in the modern world absorbs undesirable energies from pollution, computers and televisions.

Malachite improves vision, physical and psychic, is excellent for teeth and gums, encourages tissue regeneration and boosts the immune system.

Malachite is sacred to Thoth and Hathor.

Obsidian

Type: Lava/Magma

Colour: Translucent black to dark smoky grey.

Obsidian was used a great deal in funerary adornment but is also potent for healing. It absorbs and dissolves darkness of mood, energy blocks and stagnant energies in the body, mind and spirit and converts them to white light. It dissolves anger, criticism and fears, heals grief and is very protective. It is also a powerful stone for oracular wisdom and scrying.

Obsidian is relieves pain, improves circulation and heals wounds. It is sacred to Nephthys.

Quartz crystal

Colours: Transparent or clear or less commonly cloudy or opaque.

Clear quartz crystal is the ultimate transmitter of the life force, light and energies and is a pure sun stone. In Egypt, as in many other cultures, it is the manifestation of the living creative spirit.

Quartz crystal amplifies the energies of the user, drawing out negative energies and sending positive ones in their place. Clear quartz is also especially in sphere form, or as a five-faced form known as an Isis crystal.

The crystals trigger the body's own healing system to resist infection and negativity.

Round quartz crystals were used to relieve headaches or toothache by direct application to the painful spot or held in the hand to reduce a temperature. As I mentioned above the crystal sphere was a transmitter of sunlight healing. When held by both healer and patient it became an amplifier of the healer's energies through the power of the solar deities.

Quartz crystal is sacred to Ra and Isis.

Tiger's Eye

Type: Chalcedony, quartz; known also as Cat's Eye

Colours: Yellow-gold and brown stripes, burgundy striped; chatoyant, reflecting light in a wavy band. Green or blue stones are called Hawk's or Falcon's Eye.

In Ancient Egypt, Tiger's Eye was a stone of courage and a talisman against the evil eye. It brings confidence, willpower, focused thoughts and clear communication, and is a stone of balance in mind and body to guard against all excesses.

Tiger's eye aids the digestive processes, relieving stomach, gall bladder problems and ulcers.

Tiger's Eye is sacred to Khnum, the divine potter.

Turquoise
Colour: Opaque, light blue/blue-green.

Turquoise was mined in Sinai and was one of the most highly prized stones in Ancient Egypt; its name means 'delight'. Hathor was called the Lady of Turquoise as well as the Lady of Gold, giving the stone unusually a feminine association, whereas in a number of other cultures it was a male power stone. It was also linked to the sun at dawn and so is a symbol of rebirth, like lapis lazuli. The hair of Ra was made of turquoise.

The earliest examples of this semi-precious stone were found in graves dating back to the fourth millennia BCE. Absorbing all negative forces, it endows wisdom on those who wear it and increases both psychic and general communication skills, making the wearer speak the truth in his or her heart. Turquoise is said to give access to the collective wisdom of mankind.

Turquoise detoxifies the system of pollutants, relieves migraines, sore throats, rheumatism, arthritis and bone disorders as well as helping with problems to do with the inner ear and the eyes, lung and chest infections, asthma and other allergies.

Turquoise is sacred to Hathor and Nefertum.

Releasing the healing powers of your crystals and magical metals

A number of methods are described in the Papyrus Ebers and in other papyri such as the 'Coffin Texts' and the 'Book of the Dead'.Or to give it the more optimistic title, 'Coming Forth into Day'.

Sometimes these spells involved reciting an invocation over a crystal on which an amulet was drawn. For example in a goldsmith's shop in Cairo, next to a magnificent tiny ruby buckle of Isis edged with gold, I saw the following inscription adapted from the 'Book of the Dead':

'The blood of Isis, the words of Isis, the magical power of Isis, shall make me strong, and shall be protection against he who would commit hateful deeds against me.'

Apparently, the prayer was originally said over a carnelian Tjet, or Buckle of Isis amulet, but you could recite it over any red crystal you were using for protection.

Preparing for healing

▲ Collect a set of small round crystals about the size of a large coin, one in each of the main six colours of Egypt, choosing from those listed above or other crystals of the same colour. For example, sky blue howlite, which is inexpensive, is sometimes substituted for turquoise and midnight blue sodalite for lapis lazuli.

▲ Choose an item of jewellery of copper, silver and gold. It can be something small, an earring or bracelet, but by wearing it you absorb the magic of the metals (see below). You could also use coins of the appropriate colour and perhaps buy tiny real ones from a museum shop.

▲ When they are not in use, keep your healing crystals wrapped in silk in a drawstring bag made of a natural fabric and your talismanic jewellery or coins in a decorated box with a lid.

▲ Devise an incantation like the one I saw in the jeweller's before you wear your metal jewellery for the first time.

▲ Create a gentler one for reciting over your crystals before you use them for healing. For example, you might recite over the bag containing them: 'May the love of Isis and the maternal care of Isis and the healing rays of Isis fill me likewise with healing radiance.'

Individual crystal blessings

You may wish to create a chant for each of the individual crystals and write them in your Book of Egypt. This would link each crystal to its own deity. Add a simple rite if you wish.

For example, when I use malachite to remove negativity from my workplace, I set it first on the white altar cloth, sprinkle a single drop of water and a single drop of perfume (usually my precious lotus) on the crystal and say:

'The wisdom of Thoth and the joy of Hathor, shall make me joyous. The healing of Thoth and of the love of Hathor shall likewise take away all that is dark and harmful, angry or bitter from this room and from my heart.'

I then set the crystal next to my computer and when I have finished working, wash the malachite under running water. The stone really does lift the atmosphere, even if I am tired or worried, have been talking to people who are sad or ill or receive a negative response to my work. You can empower metals in the same way.

Chakra crystal healing

You can heal yourself or others using crystal on the chakras, or psychic energy points, of the body (see page 136 for diagram).

▲ Pass your crystal over the area of discomfort or the related chakra point (see pages 139–42) anti-clockwise to remove pain or discomfort and clockwise to gently energize the body.

▲ For general healing, apply a clear quartz crystal first anti-clockwise and then clockwise, circling over all the chakra points upwards and downwards, to remove pain or tension and then fill the body with the life force.

▲ Alternatively, lie on the ground or on cushions with the appropriate crystal on each chakra.

▲ These crystals work especially well in chakra healing:

Root	red jasper
Sacral	orange carnelian
Solar plexus	yellow citrine
Heart	green malachite
Throat	turquoise
Brow	deep blue lapis lazuli
Crown	clear quartz crystal

Healing protection

You can send healing to absent friends or relations and protect yourself and your family from illness by writing the name of a healing deity in the air over a healing crystal using the smoke of an incense stick.

Chant over it an invocation, such as, for example, for citrine to be sent to give a woman (named Emma for the purposes of the invocation below) energy after a bout of depression:

'May the radiant light of Ra rise on this smoke. May the golden life of Ra travel on this smoke skywards to Emma. May the sparkling sun crystal carry also the light and the life and the healing that Emma may feel joy and energy once more. Ra I write, Ra, I am. Emma, be thou likewise filled with the sun. Ra, Ra, Ra.'

Once the incense has burned through you can send the crystal to someone who is sick, or carry it yourself in a purse. You will need a supply of crystals if you use this method, but it does give ongoing healing.

▲ For extra power you can also light a candle of the same colour as the crystal and repeat the invocation while visualizing the deity in the flame.

Healing waters

▲ Soak the chosen crystal in pure mineral water in a clear glass bottle from sunrise to noon, to absorb the healing power of the sun. Place a lid or stopper in the bottle and use it in drinks. Substitute another green stone for malachite, such as amazonite or aventurine, which were also used in Egypt, as malachite can be slightly toxic.

▲ Add a few drops to a bath or splash them on your pulse points.

▲ Water plants in your home or workspace to help them protect you or scatter drops of water around your workspace in a clockwise circle. You can heal others, and even polluted places, in the same way. Sprinkle the water around pictures of endangered species or war- or famine-torn lands as well.

Crystal breathing

▲ Sit by candlelight in your temple room. Through your nose, slowly inhale the crystalline light and gently exhale any darkness as a sigh. When you can visualize yourself filled with white or coloured crystal light, softly blow it towards an absent person who may be ill, a sick child or pet or picture your own aura suffused with the crystalline healing.

Cleansing your healing crystals

If you do a lot of healing every month or so, bury your crystals overnight in the soil of a large green plant and in the morning wash them clean.

13

PYRAMID POWER

I suffer from claustrophobia and so I vowed there was no way – even in the interests of psychic research – that I was climbing down into a pyramid at Giza, on the outskirts of Cairo. But Hussam, my Egyptologist guide – a walking history book and quite the best guide I have ever met anywhere in the world – had other ideas. 'Mrs Cassandra,' he told me, 'this is a very easy pyramid: the Mother's pyramid. You are a mother and you can go inside.'

It was one of the smaller Queen's pyramids on the Giza site, the pyramid of Queen Heterpheres, mother of Khufu or Cheops.

Assisted by an elderly Egyptian attendant and the ever-enthusiastic Hussam, I began the long descent into what seemed to be a bottomless pit, down metal rungs that were attached to a wall. The terror of falling was so great that my claustrophobia disappeared instantly (and has not returned!).

Most remarkably, inside it was quite dark, but amazingly airy, fresh and quite magical. As the eminently sensible Hussam explained about the paintings around us and the oushabti figures – 'the answerers' who performed tasks for the high-born deceased in the afterlife in their stead – I felt myself floating and flying upwards; the top of the pyramid seemed to melt and become pure sunlight. The pyramid was filled with shimmering light beams and I could see the turquoise sky dissolving into pure gold. Of course, I did not mention any of this, but for the rest of the day, although it was incredibly hot and there was little shade, I was filled with energy and enthusiasm the like of which I had not experienced for many years. My euphoria lasted for several days.

Pyramid energies

Many people visiting Egypt from different parts of the world have experienced similar phenomena to the one described above, even when they know nothing of psychic energies. Mohammed is a driver and lives near the pyramids at Giza. One night he and some friends managed to gain access to the locked pyramid of Khafre. (I did not ask how and would not advise anyone else to attempt it – for legal rather than psychic reasons.) He told me:

> 'We all felt it and [discovered that we had] all had the same experiences when we talked about it afterwards. It is so amazing inside the pyramids, like being pulled by a huge magnet or a warm whirlwind. The power was so strong carrying me backwards through tunnels of time, swirling and whirling through rocks deep in the earth and then high in the sky. I saw myself inside one of the pyramids, guarding the tomb of the Pharaoh at his funeral. I smelled the rich scents of the sacred oils and the perfume of the wreaths and the smoke of the incense. I saw such bright colours, red and yellow flowers, paintings on the walls of the king and his wife in the Field of Reeds with corn far above their heads. I heard the wailing of the royal family, the

sistrum and the chanting of the priests in Anubis and Osiris masks of black and green.
Everywhere was light and I could have walked in the afterworld in those tall grasses – perhaps
they were papyrus marshes – as the tomb was sealed. I saw the goddesses waiting with their
wings and the chanting: "I, Isis, greet you. I lift you up and you are unbound. Come with me
and you shall know no fear." Her sister Nephthys said the words in a softer tone and their voices
become one. I wanted to go with my master and guard him in the afterlife. I could hear the voices
of the oushabti answerers: "Here I am."
   'I can see and hear it all whenever I think of that moment and close my eyes.'

Such experiences should not seem surprising, as the pyramid represents the first mound that
emerged from the waters over which the sun rose on the first morning, the staircase to the sun
and to the stars. This staircase can be seen most clearly at the Saqqara step pyramids, where
the brilliant noonday sun creates a white haze around the top. It takes very little imagination
to see the steps of light ascending through the brilliant turquoise blue sky into the sun.

   Formerly, the pyramids at Giza were coated in limestone so that they resembled towers
of sunlight and also had shining capstones that more exotic legends say were made of
diamonds (they were probably polished limestone or crystal quartz).

   The benu bird represents the creating sun god (see page 126), who stood on the
pyramidion – the apex of the pyramid, which represented the original mound at Heliopolis
and which is also recalled in the shape of an obelisk, a tall tower with a pyramid shape on top.
At sunrise, the sun god or the deceased Pharaoh ascends that mound and is born anew.

   There are more than 90 pyramids in Egypt, the majority being grouped together in the
northern part of Egypt around Cairo. The first stepped pyramids, which evolved from the
mastaba or rectangular bench-shaped tomb, were built at Saqqara from around 2650 BCE and
then evolved into the true pyramids, the gigantic stone shapes at Giza, from around 2500 BCE.

   If you would like to learn more about the history of the pyramids, you may find some of
the titles in the 'Further Reading' section at the end of this book useful.

What are the pyramids?

Most people who research into the subject of the pyramids do have problems with accepting
the possibility that such huge and mathematically perfect structures could be built within the
rule of a single Pharaoh. After all, each pyramid was at the centre of an elaborate palace
complex for the deceased king and his family, including mortuary temples and areas for
making offerings.

   I have already mentioned the theory that the early deities – Thoth, Isis, Osiris, Nephthys,
Set and Horus – were extraterrestrial beings who brought their wisdom to Egypt. This might
explain the great accuracy of measurement that the ancient Egyptians were capable of and
which has astounded modern mathematicians. It might also explain how the stars in the belt
of Orion were aligned to the three main Giza pyramids at the time of their creation.

   Another related theory, which I mentioned in the previous chapter, is that refugees from the lost city of Atlantis came to Egypt, bringing with them their advanced wisdom and technology, thereby enabling the Egyptians to complete the awesome architectural task of constructing the pyramids. (Plato the Greek historian was the first to write about Atlantis, in around 360 BCE.)

There have been many disagreements about the original purpose of pyramids, as some of them seem never to have contained tombs. Some theorists argue that the pyramids simply housed the mummy of the Pharaoh; others believe that they were living temples to the Egyptian deities and the divine deceased Pharaoh. More esoteric theories view the pyramids as astronomical observatories. Because of the strange nature of the surviving hieroglyphics on the walls of some of the inner chambers of the pyramids, it has been suggested that the buildings may also contain predictions of future events, including the end of the world when only Amun and Osiris will survive, in the form of serpents.

It may also be that their structure makes them repositories or transformers of cosmic energy, or even giant markers for spacecrafts. Another theory is that the pyramids were used for secret initiation rites. During the course of these rites, initiates underwent a 'death' in ritual form and their spirits, or bas, flew as human-headed hawks through celestial realms to learn cosmic truths, returning as akhs, or transformed spirits, into the bodies of the living. Even if the latter was not the purpose of the pyramids' creation, certainly rituals have been carried on within them through the ages, of which I suppose my friend Mohammed's foray was a relic.

What are pyramid energies?

Even if there is a totally mundane explanation for the building of the pyramids (and you will have to wade through countless volumes of pyramidology to draw even basic conclusions), modern research indicates that both the pyramids themselves, especially that of Khufu or Cheops at Giza, and reproduced pyramid shapes, do emit healing and psychic energies.

At the University of St Petersburg in Russia there is a department for pyramid research that has been working to understand the rationale behind these energies for many years. Organizations such as The Pyramid Energy Research Center in the USA are also seeking to unravel the mysteries of these ancient buildings. The problem is that while experiments to demonstrate pyramid power can be made under laboratory conditions and replicated, the precise nature of the energies that cause the results is not explicable within current scientific knowledge. Regrettably, this is an area of research not taken as seriously by conventional scientific bodies as it should be.

The Great Pyramid itself is aligned to magnetic north and it would seem that certain electromagnetic waves are concentrated and condensed by the particular configuration of a pyramid. The pyramid form does seem to attract the earth's magnetic forces. However, electromagnetic forces are not the whole secret of pyramid power, because similar magnetic forces housed in a building of a different shape do not produce the same effects.

One plausible theory for pyramid power is that the frequencies radiated by the earth itself (including the magnetic force lines) and cosmic or solar radiation blend within the pyramidical structure and produce a new vibrational frequency, in the same way that two piano keys, when struck simultaneously, produce a third beat frequency. This frequency could thereby create a concentrated and combined energy that contains the power to amplify the body's natural healing and psychic powers and to develop potential for growth in both plants and animals.

Creating pyramid energies

The most successful pyramid work – whether you are trying to test the energies or use them more practically for personal healing or power – work best if a scale model of the Great Pyramid of Cheops at Giza is used.

However what is significant is that the psychic and healing properties of the pyramid are as potent when an open-frame, wire-and-metal-tubing pyramid is used as they are within pyramids that have solid walls. A number of healers and psychics have concluded that the open structure needs the four base sides as well as the four upright sides to be really effective. A frame of copper tubing has been found to be particularly effective for energizing water or encouraging plants and animals to thrive, as has a copper capstone (the uppermost stone in the pyramid's structure).

Again this is not the whole story, for a hand-held or table crystal pyramid (a pyramid that may be set on a table and held during meditation) also transmits a lot of power. I use my small amethyst pyramid for energizing water by placing it in a large jug.

What is more, people who have worked in the field of healing and psychic matters for a number of years are able to amplify their psychic power by visualizing a purple or deep blue crystal pyramid over themselves. Indeed, some healers trace the pyramid shape over both them and their patient with a clear pointed crystal point to offer protection and concentrate healing energies. Tracing a pyramid over your bed, or that of a child, with a gentle amethyst is an excellent way of bringing sleep and keeping away all harm. There is currently a trend in the UK for pinning drapes to the ceiling to form a canopy round the bed-head and I have seen some beautiful deep blue and purple gauze that could be adapted to make a protective pyramid over a bed.

The experimental evidence

It may well be that knowledge of the power of the pyramids remained within Egypt long after the Roman Empire was overthrown. There is certainly still a strong healing tradition in Egypt that draws on energies focused by pyramids. In the 1930s, Antoine Bovis, a French radiesthesist (a person who works with psychic energies), was exploring the Great Pyramid of Cheops and noticed that although the bodies of animals that had become trapped in the King's Chamber had dehydrated, they had not decayed – they had become mummified. On his return to France, Bovis built a wooden model of the Great Pyramid perfectly to scale and placed a dead cat in it, in the same position that the mummified animals had been discovered in the real Great Pyramid – about a third of the distance from the base to the apex.

Rather than decaying, the cat became mummified. In further experiments, Bovis discovered that similar effects occurred with fruit and vegetables.

The next breakthrough came in the 1950s, when a Czech radio engineer – Karel Drbal – discovered that a blunt razor blade would regain and retain its sharpness within a scale cardboard model pyramid. The model had to be positioned very specifically, however, so that the sides of the pyramid were aligned with the earth's magnetic field and the blade was also aligned, along the north-south axis of the pyramid. Drbal experimented with a variety of objects, such as knives, scissors, razor blades and electric shavers, and he realized that this effect occurred in pyramids of any shape and size, not just scale models of the Great Pyramid, although these proved to be the most effective shape.

Pyramid preserving power experiments

The most exciting work in this area has been carried out by two American pyramidologists, Bill Kerrell and Kathy Coggin. During the 1970s they began a number of very successful experiments under scientifically controlled conditions and these have formed the basis for a whole field of formal and informal studies. One of their discoveries was that foods – including frozen foods – tasted fresher after being kept under a pyramid for a few hours. Coffee treated in the same way was less bitter, fruit juice was sweeter and even wine mellowed rapidly.

You can quite easily set up similar experiments yourself. For example, try pouring wine into two small bottles, corking both and placing one under an open wire pyramid structure (see below for how to make one easily) and one in a cool place. You can also try the same experiment using two halves of a bunch of grapes, or even a plant that has been split in two. You will find that if you repeat the exercise with two identical cartons of milk or yoghurt, the carton under the pyramid will not sour as quickly as the one left in a cool place.

Plant growth experiments

Pyramids have also been shown to bring about accelerated growth in plants – something that a number of gardeners know from experience but cannot explain. According to research by Kerrell and Coggin, some have reported increases of more than 150% in the growth of plants placed under pyramids.

Experiments with a variety of differently shaped greenhouses revealed that plants grew up to eight inches a day in summer in a pyramid and even grew under a pyramid frame in freezing winter weather. Tomato seeds also sprouted earlier when they were exposed to pyramid energy.

The rate of plant growth was also accelerated by the application of pyramid water – that is, water left beneath a pyramid shape overnight.

Pyramids and animal health

As with experiments on plants, those involving animals remove the risk of the suggestibility factor that is always a risk with humans – i.e. that a subject may feel healthier using a pyramid because he or she expects to do so. Anecdotal but nevertheless valuable evidence from Kerrell and Coggin included cases in which a lame dog's mobility improved dramatically while it was sleeping in a pyramid kennel. In another case uncovered by the researchers, a dog showed increased energy levels, his thinning coat revitalized and the stiffness in his legs disappeared when an eighteen-inch pyramid was suspended over his bed for a few days.

Fish and other marine creatures such as shrimps also live longer and grow to a greater size when kept in water placed beneath a pyramid than in control groups or in comparison to marine life in ordinary water.

Once the control shrimps in one experiment had died, the experimenters removed the aerating device from the pyramid water in which a second group of shrimps were living, but in spite of this the creatures survived for more than a year. Chemically the water was no different to that of the control group.

Psychic pyramid powers

From its early creation, the geometry of the pyramid has been recognized as conducive to generating supernatural powers. According to the Book of the Dead the power of the pyramid awakens the god who sleeps in the soul.

Dr Paul Brunton was a British philosopher, traveller and mystic, who spent a great deal of time visiting ancient sites world-wide and assessing their spiritual significance. He spent a night in the Great Pyramid during the 1930s, having fasted for three days so that he would be more receptive to his own psychic feelings. He stayed in the King's Chamber. Almost as soon as he settled there, he began to notice an intense cold in the chamber and as he sat in the darkness he sensed an overwhelming sense of evil. He also witnessed malformed spirit shapes floating around the chamber. After a while, the evil presences departed and two Egyptian high priests appeared. Dr Brunton felt his own spirit rise from his body and found himself floating round the chamber. He later recalled the words of one of the priests:

> 'Know, my son, that in this ancient temple lies the lost record of the early races of man... Know, too, that chosen men were brought here of old to be shown this covenant that they might return to their fellows and keep the secret alive. Take back with thee the warning that when men forsake their creator and look on their fellows with hate – as with the princes of Atlantis, in whose time this pyramid was built – they are destroyed by the weight of their own iniquity, even as the people of Atlantis were destroyed.'

In a large number of cases studied since Dr Brunton's experience, there is suggestive evidence that pyramids can serve as amplifiers of psychic powers. Sitting inside a scale model of a pyramid, or holding a symbolic crystal pyramid, improves telepathic communication, clairaudience, clairvoyance and mediumship. Sleeping with a scale model pyramid of the Giza Cheops pyramid beneath the bed not only increases energy levels the next day in a number of people, but also brings to a considerable proportion of subjects tested vivid dreams and out-of-body sensations, in particular experiences connected with past lives in Egypt. Students of the Maharishi Mashesh Yogi collected records of more than 4,000 such experiences in America during the 1970s. Those interested in this aspect of Egyptian knowledge may be interested in a key study of pyramid-related experimental work – Pyramid Power – written by American parapsychologist Dr G. Patrick Flanagan and first published in 1973. It is a good source of evidence for all kinds of pyramid work, from plant growth to meditation.

One explanation may be that sitting under a pyramid measurably increases the amplitude and frequency of alpha and theta brain waves that are naturally present in states of meditation and altered consciousness. This occurs even when subjects are blindfolded and unaware that an open pyramid structure has been lowered over them, (the blindfold ensures that the subject is not aware when the pyramid is near them, thereby reducing the possibility that they would 'expect' to feel something because of the pyramid's presence).

Pyramid healing powers

There is a great deal of circumstantial evidence to suggest that pyramids help to reduce levels of stress and tension. Many people report increased tranquillity and euphoria during meditation sessions spent inside a pyramid, as well as warmth and tingling sensations – especially in the upper part of the body. Children who know nothing of pyramid energies have independently described the same feelings as those reported by adults. As a bonus, there is evidence to suggest that hyperactive children become noticeably calmer when playing under an open pyramid structure and that the effect remains in their daily lives for a number of days afterwards. When used in meditation, pyramids also relieve insomnia, help with alcohol and cigarette addiction and enhance memory and learning abilities.

Pyramids have also demonstrated specific healing properties in a number of cases. These can be easily adopted at home:

▲ By placing a pyramid directly beneath a bed or chair pointing towards the source of a pain, many people have reported experiencing relief within a short time.

▲ Cuts, wounds and bruises heal more quickly under a pyramid, while sitting under a pyramid will reduce the pain of headaches, migraine or toothache almost instantly.

▲ Water placed under a pyramid overnight also reduces inflammation from bites and burns, when rubbed on the affected areas, and acts as a natural aid to digestion when drunk or used in a bath.

▲ In experiments, polluted water has been purified by placing it inside a pyramid for several days; it has also been demonstrated that chlorinated water treated in a similar way loses its unpleasant chlorine taste.

▲ Gargling with water kept under a pyramid has been shown to reduce the pain and inflammation of a sore throat.

▲ Women who slept nightly under a pyramid for four to sixteen weeks revealed that they did not suffer menstrual cramps and pains and that their menstruation time was reduced.

▲ Sleeping or meditating under a pyramid or pyramid frame just before PMT symptoms appears to be helpful for some women.

How to make a pyramid

Pyramids sold for meditation or healing work are frequently constructed from tubing made from copper – a natural conductor of energy and a healing metal – with quartz crystal clusters at the four corners of the pyramid to amplify natural earth energies. These pyramids can be placed over massage couches, sofas or beds, used as a meditation tent on the floor and even made into greenhouses. They can be obtained by mail order through the internet or from large New Age stores and warehouses. Small crystal pyramids are widely available.

Providing a model pyramid is constructed as nearly as possible to scale, based on the Cheops pyramid, it can be rudimentary and constructed of almost any material and any size, from a pyramid large enough to sit in or lie under to one small enough to hold in the hand and use a focus for meditation.

The King's Chamber is located approximately one third of the distance from the base of the Great Pyramid to the apex. Experiments with scale models suggest that this position in a pyramid marks a focus of the pyramid's energy. Massage couches, chairs and beds placed within a pyramid shape can be positioned so that the user is lying at approximately one third of the height of the structure's apex and is aligned to the north-south axis.

Each of the Great Pyramid's four sides measures 230 metres (755 ft) at the base, and the structure is 147 metres (481 ft) high at the summit. Based on these proportions, a scale model can easily be created. For example, you could adapt a children's tepee, or cheap frame tent, by making it 2.3 metres at the base and 1.47 metres high. Your pyramid can be made from any available material, with ventilation holes or one side with an open flap in an enclosed version. I have known people lash together four large thick garden canes on the ground in a square and add poles at each corner that meet vertically in a point in the middle – and the power does work even when the proportions are not quite right.

If you have a high enough ceiling, you can also create an open work pyramid form over your bed, using the bed-posts as a base so the top point comes about level with your stomach. You can drape it with deep blue or purple curtains if you wish. A visit to a garden centre or DIY store, especially with an enthusiastic DIY friend or family member, will soon bring inspiration.

Working with pyramids

The beauty of pyramid work is that you don't actually work yourself. You sit, sleep, read, energize your water, or your crystals, within one and allow the energies to filter into you. If it is a sunny day, or a clear starry night, you can take an open work frame into the garden – or, if you are on holiday, in a forest or on a beach when it is quiet.

You can visualize your pyramid in any way you wish. You may imagine it as a tall crystalline structure of the kind favoured in Atlantis (according to psychics who believe they have made a genuine connection with the spirits of wise men and women from that lost civilization), or as a deep cool stone pyramid with a soft grey light. You can picture yourself sitting in the shaft looking upwards at a peak – this visualization is spiritually rather than architecturally accurate since pyramids contained chambers. You can see the peak dissolving and a staircase of sunlight appearing, or at night a spiral of stars to climb, or even a rainbow on those clear moments after rain. Float or fly upwards in your mind.

In time you will not even need the pyramid frame, but will be able to build up the form around you (see below).

Crystal pyramids

My favourite focus is a small crystal pyramid. You can buy crystal pyramids in many forms, including rose quartz, amethyst and a clouded white quartz, from museum shops and ethnic gift stores or from a specialist crystal dealer.

I have an amethyst pyramid that is clouded with imperfections and in which I can see all kinds of magical pathways. You may find more traditional shiny black onyx pyramids or creamy yellow calcite ones. Calcite was used in temple building and in ritual cups, dishes, funerary items and chests to hold the jars containing the lungs, stomach and intestines of the deceased. These jars were adorned with the heads of the four sons of Horus.

The true shape of a pyramid is quite squat. However, I have become less of a purist on this point since working with beautiful taller pyramids in glass and clear crystal, including some set with plants. These form a lovely focus for meditation and visualization.

Using a crystal pyramid as a focus for meditation/inspiration

▲ The key to successful crystal pyramid work is the imagination and if you have problems relaxing into a larger pyramid, you can simply visualize it by holding your crystalline pyramid and letting it expand around you in your mind.

▲ If you are working with a crystal pyramid alone, take it into the open air if possible where it can be filled with sun, moon or starlight.

▲ If this is not possible, light a pure white candle and sit in your temple room so that the light reflects within the pyramid or, in the case of a dark pyramid, bounces off as light and shadow.

▲ Hold the pyramid between your hands. Turning it to catch different angles of light, and through half-closed eyes, slowly relax so that the rigid personal boundaries we all have begin to melt around you.

▲ Very gently inhale the crystalline light as though the air was becoming the same colour as the crystal, and then slowly blow out through your mouth so that the colour psychically builds up around you.

▲ Visualize the walls of colour building up and ascending to a peak and gradually allow yourself to breathe naturally.

▲ You may find it fulfilling sitting inside your pyramid seeing images, hearing sounds and perhaps smelling fragrances of flowers or perfume.

Pyramid visions

After a week or so, you may decide to explore in your mind's vision beyond the pyramid. This is quite safe, but you may wish to ask for your guide (see pages 19–20) or a favourite gentle deity to keep you safe.

▲ Identify a door within the base and open it. Look around and you may see Ancient Egypt or another land – perhaps the star system of Sirius and especially Sirius B from which, in modern myth, the first deities came led by wise Thoth. You may see Atlantis.

▲ When you are ready, walk a little way beyond the door. Your guide may be waiting, but if not he or she is there unseen. If you encounter groups of people listen to their words and observe around you the sights, the buildings, flowers, clothes, animals and birds. Perhaps you will come across a wise teacher or a temple procession with statues you may recognize.

▲ Because you are travelling in your mind, you cannot be seen and when you are ready you can return, following a trail of crystalline light back through the door. Thank those who have allowed you to glimpse their dimension.

▲ If you pass regularly through the door you may recognize spiritual kinsfolk who may look like you, or share your experiences, mirrored in another place and age. However, you may also visit different times and pyramid places.

▲ Though direct communication with the people you observe does not occur in this kind of experience, you will spontaneously gain all kinds of insights into your own life and decisions.

▲ You may revisit some of the crystal places in your dreams and actually talk to the people, or become part of the scene. This is another way answers will come – sometimes to issues that you had not realized were troubling you.

Crystal pyramids for contact or absent healing

On page 165 I mentioned directing sunlight through a crystal sphere as a method of healing. Contact healing does not necessarily involve touching the patient, but only requires that the person is present.

The method is basically the same for both crystal sphere healing and pyramid crystal healing. The main difference is that that pyramid healing using an amethyst, rose quartz or calcite pyramid is much gentler than crystal sphere healing and so is especially helpful for emotional wounds, for children, animals and older people or for those with chronic conditions.

▲ If it is practical, work in sunlight or light white or golden candles so the light falls on the crystal. Some healers prefer to work by moonlight and with silver candles when they are using amethyst and rose quartz crystal pyramids. Experiment until you find a method that suits you.

There are several ways of giving healing by this method.

Flowing through the crystal

▲ Both you and the person to be healed can sit side by side facing the source of light so that your healing energy, plus that of the sun, passes through the pyramid or sphere. (NB: be careful the crystal does not get too hot.)

▲ You and the patient can join your energies through the crystal if you both hold it at the same time, each with one hand.

▲ Ask in your own words that higher healing energies may flow through you and the crystal into the patient – who you should name, along with the problem – and that healing may occur.

▲ As you hold the crystal, talk. Allow words to arise about crystalline pyramids, spheres of sunlight, the brilliant blue skies and the blue Nile and you will find your patient tapping into your vision and perhaps adding images of their own. The crystal may appear full of light.

▲ Gradually you will feel the power ebbing. Allow your words likewise to trail into silence. Sit quietly and when you are ready gently take the crystal and set it on a table.

▲ Make time to talk about the experience and afterwards wash the crystal under running water. Splash water on your own hands, wrists and temples to purify yourself of any negative energy that may have passed from the patient's illness or sorrow.

Transmitting directly through the crystal to a specific body part

If you know a patient well or are healing yourself, you can – with care – reflect light through the sphere or pyramid directly on to the area above the affected body part. You can do this through clothing, but be super vigilant not to allow the crystal to get too hot and do not carry this out near your eyes, or those of the patient.

▲ As you work, again talk softly about sunny desert places and sunlight reflected on the river flowing between rich green banks.

▲ Circle the crystal or pyramid anti-clockwise to remove pain or discomfort and then clockwise to gently energize.

▲ After a time, the crystal will seem duller and feel heavy. When this point is reached, the healing is complete.

▲ Wash the pyramid afterwards and sprinkle yourself with running water.

Directing the crystalline energy

You can also use this method for children, animals or people whom it would not be appropriate to touch. Set the crystal on a table and hold your hands palms down above the pyramid until you feel them filled with light. Move your hands so that your palms are facing the subject of the healing. Gently push the healing light towards the subject, still with your palms vertical facing outwards, again talking softly.

Absent healing

Finally you can send the crystalline light over great distances to people, animals and even places in need of healing. Again, set the pyramid or sphere in sunlight, moonlight (especially for amethyst or rose quartz) or where candlelight will enter the sphere.

▲ Place a photograph of the person, animal or place or the name of the recipient on a piece of paper beneath the pyramid or sphere, so that the light is reflected downwards. Alternatively, write the name of the person and their illness or sorrow on a piece of paper.

▲ Enclose your hands around the pyramid or ball still on the table and say:

'I ask for healing for - (here, name the person, animal or place and the problem). I ask also that the healing power of this crystal may, through my hands, transmit that healing to – (here, name the location of the subject).'

▲ Close your eyes and picture the light growing brighter and more powerful, flowing into your fingertips and through your whole body.

▲ When you feel filled with light, open your eyes and extend your arms as far in front of you as you can with your hands horizontal, palms down and your fingertips taut (in the typical sleepwalking position).

▲ Now bring your hands close to you and thrust the fingers forward so you are sending out psychic rays of light in the direction of your subject.

▲ Repeat this until, after perhaps nine thrusts, you feel the power diminishing.

▲ Resting your hands once more on the sphere, say: 'Go swiftly, go true and bring healing.' You might like to add the name of a gentle healing deity (see pages 154–6). Recite this formula nine times as a gentle mantra.

▲ Sit quietly for a while gazing into the crystalline depths and visualizing the subject of your healing feeling renewed, like the first shoots of grass in a polluted place, and then rinse your hands, wrist points and temples as before.

▲ Leave the photograph or written name beneath the pyramid or sphere for a further eight hours and then wash the crystal.

▲ Wrap the name or picture in white linen and set it on the altar, opening it when you consecrate your altar each day and asking for continued healing.

▲ Repeat the healing weekly, until the problem resolves itself. For an ongoing issue, allow a period of three or four weeks and then continue the crystal pyramid healing ritual monthly or whenever you have time.

14

THE STARS AND PLANETS

'As above so below' are the opening words of the Emerald Tablet by the Egyptian sorcerer Hermes Trismegistos. The Emerald Tablet was said to contain the secrets of all magical wisdom and was handed down through the millennia in Ancient Egypt. These words established the most important occult principle, that a connection exists between the cosmic and earthly realms and that positive results might be attained on earth through the magical manipulation of these cosmic energies in ritual.

Hermes Trismegistos – whose name means 'Thrice-blessed Hermes' – expressed the belief of earlier astrologers in the influence of the movement of the stars and the planets upon the lives of humankind. He is a fascinating if elusive character, regarded as semi-divine and associated with Thoth, whom the invading Greeks merged with their messenger deity, Hermes. Like Thoth, Hermes was the god of writing, medicine and communication; he was also the father of astronomy and astrology – which were regarded as the same in the ancient world. Some evidence suggests that the thrice-blessed Hermes lived during the first century CE and after his death became worshipped as a god. Other accounts record that the legendary Emerald Tablet was discovered by Alexander the Great in the mummified hands of Hermes Trismegistos, but since Alexander invaded Egypt in around 332 BCE, this theory is inconsistent with other records concerning the birth and death of the sorceror.

The stars and the seasons
The rising of certain stars seemed to the ancient peoples to regulate the seasons. For example, the ancient Egyptians linked the coming of the Nile flood and the season of inundation with the time in mid-July when Sirius made its first brief appearance around sunrise above the horizon after an absence of 70 days. The appearance of Sirius also heralded the Egyptian New Year. This annual ten-day period when Sirius rose above the horizon around dawn was called the heliacal rising and was a time of great celebrations.

The stars and sacred geometry
It may be that the building of the pyramids, as well as the construction of certain other tombs and temples, was intended to mirror the skies. The plain of Giza has been cited as the prime evidence for this argument, with the three great pyramids representing the three stars of the belt of Orion/Osiris. The sphinx at Giza has been identified with the lion Leo constellation (though you may prefer to think of Leo as Sekhmet) and the Nile as the earthly Milky Way, the celestial Nile.

According to this theory, the purpose of such planning was – as with temple building – to recreate a representation of the universe and by channelling cosmic energy on earth, to prevent the triumph of chaos. The psychic power of the great pyramids is sometimes attributed to this stellar connection.

The moon

The moon was in no way inferior to the sun in pre-agrarian societies, for the hunter would need the moonlight to see his prey. It is therefore perhaps no accident that Thoth, one of the wisest and most historically ancient of the deities, was a lunar god. While Ra sailed the realms of the underworld at night, Thoth guarded the earth.

As the agrarian way of life along the fertile banks of the Nile became established, leading to an increasing emphasis on the importance of the sun, the lunar deity Set became increasingly marginalized in his unsuccessful ongoing fight against Horus, the God of day and light. However, Horus's left eye represented the power of the moon and his right the power of the sun, so the moon retained its status as light of the world at night, as did its guardian deity Thoth.

The sky goddess

Nut was the sky mother supreme, a woman covered in stars bending over the earth, touching the horizons with her toes and fingertips.

She was depicted in the same protective position on coffin lids, offering an ascent to the stars so that the blessed dead could return to the sky womb in the afterlife. Along the Milky Way, lay the Field of Reeds where the blessed dead lived.

Ancient Egyptian astrology

The zodiac is the system used by astrologers from Greek times onwards to mark out the relatively fixed constellations in the sky as seen from earth through which the sun, the moon and the planets appear to move in a regular pattern.

The actual shapes of the constellations we see today are not very different from those of the ancient Egyptians thousands of years ago. The reason for this is that though they are all moving relative to the sun by several kilometres a second, they are so far away that it takes thousands of years for us to be aware of any minor changes in their patterns.

Nor are constellations self-contained groups of stars. They are particularly bright stars that give the appearance of being close together and forming distinctive patterns. Over the ages these patterns have been identified as animals, deities or mythological heroes and heroines.

The sky today

However, in terms of astrology, the zodiacal positions of the 12 constellations we use for our birth signs are very different from the positions fixed by the ancient Greeks and Romans that still determine our birth signs. In fact, astronomically our birth dates are one whole star sign adrift from when the Romans set them and two signs away from ancient Egyptian times.

Why should this be? The phenomenon is called the precession of equinoxes. As the earth moves round the sun on its year-long journey, the background of the constellations changes month by month and so it appears as if the sun is actually moving through the zodiac. You cannot see the constellations during the day because the sun is too bright.

In reality, as the earth spins on its axis every day, (imagine it spinning on a rod extending from pole to pole), it is wobbling like a spinning top. Of course, at the same time it is spinning round the sun. But because of its wobble, over a period of 2,600 years its angle of spin does change, albeit slowly. (If you want to understand the nuts and bolts of this incredibly confusing astronomical principle, there are a number of good astronomy sites on the Internet and numerous good books : see page 214 for my favourites.) So when the Egyptians built their pyramids, in around 2500 BCE, the pole star was Thuban, in the constellation of Draco, the dragon. Now the North Pole points toward Polaris and in 12,000 years it will aim at Vega.

If you refer to real star maps, at the spring equinox – which we use in western astrology as the starting point of the astrological year – the sun appears to be just within the constellation of Pisces. Soon it will move into a new constellation and astrologers will hail the Age of Aquarius.

From about 4600 BCE–2100 BCE the spring equinox was in Taurus. Thereafter, until around CE 400 and while the Romans were still occupying Egypt, the spring equinox occurred when the sun entered Aries. On modern zodiac wheels, that position still remains because – as I noted earlier – that was the time when the zodiac we used today was fixed, though astronomically we have moved on a sign.

In fact, the spring equinox was not as important to the ancient Egyptians as the summer equinox. This is because the latter was closer to the flooding of the Nile, the ancient Egyptians' New Year marker (see below for the psychic influence of Sirius).

The zodiac in Ancient Egypt

The modern zodiac does not appear in Ancient Egypt until the time of the Greeks and we do not know a great deal about the precise way this zodiac was used. The first was discovered on a ceiling in a hall near Esna and is dated around 221 BCE. Certainly the Dendara zodiac, created some time after 125 BCE during the Roman occupation, on the ceiling of the temple of Hathor at Dendara, does contain elements of Egyptian mythology and astrology. The original is now in the Louvre Museum in Paris and is well worth a visit, as is the fabulous collection that fills many rooms and has some spectacular reconstructions.

The reason for the mixture of Egyptian and Graeco-Roman astrology at Dendara was to make the Roman invasion legitimate as a continuation of Egyptian culture, and the Greeks and Romans did this superbly. For example, the 12 zodiac signs can be identified with symbols of Egyptian mythology. Hathor the divine cow and later the Apis bull – manifestation of Ptah – is equivalent to Taurus, though in fact the substitution of the scarab beetle for Cancer the crab is the only difference between the Dendara zodiac and the familiar 12 zodiacal constellations. Another constellation that appears on the zodiac is Scorpio, which the ancient Egyptians linked with Serqet the scorpion goddess. At the time the pyramids were built, Scorpio rose before the sun on the autumn equinox (23 September in the Northern Hemisphere) to give another directional mark to the year.

From the fourth to the second millennium, Leo was linked with the sphinx and the hottest part of the year around the summer solstice, at the time of the Nile flood when desert lions came to drink (see chapter 6).

The Dendara zodiac also features the five planets that are visible to the human eye: Mercury, Venus, Mars, Jupiter and Saturn, as well as the moon. The major Isis/Osiris stars Sirius and Orion and the three major Northern Hemisphere constellations, Draco, the Dragon, Ursa Minor and Ursa Major are also present on the zodiac.

In each of the four corners of the Dendara zodiac – at the positions of Scorpio, Leo, Taurus and Aquarius – are four goddesses supporting the inner circle with their arms.

The Decans

There are 36 star figures on the zodiac that represent the 36 decans, the number of divisions – constellations or major stars in the Northern Hemisphere – the Egyptians made in the night sky. Each decan was said to rise for 10 days above the horizon. Within each decan were 10 stellar deities, one to rule for each day, and the queen was the deity Sopdet. Each decan held mystical powers and they were collectively known as 'the imperishable ones'. We have not been able to identify them all from the pictorial evidence on coffin lids and ceilings.

In myth, the star figures sailed across the night skies in their stellar boats. They are positioned around the edges of the zodiac circle, moving in anti-clockwise order.

Working with the Egyptian zodiac

The real problem is that the Greeks overlaid the zodiac system on the ancient Egyptian one. As a result, the information we get from the works of Hermes Trismegistos and the famous second-century Egyptian astronomer Claudius Ptolemy re-worked Greek material that altered the earlier, less organized system of the ancient Egyptians. The evidence we have of the earlier systems in Egypt is based on paintings on ceiling walls of tombs and coffin lids and a certain amount of papyri information from, for example, the Coffin Texts. However, there are few clues as to correlations between the true Egyptian system and the Greek system. Therefore, to try to create modern-style birth horoscopes or to link these to the incredibly complex system of favourable and unfavourable days is neither accurate nor necessarily helpful in trying to understand Egyptian magic from the inside.

You can link your current birth sign to an Egyptian deity or creature. This seems to work better than trying to use three different Egyptian deities for each of the modern birth signs to correspond with the 36 decans.

One advantage of adding rather than substituting Egyptian deities to the modern zodiac characters is that they can add new dimensions to your potential gifts and reveal undeveloped or unrecognized positive aspects to your personality. For the Egyptian deity qualities that correspond to the westernized zodiac represent strengths not necessarily present in the westernized zodiac descriptions.

Aries, the Ram (21 March–20 April)
Key word: Assertiveness

Those born under Aries are innovative, enterprising, free spirits with a strong sense of identity, energetic but self-centred.

Egyptian deity: Amun, in his ram-headed form, is a symbol of male potency, fierce protectiveness and the will to succeed that applies to women as well as to men. For Amun's horns are both protective and combative. As supreme deity, he also brings nobility of spirit, altruism and spiritual and moral integrity to this sign.

Taurus, the Bull (21 April–21 May)
Key word: Persistence

Those born under Taurus are patient, reliable, practical, loyal, and concerned with material comfort and security for self and loved ones, but can be possessive and materialistic.

Egyptian deity: The Apis bull of Memphis, manifestation of the creator God Ptah, as symbol of oracular wisdom, great mental and spiritual as well as physical strength, potency and a connection with tradition. This figure also symbolizes the knowledge of the past, as one Apis bull succeeded another. So he brings a dimension of oracular powers and a love of spiritual as well as historical traditions to this sign.

Gemini, the Heavenly Twins (22 May–21 June)
Key word: Communication

Those born under Gemini are adaptable, intellectual, scientific/technologically adept, inquisitive, intelligent and adaptable, but restless and inconsistent.

Egyptian deity: Isis and Nephthys, the twin sisters of Geb and Nut – in fact, they are one of two sets of twins, the other beings the twin brothers, Osiris and Set.

Isis and Nephthys represent day and night, light and shadow, birth and death and so bring balance and harmony, gentleness and healing qualities to this often restless sign.

Cancer, the Crab (22 June–22 July)
Key word: Sensitivity

Those born under Cancer are kind, home loving and nurturing – especially towards children – in short, creators of emotional security. However, they are also secretive and can become oversensitive to potential criticism.

Egyptian deity: Khepri, the scarab-headed god, associated with the rising sun and the scarab beetle, a symbol of rebirth and regeneration, so bringing optimism and renewal of energies. He opens up this lunar sign to the healing and expansive aspects of his solar connections.

Leo, the Lion (23 July–23 August)

Key word: Power

Those born under Leo are courageous, generous, noble, proud and loyal and are born leaders. They need the adulation of others, however, and occasionally can be arrogant.

Egyptian deity: Sekhmet, the fierce, lion-headed goddess of fire and the sun who destroys what is unworthy or redundant, avenges the weak and is also a healer. She brings powerful feminine energies to this masculine-biased sign as well as her tenderness to her cubs and her protectiveness to the vulnerable.

Virgo, the Maiden (24 August–22 September)
Key word: Perfection

Those born under Virgo tend to be methodical, meticulous, dextrous, perfectionists, modest and efficient. They can be critical of themselves and others, however, and worry over details.

Egyptian deity: Nefertum, the lotus god. Adding gentle masculine qualities he emerges from the lotus as the first sunrise, bringing insight into spiritual perfection, gentle healing and acceptance of weakness to this sign that can sometimes be inflexible.

Libra, the Scales (23 September–23 October)
Key word: Harmony

Those born under Libra tend to be balanced and peace loving, harmonious and diplomatic with a strong sense of justice. However, they can also be unwilling to make decisions and can be narcissistic.

Egyptian deity: Ma'at, who weighs the heart of the deceased against the ostrich feather of her head-dress. She is the symbol of the highest forms of integrity, honesty and justice without personal motivation or desire for vengeance and of order and harmony in the universe, as well as in individual lives. Therefore she gives moral fibre and strong principles, to prevent Librans being swayed by promises of gratification.

Scorpio, the Scorpion (24 October–22 November)
Key word: Intensity

Those born under Scorpio tend to be psychic, mystical, purposeful and regenerative but can be vengeful and overly introverted.

Egyptian deity: Serqet, the Scorpion goddess. Very beautiful and one of the four protective goddesses of the deceased, she brings healing and protection against spite and malice to soften her fierce side. She can bring out what is best in Scorpio by turning her vengeful side to fighting the world's injustices and shielding the vulnerable.

Sagittarius, The Archer (23 November–21 December)
Key word: Expansive

Those born under Sagittarius are visionaries, seekers after truth and meaning, flexible, open-minded, extroverted and optimistic. They can also be very outspoken and sometimes lack staying power and clear focus.

Egyptian deity: Neith, goddess of the hunt and of war, along with her bows and arrows and shields, was used as symbols of protection for both the living and the dead. She can bring focus, and – as a weaver of fate – a long-term perspective to this sign.

Capricorn, the Goat (22 December–20 January)
Key word: Prudence
Those born under Capricorn are cautious, quietly resolute, persistent, conventional and ambitious, with great self-discipline, but can also be mean and very inflexible.
Egyptian deity: Banebdjeted, sacred goat deity of Mendes in the north-eastern Nile delta, invoked for fertility and also male potency. Sometimes associated with Ptah and father of Rameses, he was also one of the judges who heard the case between Set and Horus and so is also a symbol of wisdom. He is consort of Hatmehyt, the fish goddess of Pisces.
    Banebdjeted brings emotional depth, and also passion, to this sign.

Aquarius, the Water Carrier (21 January–18 February)
Key word: Idealism
Those born under Aquarius are independent, idealistic, intellectual, inventive and humanitarian, but can be emotionally detached and somewhat eccentric.
Egyptian deity: Satis, personification of the Nile waterfalls. She was often pictured pouring water into the dry earth to revive it. She is shown as a beautiful woman with the white crown of Upper Egypt and two gazelle horns and symbolizes, healing compassion and general restoration of harmony.
    She offers a connection to humanity, tenderness and the power to give emotionally.

Pisces, the Fish (19 February–20 March)
Key word: Intuition
Those born under Pisces are sensitive, sympathetic, imaginative, intuitive, impressionable and spiritual but can be self-pitying and easily lose touch with reality.
Egyptian deity: Hatmehyt was associated with the first fish in the primordial waters and so is an ancient symbol of fertility, protectiveness and deep instinctive wisdom, knowing the right time to act or wait. She is depicted with a dolphin on her head-dress or as a fish.
    She brings depth to Pisceans and a keen instinct that can stop the tendency to be pulled two ways.

The Ancient Egyptian calendar

On pages 79–84, we worked with the energies of the different seasons: Akhet, the time of flood from mid-July; Peret, the time of growing from mid-October to November; and finally Shemu, the time of drought from March to April. Because each season was divided into four 30-day months with three 10-day weeks in each, the calendar was five and a quarter days short each year. Therefore five extra days, called epagomenal days, which roughly translates as 'extra days upon the year', were added at the end of Shemu, They represented the birthdays of Osiris, Seth, Isis, Nephthys and Horus. In spite of this, because of the extra quarter day each year, the calendar continued to slip back by a day every four years.

Because of this widening gap, Sirius only rose on the first day of Akhet every 1,461 years. This unit of time between the heliacal risings of Sirius on the first day of Akhet was called the Sothic cycle. This Sothic rising was therefore a major astrological and spiritual change point. We know that one occurred in 139 CE during the reign of the Roman emperor Antonius Pius.

Many festivities followed the older lunar rather than the inaccurate civil calendar. In about 2500 BCE, the Egyptians created a third calendar based on a civil lunar year that was not linked to the rising of Sirius and they seem to have used all three for different purposes.

Understanding Egyptian astrology

From the images on coffin lids and the ceilings of tombs, Egyptologists have learned much about the knowledge the ancient Egyptians possessed about the movements of the planets and stars.

The most detailed source for understanding ancient Egyptian astrology is what was called the Cairo Calendar, which lists every day in the Egyptian year. It records whether a particular day was favourable or unfavourable and gives the myths that account for the nature of the day and ways people should act or not act, activities that were permissible or ill advised and even forbidden foods. Each was presided over by a particular deity. If you look on the internet you will find sites that explain this in more detail and it can be illuminating – if confusing – to study it, as creativity was always the Egyptian watchword, even with time.

Working with Egyptian astrology

There is a great deal of conflicting, complex and confusing material about Egyptian astrology. Therefore it is most useful magically to use these ancient stellar and planetary symbols as a catalyst for our own spiritual potential.

Below, I have listed which of the stars and constellations are seasonal and which are circumpolar because they are closer to one of the celestial poles. Circumpolar celestial bodies are generally visible in one hemisphere of the world or the other and never sink below the horizon. However, even these divisions are arbitrary. The stars you can see vary according to the place in the world from which you view them, as well as the time of year. Near the equator you may, at certain times, see stars from the opposite hemisphere or lose sight of circumpolar stars in your own hemisphere. The Egyptians, especially those further south, did work with Southern Hemisphere constellations and therefore I have listed two of these so that readers who live in the Southern Hemisphere can work with them. You can also work with the five planets the Egyptians used.

Use a good sky map or computer programme so you can work with the actual stars, planets and constellations. The planets are rightly called the wanderers and cannot always be seen, so you may find it useful to consult a star map or globe.

On pages 196–7 I have suggested methods for connecting with the energies of these heavenly bodies or their visualized guardians.

The planets

From the Middle Kingdom come references to the five planets visible to the human eye; they were thought to sail across the skies in their barques or boats. Use a sky map or computer programme to track them in the night sky if you want to use the planet itself as a focus. Alternatively, focus on their ancient Egyptian guardian as you sit in your temple room or under the stars. I have listed the planets in order of their closeness to the sun.

Mercury

This planet was identified with Thoth, creator of the hieroglyphics, divine scribe for the deities and magician supreme. Mercury is the smallest planet and as the one closest to the sun is the fastest in its orbit through the skies.

For Mercury energies, visualize wise Thoth with his ibis or baboon head, or as a man with a scribe's writing palette. Ask him for wisdom, for inspiration, to help you juggle impossible tasks or finances that do not add up and to be clear, kind and honest in your communications.

Venus

At its brightest Venus is the most brilliant object in the sky besides the sun and moon. In earlier Egyptian times, the planet seems to have been identified with the one who crosses the skies or the god of the morning, Harakhte, an aspect of Horus, god of the morning sun with his hawk head and sun disc and with Uraeus snakes on his head.

This masculine aspect of Venus was associated especially with the morning appearance of the planet before the sun rose. The evening appearance, after sunset, was linked to the feminine guardian. This latter became Isis who, in Roman times, took on her aspect of Stella Maris, star of the sea in Roman times, and was the Egyptian guardian of Venus in all aspects.

Visualize hawk-headed Harakhte in the morning for new beginnings, optimism, shining vision that will not be clouded by others, clear focus and by the determination to seek what is of worth.

In the evening, visualize Isis, lady of enchantment, for fulfilling your dreams, especially of love, for inner radiance and the power to use your clairvoyant vision.

Mars

Mars is the fourth planet from the sun. Because of its red tinge, it was called Horus the red, or Horus of the horizon. As early as the third millennium BCE, the Egyptians noticed the distinctive retrograde pattern of Mars, which means it appears to stop and move backwards at certain times in its orbit. Astrologically a retrograde indicates a halt or reversal to plans. For this reason, the planet was called 'Horus who travels backwards' at such times.

Visualize Horus with his hawk-head scarlet against the sun, for determination to win through, for concentration and swift focused action without sentimentality, but also without cruelty – for the falcon kills for food, not pleasure.

Jupiter

Jupiter, the largest planet, is for much of the time the second brightest planet in the sky, shining creamy white and visible for continuous expanses of time. The planet was linked to Amun, the supreme unknowable god whose power might, like the Roman Jupiter, be manifested as lightning and thunderbolts. A more visible and approachable aspect was as Horus of the two lands, because the planet shone over all Egypt and protected it like a hovering hawk.

Horus represented the Pharaoh ruling the land; by extension, the planet Jupiter was regarded as one of wisdom and authority.

For nobility of purpose, authority, leadership qualities and wisdom, visualize the shimmering Amun or the kingly Horus wearing the combined crowns of Egypt.

Saturn

Saturn is the second largest planet and is famously surrounded by rings, which cannot be seen by the naked eye. It can appear slightly yellow. In ancient Egyptian times, Saturn was Osiris, god of the underworld and symbol of regeneration. He was sometimes called Horus, the bull of the sky, recalling the ancient concept of the bull son/consort, born of the mother goddess, in this case Isis in her form as a divine cow.

Visualize Osiris as vegetation god with his green face or Horus as a divine cosmic bull, for the rebirth, after loss, strength in difficulty, for oracular or divinatory power and for accepting that life runs in cycles with loss as well as gain, weakness as well as strength, but that given belief and effort, there will be an upswing.

The stars and constellations in Ancient Egypt

Draco – the dragon, a circumpolar constellation in the Northern Hemisphere, associated in Ancient Egypt, with the hippopotamus and so with Tauret, the hippopotamus fertility goddess. The constellation wraps itself protectively around Ursa Major and Minor (see page 195 for their Egyptian personas). Less positively, it has also been linked to Apep, the world serpent, with whom Ra fought nightly, but never completely destroyed because the principles of chaos were necessary for the balance of the universe.

The dragon/hippopotamus goddess was guardian of the treasure that was believed to be hidden within the pyramids and ancient tombs. It was believed that Draco's resident pole star, Thuban, offered a doorway into the world of the gods.

Tauret and Draco may have even earlier associations with Tiamat, the Sumero-Babylonian goddess mother who, as a great dragon, birthed the universe from her menstrual blood, which flowed continuously for three years and three months.

Visualize Tauret in her protective role in the family home, for all forms of protection – in particular, domestic protection – for discovering hidden treasure in yourself and others and for fertility.

Orion – a seasonal constellation seen in the winter skies of the Northern Hemisphere and the summer skies of the Southern Hemisphere, was Osiris to the Egyptians. The three stars in a straight line on his belt were important marker points for sacred Egyptian buildings.

Gentler than the Greek huntsman Orion, Osiris here represented the endurance of one's fate and therefore triumph over it. Since Osiris was once the living King, it was believed that a Pharaoh after his death filled Orion with potency so that Osiris could inseminate Sirius/Isis and thus ensure their son Horus would be manifest in the next ruler of Egypt at his coronation.

A shaft in the Pyramid of Khufu is said to represent the phallus of Osiris through which he could inseminate Sirius at her heliacal rising.

Visualize the all-powerful Osiris for personal as well as sexual potency and fertility, for strength and integrity of mind and spirit and to breathe life into a dying project, career or relationship if so you wish.

The Pleiades – a group of stars within the seasonal constellation Taurus that is visible in the Northern Hemisphere winter skies and in the summer skies of the Southern Hemisphere. The seven stars of the Pleiades dwell within the constellation of Taurus, the divine cow, Hathor. They were the seven daughters of Hathor and were the fate goddesses. At the time of the building of the great pyramids, they rose before the sun on what was then the spring equinox, which occurred in Taurus.

These are a group or cluster of seven stars that have assumed great magical significance. There are in fact many more in the cluster but seven are prominent and visible to the human eye, though the seventh is extremely hard to see without a telescope.

Visualize the starry beautiful daughters of Hathor, one much paler than the others, for healing of all kinds, gentleness, care of the environment, harmony, for magical insights and all forms of scrying and divination.

Sirius – a seasonal star in the constellation of Canis Major, a seasonal constellation in the northern winter skies and the southern summer skies. Because of its brilliance and Egypt's relative proximity to the Equator, Sirius is famed for its reappearance for 10 days around mid-July.

As I noted earlier, Sirius – or to be more precise, Sirius A – is the single most important star in the ancient Egyptian world. Associated with Isis (the Nile flood was said to be the tears of Isis), the star goddess was called Sopdet or Sothis by the Greeks and was depicted with a star on her head. Her husband was the constellation Orion, known as Sah in Ancient Egypt, and was linked with Osiris.

The star son of Sopdet and Sah, Soped was a hawk-god and personification of the eastern frontier of Egypt. Therefore Soped was the star of Horus.

Sirius's constellation Canis Major, one of Orion's hunting dogs, was associated with Anubis the dog or jackal-headed god of death.

Sopdet, or Sothis, means 'scorching' and it is the brightest heavenly body in the sky after Venus. The fact that it can be seen for the later part of the summer when the days are hottest and its brilliance created the belief that the light of Sirius combined with that of the sun to produce the intense heat of Egypt in August.

Sirius in her Isian form was said to follow Orion across the skies as on earth she searched for his dismembered form. Sirius was regarded as the guardian star of Egypt.

Visualize Sopdet with her star head-dress or Isis in a deep blue mantle of stars in her role as Stella Maris to bring healing of all kinds, for fertility, passion in all its aspects and fidelity.

Thuban – the Pole Star, a circumpolar star within the constellation of Draco in the Northern Hemisphere. We know that Thuban was an important alignment point for the pyramid of Khufu, or Cheops, at Giza as well as other sacred temples. Khufu would have chosen it because it was a powerful icon of eternal life, since it was seen shining all the year. In the burial chamber of Khufu at Giza are two shafts. At certain periods of the year in ancient times, one of these shafts would have given a view of Thuban, while the other would have provided a view of Orion (Osiris) to help the dead king to travel to them in a direct line. During the Middle Kingdom, Thuban also became symbol of the soul of Osiris.

Visualize Osiris in a robe of stars, or a star man, for fulfilling whatever is central to your happiness, for staying on course, for aiming high and for the highest forms of spiritual development.

Ursa Major and Ursa Minor – the Great and Little Bear are Northern Hemisphere circumpolar star patterns. In ancient Egyptian astrology, Ursa Major was not regarded as a bear at all, but was identified with Set when he was Lord of Upper Egypt and fought against the serpent Apep on behalf of the sun god. The section we call the Plough or the Big Dipper today was identified as the 'Haunch' or 'Thigh in the sky' in Ancient Egypt.

The creature whose head-dress Set often wore, later associated with the evil Greek storm God Typhon, was to the Egyptians the symbol of Ursa Major. This being was a mixture of animals and has a long pointed face, a long and sometimes erect tail and raised ears set at an angle. In the time before Set was demonized, his animals were identified as pulling the solar barque at night.

Ursa Minor was linked to Anubis, the jackal-headed god.

Visualize Set in the rich red robes of the Lord of the desert, or Anubis with his black jackal head, as antidotes to fear and as fierce protectors if you are afraid or suffering any kind of abuse.

Pisces Austrinus or Australis – a circumpolar Southern Hemisphere constellation that can also occasionally be faintly seen low on the horizon in the north in the summer. (A greater number of the Southern Hemisphere constellations were visible as far north as the Mediterranean in ancient Egyptian times.)

Not to be confused with the zodiacal seasonal Pisces, this constellation is a huge fish with a mouth, from which at certain times of the year spouts the water from Aquarius the water carrier's mouth. (Aquarius is, of course, Satis in the Egyptian tradition.) Pisces Austrinus/Australis is the fish that swallowed the phallus of the dismembered Osiris and so is associated with the Nile flood and with fertility and potency, as it has absorbed the power of Osiris.

Visualize a huge star-studded fish with the waters of life pouring into and out of its mouth, for relieving stagnation or an impasse in your life, for inspiration, fertility and potency in any aspect of your world and for vitality in all aspects of your life.

Argo Navis – a Southern Hemisphere circumpolar constellation. This huge ship constellation was divided by the French astronomer/map-maker de Lacaille in 1763. It was originally the great boat that sailed the Great Flood, but has also been linked with the solar barque of Ra and all of the boats of stars that sail across the heavens. One part Carina, the keel is partly on the Milky Way far south of Sirius. Vela (the Sails) and Pyxis (the Compass) are also related constellations.

Visualize Ra on his solar boat sailing through blue cosmic waters for bringing order into a chaotic period of your life, for an unbroken period of happiness, for reprioritizing your time, for restoring harmony to a situation or a place and for directing your own destiny.

Awakening your own star energies

We are all potentially star people and as microcosms, or miniature versions of the cosmos, we can use the individual stars, constellations and planets to activate hidden energies and undeveloped potentials deep within ourselves. In this chapter I have concentrated on those aspects and associations that relate to the ancient Egyptian world, but of course there are other aspects and strengths that come from the later Classical world. I have written about these in a book called *A Complete Guide to Night Magic* (see 'Further Reading').

You can, as I suggested, work outdoors on a clear night with the heavenly bodies themselves and can identify the stellar forms with any sky map or computer star globe. Then you can pinpoint the location of the guardian to whom you wish to connect. The right constellations may not be in the sky when you need their strengths, though, and so you can work under the stars by visualizing your chosen planetary or star guardian formed out of stars in the night sky.

That is why, if possible, you should always do your star work outside. Even with city light pollution, the stars do release powerful spiritual healing and restorative energies. You may work with a number of different star foci on different nights or may prefer after experimenting to focus on one or two favourites that seem to work for you. Remember, you can choose absolutely any star or constellation, including that of your birth, and weave Egyptian myths round them; in this way you are creating your own Egyptian star magic. In addition you can ask Thoth, Horus, Osiris or Isis to be the guardian of any star or constellation and as you work with different stars you will come to understand their particular properties.

▲ Sit or lie comfortably (if necessary wrapped in a blanket) on a padded mat or blanket on the ground and gaze at the sky so your focus is either above or ahead of you.

▲ If you cannot find your chosen star, pick a cluster of stars. Then, in your mind, begin to trace the outline of the guardian you seek, naming the star aloud and saying, 'As above, so below, guardian star may it be so' over and over until you are in a relaxed light trance state. You may choose to do this even if you are working directly with the actual constellation.

▲ Begin to breathe in very slowly, visualizing starlight entering your body and darkness flowing out of your mouth as you softly sigh the out breath.

▲ When you feel filled with starlight, hold your hands vertically, palms facing away below shoulder level, and rotate your hands gently clockwise nine times, moving them away from your body and progressively upwards to create a path of starlight.

▲ Next, fold your hands or rest them at your sides.

▲ While watching the star form, visualize your etheric or inner spirit self, a more ethereal version of the physical body, stepping upwards towards the chosen star or constellation until you can see yourself among the stars.

▲ Speak to your star guardian either aloud softly or in your mind, expressing your feelings, hopes and fears and the particular strengths you need.

▲ When you have finished, close your eyes and feel the healing and restorative powers passing from the top of your head down through your body, right to your feet and fingertips. You may hear words in your mind, clear and focused, but compassionate and wise like a kind, experienced friend.

▲ When these fade into silence, sit quietly for a moment and then picture your etheric self descending the path of starlight from the sky that gradually fades behind you.

▲ You may experience a gentle bump as your spirit self reconnects and a deep sense of peace and quiet confidence.

▲ Sit watching the stars for a while and if possible camp out and go to sleep. Your experiences may continue in your dreams.

▲ Draw and write about your star guardian encounters in your Book of Egypt.

- APPENDIX 1-
DEITIES AND THEIR QUALITIES

The following gods and goddesses can provide a focus for your magical rituals and invocations. I have listed their main attributes, but if you want to know more there are a number of good Egyptian deity lists available online. I have also listed two dictionaries in the suggested reading list that I found helpful. You can find out more about the mythology of the deities online or from books (see 'Further Reading').

However, the best method to connect with your chosen god or goddess is to sit in your temple place or outdoors, close your eyes and recite the deity name slowly over and over again, allowing an image to build up in your mind's vision of the chosen deity. Write down any impressions in the deity section of your Book of Egypt and sketch what you saw in your mind's vision. In this way you can connect psychically with the essential energies of the deity form.

You can collect statues or pictures of your favourite deities, or draw their image or name on a crystal, or fashion it in clay or melted candle wax and carry it for power or protection.

You can also write the deity names or draw their images on white cards and laminate them, leaving one side blank. When you have a decision, or are not sure which strength you need, shuffle them and pick one from a face-down circle (see also page 122). This will tell you the powers you need.

I have included deities I have referred to already in detail in the book for easy reference.

Ahemait or Ammet
A goddess in the underworld who devoured the hearts of those who failed to become one of the blessed dead. She is represented by the head of a hippo, the tail of a crocodile and the paws of a feline. Her image was on one of the funerary beds of Tutankhamun to protect the young king from the dangers of the afterlife.

Use her energies carefully, sparingly and with positive intent for protecting those who are vulnerable from hostility and for keeping away danger in lonely places.

Akhet
The goddess of the seasons and the sunset, sometimes called goddess of the Nile because she was the female manifestation of the annual flood. She gives her name to the first season of the year, which begins in mid-July She is sometimes pictured with an open papyrus reed on her head-dress.

Use her energies for releasing tension in your life, for clearing stagnation and for fertility.

Akusa
The goddess of the setting sun and wife of the creator god Atum, himself a symbol of sunset. Picture her surrounded by a sphere of red and orange light, with a sun disc on her head-dress.

Use her energies for quiet sleep, to leave behind any unsatisfactory or unfinished matters from the day and to heal chronic pain or sorrow.

Amaunet
The consort of Amon (an early form of Amun-Ra), Amaunet was, like her partner, a primal deity of air in the Hermopolis creation myth. She was one of the eight primordial deities – or Ogdoad – and took the form of a serpent. Like the other primordial deities, however, Amaunet was not immortal and after death, she descended to the underworld and from here ordered the daily passage of the sun and the flowing of the Nile.

Use her energies for creating order out of chaos, for starting what may seem a long and daunting venture and for moving from one life path to another.

Amenti

A goddess who was sometimes associated with Mut, the wife of Amun-Ra at Thebes. She is represented in a number of ways, with the head of a sheep, a human head and the crown of Lower Egypt or with papyrus flowers on her head-dress.

Her home was a tree at the edge of the western desert and she welcomed the newly deceased at the gates of the afterworld with fresh bread and water to sustain them. Amenti, was the land of the setting sun.

Use her energies to receive sustenance when you are tired and dispirited and for letting go of what is destructive or redundant in your life.

Amon, Amun or Amen

Creator god in the Theban creation myth, Amun-Ra as he was known, increased in power and combined with the figure of Ra to become supreme deity and the other deities manifestations of his power.

He was married to Mut, the vulture goddess.

Gradually Amun-Ra became more remote and was called the unknowable, secret god, the lord of mysteries, and represented total divinity.

Amun took on other god forms that were part of him, for example Amun-Re-Atum, Min Amun and Amun-Re-Horakhte, in the latter joining his power to that of Horus.

Amun is linked both with the goose, the Great Cackler, who daily laid the egg of the sun, and also with the fertility symbol, the Ram.

Amun-Ra was regarded from the Middle Kingdom as the father of each king, coming to the mother in a dream or superimposing himself on the body of her husband to conceive the child.

In his role as supreme king and father of the Pharaohs, he wears a crown of two feathered plumes.

Use the energies of Amun for power, for authority and leadership qualities, for male potency, for developing hidden talents and for all major creative ventures.

Anubis or Anpu

The black jackal-god who was both the god who healed the living and who prepared the body of the deceased, so that it might be preserved. He was therefore patron deity of surgeons, healers and embalmers.

In his jackal-headed form, he was son of Nephthys and Osiris and the alter ego of Horus. He embalmed and mummified his dead father and performed this role for all the deceased so that they might become as his father in the afterworld.

He is also pictured as a black crouching dog/jackal, placed to guard tombs or sacred shrines. In this role, Anubis was called the guarder of secrets.

Lord of death and the afterlife, Anubis led the deceased into the underworld where he assisted weighing the heart. He is also pictured on tomb walls wearing armour and guarding Osiris.

Use the energies of Anubis for fierce protection of yourself, your home and those you love, for increased spiritual awareness, for the rebirth of hope after a setback, for inspiring loyalty in others, for outfacing threats and for removing whatever is no longer needed in your life.

Anukis, Anqet or Anuket

Wife of Khnum, or sometimes regarded as the daughter of Khnum and Satis, Anukis was worshipped first as the goddess of the First Cataract at Aswan and later of the lower Nile. She was pictured in the form of a desert gazelle, embodying peace, swiftness and grace or represented as a woman with a high feather head-dress. Her titles include Lady of the Sky and Mistress of the Nile. A goddess who brings abundance, Anukis is depicted sometimes suckling the Pharaoh in her role as divine mother and was invoked to fill the granaries. She usually appears with her daughter Satis (see page 208).

Use her energies for getting swift results in a venture, for abundance and prosperity, for peace and for healing.

Aten or Aton

The sun disc, a supreme deity form for a relatively short period during the reign of King Akhenaten, his patron. Akhenaten introduced monotheistic worship to Egypt, forbidding all other deities.

In pictorial form, the sun disc was shown radiating light over everyone. Each solar ray ends in a hand, holding an ankh. The ankhs are being offered to King Akhenaten, divine representative of the sun on earth, and Akhenaten's wife Nefertiti. Aten was the alter ego of Apep, the chaos snake of darkness.

Use the energies of the Aten to bring light and confidence into your life, to gain total power over a situation or your fears and for healing others, especially in overcoming grief and sorrow.

Atum

The original creator sun god of Heliopolis, later identified with Re and assuming the role of the setting sun once his period of glory was eclipsed by Ra. He is depicted in human form wearing the double-headed crown of Egypt.

Atum's creatures are the snake, the bull, the lion and the desert lizard (the ancient Egyptians mummified desert lizards in huge quantities). At the end of the world, when creation is reversed and the primal waters submerge everything, he and Osiris will survive in the form of serpents.

Use the energies of Atum for permanence, for endurance, for starting over again, for resolving ageing issues and for surviving crises.

Bast or Bastet

The cat-headed or cat goddess, known respectively as Bastet or Bast, represents the gentle aspects of the lioness Sekhmet, though she was herself once a lion goddess and has retained her fertility powers.

In her fiercest form she protected the solar boat each night by wounding the serpent Apep when he wrapped himself around the boat to try to submerge it. Apep's blood coloured the sky at sunrise and at sunset.

Cat-headed Bastet was also linked with music and dancing, and was pictured holding the sistrum. She was a moon goddess and in a number of myths was considered to be daughter of the sun god Ra; she was also spiritual mother/sister of all the Pharaohs and was their divine protector. Bastet also gave protection to homes and families against disease and vermin.

Use the energies of Bastet for all forms of domestic protection, for nurturing qualities, for fertility, for lunar energies, for happiness, love and female sexuality, for healing and for protection against disease.

Bes

The Egyptian dwarf god who protected the home, children and pregnant women. With his huge head, prominent tongue and genitals, bow legs and the ears, mane and tail of a lion or cat, Bes is hardly an attractive figure. However, he is entirely benign to those whom he guards against misfortune, malevolent spirits and serpents; he may also help to increase sensual pleasures.

Bes wears a lion or panther skin but is otherwise naked. When his help is sought in matters relating to childbirth, he is depicted brandishing knives or loud instruments to drive away all harm.

Use the energies of Bes for protection of home and family, for all matters concerning babies, children and mothers, to increase pleasure and skill in dancing, singing and music to bring joy and also courage in the face of opposition.

Buto, Edjo or Uadjet

The cobra goddess, symbol of Lower (northern) Egypt, whose sacred place was he prehistoric town of Buto. She is sometimes depicted as a cobra on the crown of the Pharaoh with her sister Nekhbet the vulture Goddess. Buto is called mother of the sun and moon and is linked with the eye of Ra, fixing the enemies of the Pharaoh with her fiery eyes and then spitting poison into their faces. She also administers the death sting to the Pharaoh when his time on earth is ended and did so for Cleopatra (see page 213).

Sometimes she appears as a winged, crowned cobra or in the form of a snake with the face of a woman.

Use the energies of Buto to repel hostility, to repel spite and malice, for nobility of spirit and for giving tough love to one's family or partner.

Geb or Seb

The earth god. Like his sister wife, Nut the sky goddess, Geb was regarded as the offspring of Shu – God of Air – and Tefnut – Goddess of Moisture – in the creation myths of Heliopolis and Hermopolis.

He is shown as green with papyrus flowers growing from his body, reclining on one arm so that his body forms the undulating land. He usually has an erect phallus extending towards Nut to indicate his potency and his connection with the growth of land and the crops. In the Hermopolis creation myth, Geb was associated with laying the primordial egg.

For this reason some images depict him in human form with a goose on his head-dress. Use Geb for all matters of gradual growth, for care of the environment, for potency and for gentle fathering qualities.

Hapy or Hapi

The god of the Nile flood, Hapy was depicted as a corpulent hermaphrodite human figure with a huge stomach and breasts like those of a pregnant woman. He wears flowing papyrus and lotus flowers on his head, carrying a loaded offering dish with wine, food and lotus blossoms.

His appearance symbolized the abundance of the Nile at this time, teeming with fish and marsh birds – of which he was Lord – promising a good harvest.

He was occasionally shown with a double goose head-dress and had a court of crocodile lords and frog ladies to serve him.

Use the energies of Hapy to attract prosperity and abundance into your life, for fertility, to bring new life and enthusiasm to projects and situations and to wash away what has become fruitless and pointless.

Hatmehit or Hatmheyt

The fish goddess was called the first fish and was associated particularly with the Nile perch, which swallowed her own eggs to keep them safe. She is depicted with a dolphin on her head-dress or as a fish and was worshipped in the Nile Delta around Mendes. She is linked to the first fish in the primordial waters of creation and so was an early goddess. Occasionally she is identified as the fish that swallowed the phallus of Osiris, thus reabsorbing his generative power.

Use the energies of Hatmehit for healing, for fertility, for protection and for allowing ideas or plans to lie fallow until the time is right to put them into practice. You can also appeal to her for help with listening to deep instinctive inner wisdom that can become drowned out by the opinions of others.

Hathor

The goddess of happiness, love, dance, music and joy, fertility and marriage. A domestic goddess, she was worshipped on family altars as well as those at her great temples, including those at Memphis and Dendara, and women would make offerings for a good husband or leave fertility images in order to conceive a child.

Like Isis and Nut, Hathor was one of the primal mother goddesses. Therefore she assumed a maternal role towards the Pharaoh and is sometimes pictured as a cow suckling him.

Originally Hathor was seen as the mother of Horus, when he was regarded as the brother of Seth, but in some later legends she became Horus's wife. She was also the sister and gentle aspect of Sekhmet. Like Sekhmet, Hathor was the daughter of Ra, though at times she was regarded as his consort.

Although frequently portrayed as a cow, Hathor was also represented as a beautiful woman, wearing a crown of cow horns with the sun disc between them. At some temples, including the one at Memphis, her head was adorned with cow ears and was positioned emerging from a pillar.

Use the energies of Hathor for protection, for nurturing and all mothering issues, for marriage and committed love affairs, for harmony, fertility, inspiration, joy and for protection.

Heket or Heqet

These are sometimes regarded as separate frog goddesses, but in practice their identities have merged into the frog-headed or frog wife of Khnum, the divine potter who made humans from the clay or mud of the Nile.

As a creating goddess, she breathed life into the clay figures her husband made and was also goddess of fertility and childbirth. Heket helped Isis to restore life to the dead Osiris for one night so that Isis might conceive Horus.

Use the energies of Heket for fertility and abundance, for putting plans into action or ideas into practice, to aid all practical endeavours and creative ventures that have a practical application.

Horus

One of the most complex but popular gods, Horus appeared in a number of forms. Originally, Horus the elder, son of Hathor, brother of Set, was a distinct deity who was hawk-headed, or took the form of a hawk – a solar image. Horus was a sky god, associated with the sovereignty of the king. His two eyes were the sun and moon. In these myths in the battle between Horus and Set, Horus became lord of Lower Egypt and Set the lord of Upper Egypt.

The second young Horus, the son of Isis and Osiris, was portrayed as a young man who fought and overcame Set, his evil uncle. After many arguments among the gods Horus was declared king of his murdered father's lands, lord of all Egypt and a manifestation of the living Pharaoh.

He was seen also as a young naked child, called Harpocrates, with a lock of hair hanging down and a finger touching his lips – the young god of silence. Like Nefertum he was sometimes pictured sitting in the opening lotus. On healing tablets he was portrayed as a naked youth treading on crocodiles and scorpions to symbolize his mastery over what had threatened him when he was hidden as a child in the marshes.

The two forms, the elder and younger Horus, merged and he became linked with the sun god.

In his solar form, he was known as Horus on the horizon – Horus Harakhte – and was identified with the rising sun. He was also seen in the form of a hawk riding in the solar boat and as a hawk-winged sun disc to symbolize him soaring in front of the noon sun – this linked him with the winged ba spirit that flew from the deceased after death.

Invoke Horus for courage, for overcoming children's illnesses and fears, for healing of all kinds, for focus, clear vision and the ability to soar above the mundane world mentally and spiritually.

Imhotep, Imenhotep or Imouthes

Once the scribe of King Djoser, Imhotep created the step pyramid for his master. Imhotep was also skilled in medicine and healing and performed a number of healing miracles. After his death he was made a god and continued to be a source of healing at his temple near Memphis (see also page 107), where people came to sleep in order to receive healing in dreams. In time he became known as the son of Ptah and Nut and was pictured as a youth wearing a skullcap and carrying a scroll.

His worship during the Ptolemaic period became combined with that of Thoth. Mummified ibises bearing the name of Imhotep were brought to the temple as offerings, as were clay models of parts of the body where there was pain or disease.

He was also identified with the Greek healer god Aesculapius in whose honour the Greeks and later the Romans built healing dream temples throughout the Empire.

Invoke Imhotep for spiritual healing, especially in sleep, to bring fertility of all kinds, and also to help before conventional medical or surgery takes place.

Isis

Isis is the best-known and most enduring Egyptian deity. Indeed, she became so popular in the Roman Empire that her worship almost surpassed that of the Virgin Mary.

She was worshipped by ordinary people and in homes as well as at her great temple on the island of Philae near Aswan. Isis was the devoted wife of Osiris. In a statue of the pair in the British Museum, Isis's wings are outstretched and Osiris is smaller than she is; she shields the image of her mummified husband, whom she resurrected using magical spells.

Her name means 'the earth that bears corn' and her fertility aspects are also important, as the mother of Horus. Isis is the source and inspiration of the mother and child statues of Mary and baby Jesus.

She is also a mistress of enchantment, magical healing and magical spell-casting and a solar and lunar goddess. Her images reflect her different roles: a throne on her head-dress acknowledges her status as the Queen of Heaven and Earth, while with cow horns and a solar disc she is the divine mother of the Pharaohs. She is also portrayed with a lunar disc in her role of the moon goddess, which she has maintained to the present day.

In death, Isis is one of the four protective goddesses along with Nephthys, her sister and alter ego, Neith and Serqet, the scorpion goddess.

Use her energies for help with marriage or permanent love commitment, fidelity, mothering issues, healing, protection and developing psychic and spiritual powers.

Khepri or Khepera

The god of the sun at dawn, Khepri literally means 'he who rolls'. He was said to roll the ball of the sun across the sky like the scarab beetle rolling the ball containing her young, so bringing each new day – hence his depiction as a scarab-headed man.

According to myth, Khepri was a god who came from himself without being created and rose from the womb of Nut on to the eastern horizon on the first day. This gives Nut a prominent role in creation.

Use the energies of Khepri for better times, for beginning again, for perseverance, for optimism, for new enthusiasm and for reaping the fruits of effort or patience.

Khnemu or Khnum

The creator god, who made men and women from Nile clay on his potter's wheel. He was depicted in the form of a ram and was worshipped as a creator god in Upper Egypt from pre-dynastic times.

Over time he acquired a human form with a ram head. He was the husband of Heket, the frog who assisted him in creation. The finished human, complete with ka, was set in the mother's womb at conception. He was also the lord of the first cataract of the Nile, the deity to whom prayers were offered to ensure the right amount of water was released for a good flood. In this role his wife/daughter was Anukis.

Use the energies of Khnum for energy, for creativity, for shaping your own destiny if others seem to control it, for sexual passion and for fertility.

Khonsu or Knensu

The moon god, son of Amun and Mut; together they made up the triad of Thebes, the city in which he was particularly venerated. Khonsu was the alter ego of Horus, and sometimes joined with Thoth, the other major lunar deity, especially at Hermopolis.

His name means 'to cross', because he crossed the heavens every night in his lunar boat. He is depicted in human form with a crescent moon supporting the full moon disc.

At Thebes, Khonsu's statue was set between those of Amun and Nut; he was the divine child with a side-lock of hair. In earlier, Old Kingdom times, Khonsu was still connected to the remnants of what may have been his pre-dynastic role as the light by which kings pursued their enemies and hunters hunted their prey. He was invoked for driving away malevolent spirits. He was also sometimes combined with Horus, his alter ego.

Use the energies of Khonsu for rituals at night and by moonlight, for increasing psychic and intuitive powers, for bringing slow-acting projects to fruition, for tapping into slower rhythms of time if your life is frantic and for keeping away nightmares, night terrors and worries that keep you awake all night.

Ma'at

Ma'at embodies the principle of cosmic balance, order and justice and is the female alter ego of Thoth. She also rode on the solar boat and, like Thoth, was present on the boat at the first sunrise. Some myths say that Ma'at – again, like Thoth – was also instrumental in the creation of the world by Ptah. She is sometimes called the daughter of Ra, though she is regarded as one of the elder goddesses.

In temple ritual, from the time of Thutmoses II around 1479 BCE right until the Roman period in Egypt, a feather or tiny statue of Ma'at was offered by the king or high priest as a pledge to uphold order and justice. Indeed, the principle of Ma'at formed the basis of law in Ancient Egypt.

Ma'at is depicted with a single ostrich plume in her head-dress. In the afterlife, she weighed the hearts of the deceased against this feather, to see if they were free from sin.

Use the energies of Ma'at for justice, truth, good conduct in the lives of self and others, integrity, to protect against dishonest dealings and for balance and harmony.

Menthu or Montu

A Theban deity, Menthu was god of war and was therefore especially important at times of invasion or division in the kingdom. By the time of the New Kingdom he was depicted at the side of the Pharaoh when he went hunting as well as into battle. Many images of Menthu would have been visible in ancient Egyptian society; it was believed that if the King was pictured victorious with Menthu at his side, then he would succeed by magical means, because the images had brought success into being. There were also representations of Menthu on the tombs of dead kings, depicting their victories and showing them trampling on enemies. Menthu was shown as hawk headed, with a sun disc surmounted by two feathers. He also carried a curved sword and an ankh.

Use the energies of Menthu when you are find yourself being forced to fight for survival or for your principles, to increase self-confidence and assertiveness for protection in potentially hostile situations (he is a good travelling companion).

Min

Min was the most important of the fertility deities, for plants, animals and people. His most distinctive feature is his erect phallus, images of which were carried in processions or worn as amulets to ensure the fertility of the land and the people. Min was depicted as human, with his right arm holding a whip or flail raised high behind his body. He wore two tall plumes on his head, from which a cord hung down. He was often combined – especially in later times – with Amun, who is shown with the same head-dress to emphasize the procreative role of the supreme deity.

His sacred symbols were lightning and lettuce, the oil of which was a powerful aphrodisiac and is still made. He protects miners and travellers.

Use the energies of Min for all aspects of fertility and sexual potency, for bringing fresh energies or new perspectives into your life, for power to clear away stagnation and for protection when travelling.

Mut

Mut's name means 'mother'. She is regarded as the archetypal mother goddess, the feminine and nurturing aspect of her creator husband Amun. With their son Khonsu, they were often shown as part of an idealized family group. The vulture was her symbol (it was also associated with Isis, see page 71). Worshipped with her husband at Thebes, she was also regarded as a mother of Pharaohs. She wore a vulture head-dress and above that the double crown of Egypt and she carried the sceptre of Upper Egypt. She is also pictured as lioness-headed. Her dress was usually red or blue and patterned with feathers.

Use her energies for protection, for family togetherness and loyalty, for resolving issues of mothering and being mothered, for supporting others in need and for creative giving.

Nefertum or Nefertem

The young god of the lotus flower from which he is pictured emerging (see image on page 81). Nefertum represents the first sunrise He was the son of Ptah and Sekhmet and with them formed the Memphite triad – another happy family unit.

He is Lord of the lotus and of all perfumes and oils. His name is linked with the hieroglyph Nefer, the Ancient Egyptian oud, and the musical instrument that symbolizes harmony. He represents perfection.

Nefertum is depicted in a variety of ways: as a beautiful head rising from a lotus flower, a child with a side-lock sucking his thumb, seated inside the lotus flower or as a youth with a lotus head-dress.

Use the energies of Nefertum when striving for harmony or perfection, for tentative new beginnings, for all perfume, oil and incense magic, for soothing children's fears and for healing sorrow and abuse, especially when these emotions are left over from childhood.

Neith or Neit

Neith, whose name means 'the heavens', has two functions. As a weaver goddess of fate, and also weaver of the protective bandages of the mummy, she is linked with the first creation as wife of Khnum (yet another of his wives) and is sometimes called mother and father of the gods and mother of Ra. She was also the mother of Sobek, the crocodile god. Neith is one of four protective goddesses who guarded the tombs of the pharaohs.

Neith is also a goddess of the hunt and war, and her bows, arrows and shields were used as symbols of protection for living and dead. She was depicted wearing the red crown of Lower Egypt, holding a bow and crossed arrows or a shield with crossed arrows on it.

Use the energies of Neith for changing your life path and for controlling your own fate, for weaving together people in peace, for fierce protection of those you love and for aiming true towards fulfilling your dreams.

Nekhbet or Nekhebet

The protective deity of Upper Egypt, whose image was worn on the forehead of the Pharaoh along with the cobra of the North. She is sometimes linked to Isis. Nekhbet was said to give her maternal milk to the Pharaoh. The vulture symbol was worn by the queen mothers of the pharaohs as a head-dress, to show their link with the Divine Mother.

Nekhbet became also a protective deity for ordinary women, especially mothers who asked her for fertility and protection of their children. She is also the patroness of snake charmers. Her image is that of a vulture with wings outspread for protection, or as a woman with a vulture head or snakeskin on her head-dress.

Use the energies of Nekhbet for protection of family and children, for abundance and prosperity and for nurturing yourself, especially if you give a great deal emotionally to others.

Nephthys

The twin sister and alter ego of Isis and sister wife of Set, her role is invariably benign. She searched with her sister for Osiris's body, helped her to reassemble the body that Set had mutilated and assisted Isis through her pregnancy and early days.

However, she is often most remembered for her underworld protective role, standing behind Osiris as the heart of the deceased is weighed. Like Isis she helped to protect and comfort the dead and was one of the four protective death goddesses. Nephthys represented sunset and both she and Isis rode on the solar boat at the first sunrise.

As the shadow alter ego of Isis, Nephthys symbolized darkness, silence, hidden mysteries and what was invisible. Above all, she is a symbol of hope.

As Lady of the Desert she is the mother of Anubis by Osiris.

She is shown as a woman with a pylon – a tower surmounted by a dish on her head-dress, the symbol for a mansion – and in her protective role she has outstretched wings.

Use the energies of Nephthys for compassion, gentleness, reconciliation, acceptance of what cannot be changed, for soothing sorrow, for support in difficult times and for endings that lead to beginnings.

Nut

The creating sky mother, Nut was mother of Isis, Osiris, Nephthys and Set and also the mother of Ra. Ra passed into Nut's womb each night, to be reborn through her thighs at dawn.

Mother of the sun, moon and all heavenly bodies and stars, Nut is depicted as a deep blue woman covered in stars stretched over the earth god Geb, her husband, her fingers and toes touching the earth. Many representations of her star-covered body survive from Ancient Egypt. This image was painted on tomb lids in the hope she would grant rebirth, as Ra was reborn.

Use the energies of Nut to aim for the stars to fulfil your dreams and desires, for protection against fear, to rise above pettiness and material concerns, for star magic and for learning to love the night.

Osiris

The teacher of humanity, appointed to rule the earth by his father the earth god Geb. It was Osiris who gave humans agriculture and as an early fertility and vegetation god, he was regarded as an embodiment of the corn even before his murder.

After his murder by Set, Osiris descended into the underworld where he became the embodiment of the deceased king, just as his son Horus represented the living one.

For this reason he is portrayed as a mummified figure wearing the crowns of Egypt and carrying the ceremonial crook and flail and with the curved beard that denotes a Pharaoh who has become divine in death. Sometimes he wears the atef, a tall cone-shaped head-dress, flanked by ram horns, with two plumes that links him with Amun.

He represents the annual growth of the corn, watered by the tears of Isis, the Nile Flood, and so ensures the continuation of the cycle of life, death and rebirth, as the corn is cut down but sprouts again. In this he complements the ordered passage of the sun god.

Osiris was an important god because it was believed he could claim a place in the heavens for all those who followed him, even ordinary people.

Use the energies of Osiris for regeneration – perhaps of the rekindling of hope and enthusiasm, or of a relationship, or as a means of providing yourself with the energy to start over again after a loss. You can also use his energies for fertility of all kinds, for male rituals of all kinds, for nobility of purpose and for setting in motion projects that will bear fruit months ahead.

Ptah

The creator-god of Memphis, the divine artisan or fashioner of gods and vegetation.

Brightly coloured hollow wooden images of Ptah-Seker-Osiris (Seker was a hawk god of the dead) were buried in coffins, with prayers from the Book of the Dead in the hollow, to ensure magical resurrection and sufficient nourishment in the afterlife.

Ptah is shown with the body of a mummy and a shaven head, like that of a priest, to indicate his holiness, or with a blue fitted cap and a robe that reveals only his head and hands. He holds a sceptre that consists of a forked, dog-shaped end, engraved with the backbone of Osiris, the Tet or djed amulet. The sceptre was called an uas or user. He is also sometimes shown as the potter's wheel.

Use the energies of Ptah for all creative ventures, for major life changes, for abundance and for inspiration when you need to take the initiative.

Ra or Re

Some authorities say that Ra was the first deity to be worshipped and that his origins are lost in prehistory. He seems to have emerged around the Fifth Dynasty in the Heliopian legends and replaced Atum as father of the gods, though Nut remained his mother. In some creation myths, the cosmic egg contained Ra, the sun god, and his birth set time in motion. Over the centuries he became linked with the major creator deities, with Ptah and as Atum-Ra and Amun-Ra. In time too his role as father of the gods became undisputed.

He was identified as the sun at its full power and is depicted by the symbol of the sun and also in his solar boat. Ra is shown variously as a man with a curved beard and the sacred serpent coiled around a sun disc or a hawk-headed man, crowned with the sun disc and sacred Uraeus serpent and with the uas, dog-headed rod of power (see Ptah, page 207).

Use the energies of Ra for power, nobility, and leadership, for fulfilling ambitions, for self-confidence, for illumination in every aspect of your life and for making the most of time.

Sati or Satis

Lady of the Nile waterfalls and consort or daughter of the ever-potent Khnum in the myths of Upper Egypt. She was often pictured pouring water into the dry earth to revive it. Ancient Egyptian imagery portrays her as a beautiful woman with the white crown of Upper Egypt and two gazelle horns. Satis is also linked to an archer huntress goddess. She appears frequently with her mother/sister Anukis (see page 200) and like Anukis was invoked to fill the grain stores.

Use the energies of Satis for healing, for succeeding through showing gentleness and compassion, for reviving an arid or stagnant relationship or situation, for abundance and prosperity and for the restoration of harmony.

Sebek or Sobek

The ancient crocodile god whose temple and lake, filled with jewel-covered sacred crocodiles, were at Faiyum. Crocodiles were mummified with their eggs as symbols of fertility and prosperity. Sobek displayed both destructive and protective aspects.

The crocodile was a fierce predator of humans as well as animals, but also appeared in great numbers at the time of the flooding of the Nile and so was associated with abundance. As Sobek Ra, he was regarded as a primordial creator god.

Sobek was pictured as either a crocodile or crocodile-headed human.

Use the energies of Sobek for protection against emotional as well as physical predators in your life, for abundance, male potency, fertility of all kinds and for the determination to fight off destructive or negative influences.

Sekhmet

One of the most powerful and ancient deities was the lion-headed solar goddess Sekhmet, whose cult centre was at Memphis. She was both a fierce avenger and a protectress of the living and the dead – particularly of the Pharaoh. Sekhmet was goddess of both war and healing and doctors practised in her name.

Sekhmet is sometimes called the 'eye of Ra' warrior, a reference to her father/consort, though her main marital link was with Ptah.

Known also as a lady of magic, especially magical healing and protection, Sekhmet is frequently pictured with the head of a lioness, the sun disc on her head and the sacred cobra – protectress of the Pharaohs – on her brow. She can also take the form of a lioness. In her more usual lioness-headed form she carries an ankh or sistrum.

Use the energies of Sekhmet for courage, for defence, for fire magic and for healing, but never for revenge.

Selkit or Serqet

The beautiful scorpion goddess, with the dual function of protector and attacker. Fiercely vengeful for those who are unworthy or destructive, she nevertheless cures the innocent who are wounded by the spite and malice of others. A fire goddess associated with the blazing heat of the noon sun, Serqet is one of the four protective goddesses. She is shown as a woman with a scorpion on her head-dress.

Use the energies of Serqet for repelling spite and cruel words, for the fierce defence of those you love who are vulnerable, and for kindling or rekindling your inner flame of inspiration.

Seshat

Seshat is the one who writes in the books of fate and, as a fate goddess, attended the coronation of kings and major festivals. Seshat also marks out the dimensions and directions for a new temple and for all sacred buildings. Mistress also of writing and of all books, she wears a seven-pointed star above which is a bow or sickle shape and a panther skin over her robe.

Another of Seshat's symbols is a long palm branch she carries, with notches that mark the passing years, which ends in the tadpole-like symbol for 'countless number'.

Use her energies to acquire formal knowledge, especially from books, to keep track of time, to make the most of every moment and to give blessings for all family celebrations and landmarks in your life.

Set or Seth

The ancient brother of Horus the elder, lord of Upper Egypt and originally defender of the solar boat against Apep the serpent, Set became demonized as the evil uncle of Horus the younger and assassin of his brother Osiris. Associated with the desert and the desert sandstorm, Set came to symbolize all that was arid, destructive and infertile. He had no child with Nephthys and so stood for barrenness in a relationship although occasionally he was invoked as an antidote for sterility.

As representative of the forces of chaos, he had a vital role in the ancient Egyptian world in ensuring that the forces of change could operate. For this reason, though defeated by Horus, he was never killed.

Set was also associated with foreigners, who were regarded as enemies by the ancient Egyptians. He was also associated with the pig, donkey, crocodile and male hippopotamus. Set was shown with a human body and the head of the Set animal, a strange mixture of animals that include a long tapering snout, large erect ears and bulging eyes.

Use the most positive aspects of Set for removing what is destructive or redundant in your life, for facing your own negative aspects and acknowledging them rather than projecting them on to others and for accepting that in some situations you cannot win and so should move on.

Tauret, Taweret or Thoueris

This benign and protective goddess was a variation of the mother goddess Mut. She was shown as a pregnant hippopotamus with huge breasts and sometimes the tail and back of a crocodile.

Blue faience hippopotamus amulets decorated with papyrus plants were one of the earliest amulets and indicate that Tauret was a very ancient goddess. They were a symbol of the fecundity of the Nile.

Tauret was mainly a household goddess protective of the home, the family, pregnant women and those in childbirth and babies and children. She was frequently depicted holding knives to drive danger away from those she protected.

Use the energies of Tauret to protect your home and your family, especially children, for fertility of all kinds, for putting ideas into practice and for bringing dreams into reality. Above all, use her for valuing the inner person rather than external beauty.

Thoth

Sometimes regarded as the father of the deities and present at creation – for example in the Memphite myth. Thoth was the god of law, writing and the spoken word, medicine, healing and mathematics and had command over magical knowledge. He brought creation into existence by uttering the thoughts of the creator and was later called the heart and tongue of Ra (i.e. he translated thought into word and so animated the sun).

Though he was a lunar god, Thoth rode in the solar boat with Ra. In this function, he ordered the measurement of time and was regarded as the mind behind cosmic order, sometimes being considered self-created and therefore coming into existence before creation.

As an elder god, Thoth taught Isis the magical incantations to restore life to the body of Osiris, as well as a number of her healing powers. He himself was cured of a headache by her.

Depicted with an ibis or baboon head, or as one of these creatures with a crescent or full moon disc on the head, he is also seen as a scribe with his magical palette, recording the words and commands of the deities and writing the laws for humankind.

Use the energies of Thoth for all forms of wisdom, learning and knowledge – including magical knowledge – for order in your life and in the world, for oratory and divinatory skills and for creative ventures.

HISTORY, ERAS AND DYNASTIES

Dynasties and kingdoms

Ancient Egyptian history is divided into three main eras or kingdoms. Within these are a total of 30 different dynasties, or families, or royal houses of rulers. Some dynasties lasted for more than 200 years, such as the Sixth Dynasty, while other dynasties survived only for a very short period – like the 24th dynasty, which survived for only six years. Our information about Egypt's ancient history has come from an Egyptian historian priest called Manetho who wrote during the third century BCE. He said that the information had been handed down through the priesthood.

The Pharaohs

I have used the term Pharaoh and king interchangeably throughout this book, although in fact the term Pharaoh, which means 'the great house', was not used until the New Kingdom, from about 1570 BCE. Like the kingdoms, the dynasties followed a period of ascendancy, stability and decline and between each of the main eras or kingdoms there were intermediate periods when the king was weak and during which nobles, priests or outside invaders fought for supremacy.

Pre-dynastic Egypt

This era spans the late Neolithic period in Egypt – dating from about 5,000 BCE until 3,000 BCE. It was the period before the unification of Upper and Lower Egypt, when people farmed the banks of the Nile. Hieroglyphs have been found dating from about 3200 BCE but may have been used even earlier. The most significant part of this time is known as the Late Pre-dynastic period, from 3250–3050 BCE, when between nine and fifteen kings ruled from Hierakonpolis in Upper Egypt. They were the first to use the name 'Horus Kings'. The most famous rulers in this period – called Dynasty 0 – was the Scorpion King and King Narmer, who is credited with the unification of the two kingdoms in about 3100 BCE.

Early dynastic period

This was the period of the First and Second dynasties and lasted from 3100–2686 BCE. Horus-Aha, Narmer's son, was the first king of the First Dynasty and made his capital of Egypt at Memphis in Lower (Northern) Egypt, not far from modern-day Cairo. Here, he dedicated a temple to Ptah. Memphis remained a major centre of religion and administration on and off for the new two millennia.

Old Kingdom

This era extended from the period of the Third to the Sixth dynasties and lasted from 2686–2181 BCE. The kings of the Old Kingdom were also called the Horus Kings and were depicted with a falcon behind their thrones. By the time of the Fifth Dynasty, Ra was regarded as the father of the king. It was the period of the great pyramids, beginning with the step pyramid at Saqqara for the Third Dynasty King Djoser. The step pyramid is believed to be the first stone building anywhere in the world. By the Fourth Dynasty, the great pyramids at Giza had been created. This era is often described as the golden age of Egypt. Heliopolis became the centre for the worship of Ra, incorporating the earlier solar creator god Atum.

Pepi II was the last king of the period and lived until he was 95. His death marked the beginning of the end for central control in Egypt.

First Intermediate period

This was the period of the Seventh to Tenth dynasties and lasted from 2181–2040 BCE. At the time, the country was ruled mainly by local governors of the provinces, known as Nomes. The kings were unable to maintain central control and so were quite numerous, with short reigns. There were poor harvests at the time, which led to famine. Memphis was still Egypt's major city, but later during the period, Heracleopolis in the north and Thebes in the south produced challenges to the main ruling centre and fought each other.

Middle Kingdom

This was the period of the 11th and 12th dynasties and lasted from 2040–1782 BCE. Stability returned and Egypt was centrally governed again by the time of the 11th Dynasty ruler Mentuhotep I, whose power base was in Thebes (modern Luxor). By the 39th year of his reign he was in full control of all Egypt and ruled from Itj-tawy, a town near the Faiyum Oasis, south of Memphis.

Mentuhotep III was overthrown by Amenemhet I, one of his high-ranking officials. Amenemhet's reign marked the beginning of the 12th Dynasty, which saw the rise in popularity of Amun-Ra.

Second Intermediate period

This era spanned the 13th–17th dynasties and lasted from 1782–1570 BCE. It was another unstable period, during which the Hykos people invaded from Asia, moved to the Nile Delta and took control of Egypt.

Around 1570 BCE, a leader called Ahmose and his followers led a rebellion from Thebes that resulted in the expulsion of the invaders.

New Kingdom

This spanned the 18th–20th dynasties and lasted from 1570–1070 BCE. Ahmose I went on to reunite Upper and Lower Egypt and Egypt expanded its frontiers during this long period of peace.

Memphis became the centre once more and the term Pharaoh came into usage.

Among the more colourful rulers was Queen Hatshepsut, the stepmother of the young Tuthmoses III, who usurped power as regent and kept him in the background until her death, some say by assassination, in 1481 BCE. She was a great peacemaker and trader but after her death, Tuthmoses III had nearly all references to her removed and her statues destroyed or disfigured.

The Pharaohs were buried in the Valley of the Kings near Thebes, while their wives, mothers and daughters were laid to rest in the Valley of the Queens. Most famous of all the resting places was the tomb of the boy King Tutankhamun, because it lay undisturbed until 1922. It provided an unrivalled store of rich treasures and provided archaeologists with an unrivalled opportunity to learn much more about the nature of the ancient Egyptian beliefs in the afterlife.

Amun-Ra was supreme god and his priests and temples remained very powerful throughout Ancient Egypt, apart from the brief reign of Akhenaten who, during the 14th century, established the religion of the Aten, the sun disc.

Rameses II, of the 19th Dynasty, ruled for 67 years from 1279–1212 BCE and was famed for the widespread restoration and construction of temples that he inaugurated – not least to glorify himself, as shown by the colossal statues he created in his own memory. He was also famed for putting his own name on the statues of his predecessors. His huge statue can still be seen at Memphis.

However, the Pharaoh's powers diminished as the period wore on. New pressures came to bear on him, in the form of invasions from the sea and a rise in the power of the Amun priests, who were ruling Upper Egypt by the end of the New Kingdom. The term 'Peoples of the Sea' was applied to various invading forces at the time, including the Lukka people from the south-western coast of Asia Minor and coalitions of invaders from around the Aegean Sea.

Third Intermediate period

This spanned the 21st–26th dynasties and lasted from 1070–525 BCE. As a result of the split-rule in Egypt, by the 22nd Dynasty Libyan pharaohs were able to take control of the north and succeeded in briefly reuniting the country.

During the 25th Dynasty, the Nubians from the land south of Egypt – who had been invaded and plundered for minerals for centuries by the Egyptians – seized their chance to rule Egypt. They re-established the cult of Amun in Thebes.

By 671 BCE, the Assyrians attacked and they fought with the Nubians for control of Egypt. Psamtik, an Assyrian, assumed supreme kingship and re-established the grandeur of the Old Kingdom. By 653 BCE, Psamtik had created an independent Egyptian state once more.

Late Dynastic period

This era spanned the 27th–31st dynasties and lasted from 525–332 BCE. Persian invasions marred the whole period. The final incursion took place in 343 BCE, during the reign of the last true Egyptian pharaoh, Nectanebo II.

Greek/Ptolemaic Period

This period covered the years 332–30 BCE.

Macedonian Dynasty: 332–304 BCE

In 332 BCE, Alexander the Great invaded Egypt. The Egyptians considered him a favourable alternative to the Persians and he was duly claimed as the son of Amun. Alexander subsequently restored the temples and created the city of Alexandria on the Mediterranean coast as one of the finest centres of learning in the history of humankind. Egyptian culture thrived, though it became mixed with the mythology and deity names of the Greeks. However, neither Alexander the Great (Alexander III) nor his half brother Philip, nor his son Alexander IV lived in Egypt – instead, they ruled from Babylon.

The Ptolemaic era

In 305 BCE, the Macedonian general Ptolemy, a friend of Alexander Great who had been ruling Egypt on his behalf, assumed the role of Pharaoh. His reign started a line that continued until the time of the ill-fated Cleopatra VII, who committed suicide in true Pharaoh style by allowing the sacred Uraeus snake to administer the death sting (see page 123) in 27 BCE. The Ptolemy reign ended after Cleopatra killed herself, following her ill-fated love affair with Mark Antony and their defeat at the hands of Julius Caesar's heir Octavian.

Roman Period

The period of Roman rule in Egypt spanned 30 BCE–CE 450. During this time, Egyptian culture continued to flourish, although it was now mixed with a Roman influence as it had been earlier by Greek culture. The major change came in CE 384 with the spread of Christianity, when many temples were closed and statues destroyed. The Roman Emperor was Pharaoh during this era, though prefects ruled the country.

Ten years later the Roman Empire divided and Egypt became part of the eastern Byzantine Empire until the dominance of Islam in CE 641. Today, although the country is predominantly Moslem, Jewish synagogues and Coptic Christian churches stand alongside the famous mosques. As I discovered myself, however, the old world of deities and magic still exists today – not only in the form of artefacts, but in the folk practices of a number of Egyptians.

FURTHER READING

Ancient Egypt – General

Baines, John and Málek, Jaromír, *The Atlas of Ancient Egypt, Facts on File*, New York/Oxford, 1980

Brier, Bob, *Ancient Egyptian Magic*, Quill Press, New York, 1981

Brodrick, M. and Morton, A.A., *A Concise Dictionary of Egyptian Archaeology*, Senate, New York, 1996

Budge, Wallis E.A., *Egyptian Magic*, Routledge, London, 1901 (reprinted several times and still available)

Dee, Jonathan, *Chronicles of Ancient Egypt*, Sterling, New York, 1998

Faulkner, Raymond O. (ed. Andrews, Carol) *The Ancient Egyptian Book of the Dead*, British Museum Press, London/University of Texas Press, Austin, 1989

Forman, Werner and Quirke, Stephen, *Hieroglyphs and the Afterlife in Ancient Egypt*, British Museum Press, London, 1996

Harris, Eleanor L., *Ancient Egyptian Magic and Divination*, Samuel Weiser, York Beach, Maine, 1998

Hart, George, *Egyptian Myths*, British Museum Press, London/University of Texas Press, Austin, 1990

Hart, George, *Dictionary of Egyptian Gods and Goddesses*, Routledge & Kegan Paul, London, 1996

Jacq, Christian, *Magic and Mystery in Ancient Egypt*, Editions du Rocher, Monaco, 1983/Davis Janet M. (trans.), Souvenir Press, London, 1998

Kemp, Barry J, *Ancient Egypt: Anatomy of a Civilization*, Routledge, New York, 1989

Lemesurier, Peter, *The Great Pyramid Decoded*, Element, Shaftesbury, 1989

Quirke, Stephen, *Ancient Egyptian Religion*, British Museum Press, London/Dover, New York, 1992

Quirke, Stephen and Spencer, Jeffrey, *The British Museum Book of Ancient Egypt*, British Museum Press/ Thames & Hudson, London, 1992

Russman, Edna R. and James, T.G.H., *Eternal Egypt - Masterworks of Ancient Art from the British Museum*, University of California Press, Berkeley, 2001

Shaw, Ian, *Oxford Dictionary of Ancient Egypt*, Oxford University Press, Oxford, 2000

Tompkins, Peter, *Secrets of the Great Pyramid*, Harper & Row, New York, 1971

Wilkinson, Richard H., *Symbol and Magic in Egyptian Art*, Thames & Hudson, London, 1994

Hieroglyphics

Ardagh, Philip, *The Hieroglyphics Handbook*, Faber & Faber, London, 1999

Budge, Wallis E.A., *Egyptian Language*, Routledge & Kegan Paul, London, 1983

Collier, Mark and Manley, Bill, *How to Read Egyptian Hieroglyphs*, British Museum Press, London, 1998

Jacq, Christian, *Fascinating Hieroglyphics*, Sterling, New York, 1999

Amulets and Talismans

Gonzalez-Wipler, Migene, *Complete Guide to Amulets and Talismans*, Llewellyn, St Paul, Minnesota, 1991

Astrology/Astronomy

Cornelius, Geoffrey, *The Starlore Handbook*, Mitchell Beazley, London, 1997

Alternative Theories

Hope, Murry, *The Sirius Connection*, Element, Shaftesbury, 1996

Atlantis
Brennan, Herbie, *The Atlantis Enigma*, Piatkus, London, 2000

Chakras and Auras
Eason, Cassandra, *Chakra Power*, Quantum, Slough, 2001

Crystals
Gienger, Michael, *Crystal Power, Crystal Healing*, Blandford, London, 1998
Eason, Cassandra, *The Crystal Handbook*, Vega, London, 2003

Dreams
Delaney, Gayle, *All About Dreams*, HarperCollins, London, 1998

Herbs
Manniche, Lisa, *An Ancient Egyptian Herbal*, British Museum Press, London, 1993

Incense
Cunningham, Scott, *Complete Book of Oils, Incenses and Brews*, Llewellyn, St Paul, Minnesota, 1991

Oils and Perfumes
Fletcher, Joanne, *Oils and Perfumes of Ancient Egypt*, British Museum Press, London, 1998

General Magic
Eason, Cassandra, *A Complete Guide to Night Magic*, Piatkus, London, 2002

INDEX